BASEMENTALITY

HOW THIS ENTREPRENEUR DROVE HIS FIGHT
AGAINST BIG SUGAR AND ROSE FROM THE
BASEMENT TO A $1.7 BILLION BRAND

BEN WEISS
WITH ERIC QUIÑONES
FOREWORD BY ZAC BROWN

Copyright © 2020 by Ben Weiss. All rights reserved.

Photography by Brian Tice. Cover design by Mike Boos. Interior artwork by Alyssa Adoni.

ISBN 978-1-7347325-0-4 (Hardcover)
ISBN 978-1-7347325-1-1 (Ebook)
ISBN 978-1-7347325-2-8 (Audiobook)

Published by Sun Owl LLC

Limit of Liability/Disclaimer of Warranty: While the author has used his best efforts in preparing this book, he makes no representations or warranties with respect to the accuracy or completeness of the contents of this book and specifically disclaims any implied warranties of merchantability or fitness for a particular purpose. No warranty may be created or extended by sales representatives or written sales materials. The advice and strategies contained herein may not be suitable for your situation. You should consult with a professional where appropriate. The author shall not be liable for any loss of profit or any other commercial damages, including but not limited to special, incidental, consequential, or other damages.

Quotes from interviews published in this book have been edited and condensed for clarity.

Bai® is a registered trademark of Keurig Dr Pepper (KDP). KDP was not involved in the production of this book.

To Danna, Jack, and Shayna, for dreaming alongside me in basements and on brown couches, for filling our lives with love and laughter, and for the shared moments still to come.

To Mom, for coffee-breath kisses and setting the example.

With all my love, always.

Every great story has a beginning, middle, and end. These two guys are the bookends to my Bai story. They both took a chance on me, each for their own reasons, and I hope that I delivered. Because without them, Bai would not have become my biggest breakthrough business. The two smiling faces at the heart of this photo might look like brothers, but their paths never would have crossed if not for the special company that they uplifted in their own ways. One was there for me at the start and the other at the finish of my Bai quest, which I'm proud to share with you in this book. Everyone else in the photo? They're the middle of that amazing story, the ones whose dedication and drive helped me create a full-blown bevolution and an unforgettable journey.

My stepfather, Ray (left), and Dr Pepper CEO Larry Young celebrate Bai's adoption (2016)

CONTENTS

CO-AUTHOR'S NOTE..9
FOREWORD...11
INTRODUCTION...15
CHAPTER 1: Am I Ready for This?......................................19
CHAPTER 2: Windows..29
CHAPTER 3: Two Tickets for the Roller Coaster.............47
CHAPTER 4: Seeing the Bevolution....................................89
CHAPTER 5: $60 Million Shoulders...................................123
CHAPTER 6: Targeting the Enemy....................................143
CHAPTER 7: Royals, Rebels, and Randoms...................165
CHAPTER 8: Putting the Cult Back in Culture................195
CHAPTER 9: The End Is in Sight..223
CHAPTER 10: I've Got Nothing Left...................................245
CHAPTER 11: The Aftermath...273
EPILOGUE..297
ACKNOWLEDGMENTS..299
PHOTO CREDITS...301
INDEX...303
ABOUT THE AUTHORS..307

ERIC QUIÑONES
CO-AUTHOR'S NOTE

I met Ben Weiss in our old neighborhood in Princeton, New Jersey, in the spring of 2006, when our four-year-old boys came upon each other while riding their scooters in the cul-de-sac outside Ben's town house. We became fast friends, but I quickly recognized one big difference between us—Ben was an entrepreneur and a risk-taker, while I, like most people, craved safety and security.

About three years later, after his latest business had fizzled out, Ben approached me and said, "Come with me for a moment. Let me show you what's going on in the basement." That's when I got my first glimpse at his new concept, an antioxidant beverage called Bai. I admired Ben's ability to bounce back and jump right into a new venture, something I wouldn't have had the stomach to do.

By then, I had been in my job as a writer for Princeton University's communications office for about seven years, following several years as a journalist for the Associated Press. One night, over a beer at a venerable pub called the Yankee Doodle Tap Room, I confessed to Ben that I struggled with calling myself a real writer because I had never written a book.

"What about doing a book on Bai someday?" he said. "It will take some time, but I think we can write a hell of a story together. Wouldn't that be great?"

I smiled at his ever-present confidence and agreed that, yes, it would be great. Did I think it would ever happen? Not at all. But I've since come to expect the unexpected from Ben. He turned Bai into an astoundingly successful brand, changing the lives of so many people he convinced to come along for the ride—myself included.

Now, here I am, helping him tell the tale of his journey, not so long after he introduced me to Bai that day in his basement—the place where his dreams took root. And it turns out that we did, indeed, write a hell of a story.

The boys who brought the co-authors together, Benny Quiñones and Jack Weiss (2012)

ZAC BROWN
FOREWORD

I was the eleventh of twelve kids born into a traditional, clean-cut southern family. Khakis, polo shirts, and Weejuns loafers were the Brown boys' uniform. Then I came along with my dreadlocks and tattoos and piercings, and everyone in my family looked at me like, "What are you?" So from an early age, I've been used to being around people who are different than me. And I've learned to judge people by what's on the inside.

On the surface, a Georgia-bred country singer like me and a beverage guy born and raised in New York like Ben Weiss might seem like an odd match. But we've found a true kinship—two guys who are trying, in our own ways, to leave the world better than we found it.

I was on a hunting trip in Florida in 2012 when I first tried Bai. My friend Chris brought it along because he was on a low-sugar diet after being diagnosed with cancer. I was blown away after reading the label and taking my first sip. As a parent and as the founder of a camp for developmentally challenged kids, I've been frustrated by how American diets are dominated by sugary, artificial food and drinks. I thought Bai offered a real solution to this problem, so I reached out to Ben.

I learned quickly that there's more to Ben's (and Bai's) story than the quality of the drink. It's about being passionate and rebellious and relentless. I like to call people like Ben a maverick or an outlier. He uses the term black sheep. Whatever you call it, we share the same philosophy: follow your dreams, no matter how crazy they may seem, and

Zac with the family (2019)

surround yourself with people who care as much as you do and who bring you joy.

Every time Ben and I sit down to talk, we learn things from one another. It took my band a solid decade of touring and recording before we started to hit any commercial success. Ben had many years of ups and downs before Bai took off. We've both learned that persistence is your greatest ally. You just have to be dumb enough to keep going and going until what you're doing starts to gain some momentum.

We've realized through our experiences that even when you don't understand everything about where you're going, you just have to move forward. You can't hesitate. You can't make decisions based on fear.

Trust your intuition, put your head down, and go. That attitude has led us both to some incredible places. And that's why I think you'll benefit from reading about Ben's journey and how he created a great brand in Bai while keeping his focus on the right things in life. If you're already a maverick, an outlier, or a black sheep, or you aspire to be one, you'll see a little bit of yourself—or the person you want to become—in his story.

INTRODUCTION

Toward the end of my time with Bai Brands, the company I founded in my basement in 2009, I received a wonderful gift from our chief creative officer and my dear friend, Chad Portas. It was a forty-pound ceramic black sheep that now sits in the corner of my home office and scares the shit out of our family dog, Bali, on a daily basis. It's not the kind of thing you see in every office. And that's exactly the point.

Chad understood that I took great pride in being known as a black sheep of the beverage industry. I never wanted to just be one of the flock, selling long-established brands whose best days were behind them or coming up with derivative products that simply cluttered the marketplace. To me, those brands were the white sheep—the uninspired crowd.

My black sheep mentality allowed me to assemble a great team to battle the industry's Big Three—Coca-Cola, PepsiCo, and Dr Pepper Snapple Group—and build Bai into a truly disruptive force. That mentality allowed me to reach a $1.7 billion deal to sell Bai to Dr Pepper just seven years after we launched. And that mentality ultimately got me fired from Bai.

As part of our sale agreement, Larry Young, Dr Pepper's chief executive, gave me the title of chief disruptive officer and empowered me to run Bai as an independent division of his company. Eight months later, he fired me, and a week later I tearfully walked out of Bai's office for the last time.

I hold no ill will toward Larry. He did what he felt he had to do to ensure the future of his business. In fact, I still consider him a great friend and mentor—and you'll hear from him later in this book. But the truth is that this black sheep couldn't play well with others in the pen of a Fortune 500 public corporation.

In 2018, a year after closing his acquisition of Bai, Larry sold Dr Pepper to another beverage behemoth, Keurig Green Mountain, for nearly $19 billion to create a new company called Keurig Dr Pepper. Today I'm on the outside of Bai, watching an unfamiliar conglomerate lead the brand that I created and hoping that it continues along the path we set. But thankfully, I've had the opportunity to reflect upon what defined my ability to succeed. As I considered what I lost, I also came to realize what I'd gained. I know now what it means, and what it takes, to be a black sheep and find your competitive edge. And it all starts in the basement.

When I began working on Bai toward the start of 2009, the US economy was still reeling from the Great Recession and I was coming off the failure of my latest venture, Boosta Shot, a natural energy ingredient for beverages. It was not the ideal time to start a new business from scratch. But after years of riding the ups and downs of life as an entrepreneur, I only knew one approach: move forward with no fear. So I picked myself up and went back down into the basement.

In my windowless office, I was insulated from the noise of news reports about the weakened state of the American economy. I didn't waste time licking my wounds and feeling sorry for myself after Boosta Shot's demise. I just got back to work, inspired to bring my newest idea to life

As an intuitive doer, I never had a playbook for how to win in business. I took action instinctively, starting in basements and cramped studio apartments as I sought to find my edge. Over the years, I developed the ability to view business through a bifocal lens—looking up to see what others can't see far in the distance, while still focusing on what needs to get done right in front of you. In the earliest days of Bai in my basement, I committed to do the work necessary to get the business off the ground. As that work progressed and I started to see results, my hazy vision for

Bai's future came into focus and I put on my bifocals to ensure I kept our long-term goals in view while staying focused on the day-to-day battles necessary to get us there. I harnessed what I call my Basementality to kick off what would become the most successful venture of my life.

My Basementality has guided me throughout my career. It's not just about coming up with a great idea or enjoying those early moments of inspiration in the basement or wherever you start your quest. It's about embracing a mindset that blends foresight, scrappiness, flexibility, and passion throughout your journey, empowering you to turn vision into reality and achieve success.

The truth is you can only stay in the basement for so long, because to find true success you must outgrow it. You must charge bravely into the world, unafraid of failure. You must find others to run alongside you with shared purpose. You must fight your way out of the basement as you find the edge that will lead you to true success.

But even after you leave the basement, it must always stay with you. You must seize every day with the same hunger and focus you had on Day One. You must never lose sight of your humble beginnings and the tireless work it takes to rise up. You must combine desire with discipline and big dreams with painstaking effort. That's the essence of Basementality. The basement was not only the place where Bai was born, it was the inspiration for seven-plus years of blood, sweat, tears, and joy. It was the foundation for how I found my edge and became the black sheep of the beverage business.

Today, as I write this, our country again faces economic uncertainty in the wake of the global coronavirus pandemic. I can understand why anyone would think it's not the right time to start a new business or chase their dreams in some way, especially because that's what I'm doing right now. Just like I did with Bai during the Great Recession, I've started a new journey at what might seem like a terrible time. My new venture, Crook & Marker, is an organic alcohol brand that I believe can have as much of a disruptive impact on the alcohol business as Bai did in the non-alcohol space—if not more. Sure, after the success I enjoyed with Bai, I could have rested on my laurels. But my Basementality wouldn't allow it.

In the months after I was fired from Bai, I would stare at that ceramic black sheep in my office and think about why Chad chose to give it to me. I didn't revel in being considered a black sheep just because I liked to break the rules. It was because I was driven to right the wrongs of the giant soda companies that were filling our store shelves and refrigerators with sugar. After my time with Bai, I saw the same thing happening in the alcohol space, where "better for you" brands loaded with sugar and calories are allowed to hide their ingredients from consumers. I saw another war begging to be waged. As I wondered if I had the motivation and energy to jump back into a new fight, that sheep staring back at me responded with a resounding "hell yes!" And now I'm back in the basement again.

I believe that the true black sheep among us have the ability to find their edge even when the challenges may seem insurmountable. I wanted to share my experiences and reflections in this book to help others on their own quests. This is a story about bloody knuckles, sacrifices, and a two-decade roller-coaster ride in business. It's a love story about my journey with a special company and an iconic brand that I was fortunate to build alongside people who cared deeply about trying to make a difference in the world in their own way, many of whom you will hear from in this book.

At the end of each chapter, I share one of my Basementalities, the lessons from my fights to get out of the basement and find success. I hope each of these Basementalities can inform and empower you along the steps of your own journey—and that, as a collection, they can help guide you to heed your instincts, fight for your beliefs, pursue your dreams, and ultimately find your own edge.

CHAPTER 1
AM I READY FOR THIS?

"You're ready to sign."

On a Sunday afternoon in November 2016, I was sitting at my home in Princeton, New Jersey, half-heartedly flipping through TV channels and talking with my kids as my wife, Danna, began preparations to host fifteen people for Thanksgiving four days later. But my mind was fifty-five miles north of Princeton, wondering how the negotiations were going.

My phone rang, snapping me to attention. On the line was Ari Soroken, the chief financial officer of Bai Brands, the company whose growth had consumed my life for the past seven years.

"It's time for you to come in," Ari said. "We have a few things left to finalize, but we're getting really close." Then he said the words that would not stop ringing in my ears for the next two hours. "You're ready to sign."

My stomach tightened as I hung up the phone. I rose from my seat and told the kids that I needed to leave to take care of some business. I hugged my son Jack, who was already taller than me at age fifteen, and I thought about how the company I was preparing to sell was such a huge part of his young life. I kissed my daughter Shayna, who, at eleven years old, really didn't know life without Bai in our family.

The kids followed me into the kitchen as I gave Danna a kiss goodbye. No one understood what was going through my mind as well as she did. Danna knew what Bai meant to me. We spent countless late nights together dreaming on our couch about this business. She sacrificed our time together as I traveled across the country week after week for years, fighting to get our brand on store shelves. And Danna knew why I was about to sell Bai.

I didn't say much to the three of them as I left to deal with one of the most important moments of my life.

"I'll be back later this evening," I said as I grabbed my keys. "And I should have some good news."

I hopped into my car to drive to our lawyers' offices in Times Square in Manhattan. As I maneuvered through Princeton, where the last vestiges of autumn clung to the trees lining the streets, my mind began to race through memories of launching Bai in our postcard-pretty hometown. Trying to clear my head, I flicked on the car radio. As a long-suffering New York Jets fan, I can typically find a few hours of frustrating distraction by tuning into football on Sundays in the fall. But the Jets (with their 3–7 record) had a bye that week. I put on some music, but it was really just background noise. Heading north past the strip malls on Route 1 and the industrial panoramas of the New Jersey Turnpike toward the Lincoln Tunnel, all I heard was Ari's voice echoing in my head.

"You're ready to sign."

***

When I started working with Ari in early 2010, Bai was a seedling of an idea just starting to come to life. After nearly twenty years in the coffee industry, I had come to learn about the coffeefruit—the ruby-colored flesh that surrounds the coffee bean, which is typically discarded during the harvesting process as farmers collect and sell their beans. The coffeefruit is high in antioxidants, and in countries like Indonesia, farmers would chew on the fruit because it was known locally as a natural, healthful source of energy. But no one had yet innovated a widespread commercial use for the coffeefruit, so mounds of the discarded fruit were left to rot in fields.

By the time I learned about the coffeefruit in 2009, my years in business had taught me that losses were just as frequent (if not more frequent) as wins. With Danna's encouragement, I wanted to try creating a bottled beverage for the first time to find a new path to a win. I knew it would be risky, but I wondered if the coffeefruit would work as a key ingredient in a new type of beverage.

That question wound up changing the course not only of my life, but the lives of hundreds of people who would become a part of the Bai journey.

The functional beverage category was thriving—particularly in the wake of Vitaminwater's eye-popping $4.1 billion sale to Coca-Cola in 2007—as Americans became more health-conscious and were increasingly drawn to drinks that claimed to offer some form of lifestyle benefit. I thought the antioxidant-rich coffeefruit would be my ideal launching pad into this market. First, I needed to tackle the most important elements of starting any new beverage business: to make a drink that tasted good and looked good. So I spent my days in the basement of our town house developing this new product idea, pitching different concepts to family and friends for feedback and working with two talented guys, flavor scientist Paul Sapan and designer Chad Portas, to bring the drink's flavor and brand to life.

In the evenings, I hunkered down with Danna, Jack, and Shayna on the brown chenille couch in our living room, where we would dream together—coming up with potential names and flavor combinations, imagining the possibilities of creating a successful new brand. Ultimately, we agreed to call it Bai, which is Mandarin for "pure." Those moments of dreaming alongside my loved ones were precious—and fortunately, there were many more in store.

I thought back to that basement and that brown couch as I crawled through bumper-to-bumper Midtown Manhattan traffic (even on a Sunday) en route to meet Ari and our legal team at our law firm's offices. We had come so damn far.

I officially launched Bai in August 2009, with a sales force of my stepfather, Ray, and myself. Ray sold Bai in the Princeton area, and I tackled New York City. By November 2016, we had roughly four hundred employees across the country, and Bai was the fastest-growing brand in the beverage industry, with an annual revenue approaching $250 million. But along the way, Bai developed something that was much more important to me than triple-digit sales growth — we found our fight.

I've never been a huge proponent of focus groups, pretesting, and overthinking product launches, as any of my often-frustrated marketing colleagues would surely tell you. I believe if you have a good idea for a product, you get it in people's hands as quickly as possible, see how it performs, and either double down or regroup, depending on the reaction. When we first started selling Bai to delis and markets in Princeton and New York City, we would set up a card table outside a retail location and ask entering customers to give it a try. And we quickly noticed people turning the bottle around to examine the label. They weren't as interested in our messages about the coffeefruit and antioxidants as they were in what else was in the bottle — namely, sugar and calories. We originally made Bai with organic evaporated cane juice, and the beverage contained about seventy calories per serving. So when we developed a five-calorie version without artificial sweeteners to respond to what people told us they wanted, Bai took off! We had stumbled onto what I called the solution to the "diet dilemma." And Bai's true purpose took shape.

I looked across the beverage landscape and saw an industry dominated by giant soda companies that sold billions of dollars of high-sugar, high-calorie drinks and diet beverages filled with artificial sweeteners that consumers were starting to reject. As Bai started to enjoy greater demand

and I sought ways to get it in more people's hands, I learned that those same soda companies dominated the beverage distribution game. They control the routes into retail stores big and small, into pizza joints, sports arenas, schools, airports, and everywhere else someone might be looking for a beverage. These two realities infuriated me.

I was appalled by how many beverage brands, even those purported to be good for you, were filled with sugar or artificial sweeteners—and yet there was a graveyard of good brands that couldn't figure out how to navigate through distribution. As a lifelong entrepreneur who doesn't like being told I can't do something, I was frustrated by the control that the Big Three—Coca-Cola, PepsiCo, and Dr Pepper Snapple Group—held over my ability to deliver Bai to a bigger audience. Bai's mission crystallized: to fight against the giants of the beverage industry, to take down Big Sugar, and to give people better choices to quench their thirst.

Yet there I was on that Sunday afternoon, ready to sign my baby away to one of the Big Three.

When I walked into our lawyers' offices, I found Ari and our legal team entrenched in the final stages of negotiations with Dr Pepper on a deal to acquire Bai for $1.7 billion. I didn't realize when I arrived that another twenty hours of drama would ensue before the deal was finalized and that I actually wouldn't make it back home to Princeton that night. When the time finally came for me to sign that contract, it was the most bittersweet moment of my life.

"Am I ready for this?" I thought.

I can imagine you thinking right now, "Wait a minute!" Here I just told you that I was driven by our fight against the giants of the beverage industry, and now I'm about to sign a deal that would hand over control of Bai—my vision, my baby—to one of them?

Well, that's all true. As I sat at that conference room table with pen in hand, I knew signing that paper would make me a rich man after twenty-plus years of ups and downs in business. And I knew that this deal would enrich lots of others who had played key roles along Bai's amazing journey with me, including dedicated employees, family members, friends, and investors who had put their trust in me. I was thrilled to be able to reward those people for their faith and hard work. But I didn't feel excited at that moment. Quite the opposite, actually. I was sad.

All of the memories came rushing back—vivid scenes of dreaming and working and building Bai alongside so many people I loved. I knew the mission that got me out of bed every day, energized to get to work—our fight to slay the dragons of the soda business—would never be the same.

I was ready to sign, but I wasn't happy about it.

If that fight meant so much to me, why did I make this deal? Cynics would call me a sellout. But I was forced to face reality: I had to sell Bai to keep the brand alive. We had done all we could do on our own. The beverage industry has no barriers to entry—anyone with an idea can jump in and try to do what we did with Bai. Thousands of brands have been launched by entrepreneurs who started in basements just like I did. But there are enormous barriers to scaling up because the Big Three control the routes to making your brand a national household name. Ultimately, you have to be on their team to win big in this game.

On one hand, I agreed to sell Bai to Dr Pepper because I was faced with the harsh truth of the business. On the other hand, I've always been a black sheep, determined to fight against conventional wisdom and do things my own way. So in my mind, I wasn't simply handing over control of my dreams to Dr Pepper—I was creating a new reality. I thought I was joining hands with a partner who would travel alongside me toward that envisioned future. In fact, in announcing the deal to the Bai team, I didn't call it a sale—I called it an adoption. I truly felt that I would work hand-in-hand with Larry Young to not only take Bai to unprecedented heights but to change the model for what it meant to be a huge player in this industry.

Nearly twenty-five years of fighting and dreaming had led me to this moment. As one of the lawyers slid the agreement in front of me, I gazed down at the blank signature line on that lifeless sheet of paper and took a breath so deep that I shook when I exhaled. I never thought a pen could feel so heavy in my hand.

BASEMENTALITY

MAKE THE JUMP

Your hard work will lead you to a moment at the edge, where you have to jump. Delay and you miss the opportunity. But as the edge beckons, a voice echoes in your head, "Really? Are you sure?" A true black sheep will shake off the doubts and make the jump. But the jump itself isn't the victory. It's what happens after the jump—minutes, days, months, even years later. That's the real edge.

CHAPTER 2
WINDOWS

"Somewhere, my husband is out there."

That's what my wife, Danna, used to say as a child, as she stared out her window. "What do you think he's doing right now?" Danna would ask Jill, her older sister.

Jill never had an answer for that question, but Danna always asked anyway. Like me, from an early age, Danna constantly looked toward the horizon, wondering what the future had in store for her. Little did Danna know as a young child, that just forty miles away, someone else was looking out a different window. She didn't know that person would be her husband and that, once we connected, we would be each other's partner and guide as we chased the future that those two kids saw, however faintly, off in the distance through their windows.

I spent a lot of time looking out a window at my home in Staten Island, and the view of my future seemed to change frequently because I had lots of different ideas for what I wanted to be when I grew up. When I was very young, I imagined becoming an astronaut and exploring the universe. As I got a bit older, I fantasized about playing for my favorite baseball team, the New York Mets, patrolling the outfield at Shea Stadium in blue and orange pinstripes as planes flew deafeningly to and from LaGuardia Airport. By the time I was in high school, I realized I wasn't going to play in the big leagues, and I started to become interested in the idea of entrepreneurship. All three of my parents, as you will see, had to do with that.

***

My parents, Ken and Pat, were both born and raised in Brooklyn, where I was also born in 1970. Six years before I was born, the Verrazzano-Narrows Bridge's opening launched an exodus of Brooklynites to Staten Island in search of an affordable suburban life. So in 1972, when I was one-and-a-half and my sister, Candice, was three, our parents followed suit. They scraped together a down payment on a $57,000 three-bedroom ranch house with a one-bedroom apartment, which they rented out to help cover the mortgage.

We moved into a brand-new development in Bulls Head, a neighborhood in the west-central part of the island. Our house was on Berglund Avenue, an L-shaped street with ten houses full of young working-class families. A new elementary school, PS 60, was built just a few blocks away. Candice started kindergarten when the school opened, and I followed a year later. My mother and sister look back at that time and place as an idyllic suburban setting, with kids playing ball in the street and friends piling into our house to eat and hang out in the basement. I can't dispute their description, but at the same time, I've never felt any lasting, warm connection to the neighborhood where I grew up. I had good friends and plenty of good times, but by the time I was in high school, I yearned to get out and explore the world beyond Staten Island. For as long as I can remember, I've felt an intense pull to move forward—even when I didn't know exactly where I wanted to go. That feeling intensified as a teenager and has stayed with me throughout my life in business as I've chased dream after dream.

When I was six years old, my parents divorced. It really wasn't a surprise when they split up because I heard them fighting all the time. In fact, I barely reacted. The day my father, Ken, moved out of the house, I was watching my favorite show, *Batman*, and he came walking down the steps into our sunken living room to tell me he was leaving.

I simply said, "Okay, see you later," and went right back to watching the Caped Crusader fight the Joker. I didn't even look out the window to watch him go and think about what it meant for my future. The fact that my father was moving out just didn't sink in as a huge deal at the time, even though it had an indelible impact on my life.

My mother had started dabbling in real estate while she was married to Ken, working weekends to supplement his income and taking care of Candice and me during the week. After their divorce, she went to work full time. The housing market on Staten Island was still surging in the 1980s, and my mother found that selling new construction was a perfect outlet for her passion and work ethic. She loved helping families find their ideal home—not just a house, but a true home in a community where they could live for years. She was tireless, working days, nights, and weekends not only because she needed to make ends meet but because she loved what she did. I learned so much from her example. Although she never phrased it this way, she taught me that there is no substitute for hard work and that you must pursue what you love. Those lessons were windows into my future. They would become defining principles for me and others as I imparted them to everyone who traveled alongside me in my career. (Later, when Bai started to take off, the lessons I learned from my mother inspired the core values that we formally adopted to guide our company.)

Even though I was proud of my mother, I wasn't happy about how much she worked. I was definitely a mama's boy as a kid, and I worried when she was out late showing houses and meeting with clients or builders. Many nights, I would sit on the ledge of the bay window in our living room, looking out onto the street and waiting for her to come home. When I saw the headlights of her car coming down the street, I would run back down the hall and jump into my bed, pretending to be asleep but waiting for her goodnight kiss. She would come into my room, plant a kiss on my cheek, and the aroma of her late-night cup of coffee would fill the air for just a moment. That distinct aroma reassured and comforted me. I felt safer when she was home—for myself and for her. And that memory of her tender goodnight kiss sparked my own love of coffee (which, as you will see, led me to get into that business after college).

Pat Schlaefer (mother):

Ben had certain traits as a young kid and a teenager that carried over later in life as he became an entrepreneur. He was artistic—he loved to draw the characters from the cartoons on TV and in the newspaper. That's the creative side he got from Ken. He also liked to solve problems, and he was always a worker. In kindergarten, he started a pencil club for kids who didn't have their own—he would give them out and collect them at the end of the day. It wasn't a business per se—there was no charge for the pencils—but he saw an opportunity to fill a void in a meaningful way, which is something he's tried to do with all of his businesses. Growing up, he was friends with different types of people from different groups who confided in him and wanted to be close to him. It makes me think of all the people Ben brought into Bai without formal interviews or perfect credentials—people who wound up making big contributions to the company and who got their start because there was just something he saw in them. He loved being around people who wanted to make a difference and wanted to have fun, and so many people worked so hard for him because they wanted the same thing.

***

Here's where I went from one dad to two. I refer to them both as my father because Ray, my stepfather, shouldered the commitment and responsibility of raising me and my sister in a way that Ken never did. So for the sake of clarity, I'll refer to them both by their first names in this book.

A couple of years after my parents split, my mother met Ray, a Staten Island native who was working as a technician for the Con Edison power company. They married in 1980, and he moved in to our house on Berglund Avenue.

Ken remarried and had a daughter with his second wife, eventually returning to Brooklyn. Candice and I started spending weekends with Ken, who was a walking contradiction. He was a guy who acted like a hermit most of the time but was also a great dancer who moonlighted as a bouncer at a popular disco in Brooklyn, called Gazebo, where he met his second wife.

Immediately after our parents' divorce, Ken rented a small garden apartment on Staten Island, where he always made us the one dish he had perfected: minute pepper steak. His apartment was all black—walls, sheets, curtains, everything. He lived like a vampire. It was definitely not a welcoming place for kids.

Once, when Candice and I were still in elementary school, Ken took us to spend a weekend in Upstate New York, where we stayed in a motel with a big pool in front. That trip is one of the most endearing memories I carry of him, though I can still vividly remember how uncomfortable he was in the pool, swimming with his shirt on. Ken was a big guy, standing six feet three inches tall and weighing more than three hundred pounds. He usually dressed in all black (like his apartment), trying to make his hulking frame look a little slimmer. To me, he always seemed incredibly unhappy in his own skin. Unfortunately for my sister and me, his insecurities made him unpredictable—sometimes quiet and inattentive, sometimes explosively tempered and verbally abusive. He would scream at us one minute, then feel remorseful the next minute and go off to cry and stare into space. As I said, a walking contradiction.

After Ken remarried and moved back to Brooklyn, our weekends with him turned into weekends with his mother, Millie. Our grandmother was a wonderful woman who lived in Trump Village, a seven-building complex in Coney Island built in the 1960s by Donald Trump's father, Fred. On Friday evenings, Ken would pick us up on Staten Island and drive back over the Verrazzano and drop us off with his mother, then shoot up Ocean

Parkway to be with his new wife and daughter. We didn't have anything to do with his new family. Instead, Candice and I had great fun with our sweet and loving grandmother.

Millie lived in a corner apartment on the sixteenth floor, where you could get a great view of Brighton Beach—that is, if you could make it up there without the elevator breaking down. On Saturday mornings, we would take her little fold-up shopping cart and walk to get groceries at the Waldbaum's supermarket, where the local yentas would sit outside and talk for hours. Everyone gathered in the courtyard in Millie's apartment complex, where the kids would play and the adults would chat. Most of the residents of Trump Village were Jewish, and several of the older people were Holocaust survivors. They would often give Candice and me a few dollars and have us run to the market for them when they needed bread, cold cuts, or pickles. A few times, Millie took us into Manhattan to see the Twin Towers, and she always gave us the freedom to walk down to the Coney Island boardwalk to play and hang out. We adored our weekends with her.

While Candice and I were in Coney Island, Ken might come by to see us for an hour or two on Saturday, but usually, we didn't see him again until Sunday evening, when he would pick us up and take us back to Staten Island to our mom. And you know what? For all of Ken's instability and dysfunction, I would still come home on Sunday night crying because I wanted to be with him. Not because I didn't want to be home with my mother but because I simply wanted my father around. Now that I have kids of my own, I have a better understanding of a father's impact on his children and the work it takes to care for them. That's why I look at Ray—who embraced Candice and me as his own and gave us unconditional love and support—as more of a role model than Ken in terms of fatherhood.

This is not to say that Ken didn't try to support us in his own way. In fact, Candice and I both worked in his office early in our careers. But his volatility created a toxic environment. Ken's company, Silverado, specialized in creating retail displays, posters, and other point-of-purchase materials

With my sister, Candice, my sidekick in childhood and later at Bai (1974)

for premium liquor brands such as Seagram's, Tanqueray, Johnnie Walker, and Rémy Martin. He started his business at home before moving into an office on Staten Island and later in the Flatiron District of Manhattan, on East Twenty-Second Street between Broadway and Park Avenue. Ken was a talented creative artist who was well regarded in his industry, winning a bunch of Point of Purchase Advertising International (known as POPAI) awards. But when it came to running a business, he was a disaster.

When I look back at my father's career, I can see that we shared the ability to envision an idea, obsess over it, and bring it to life. Ken thought outside the box, but he was not a true black sheep because he wouldn't do the work necessary to find his edge—and that's the key difference between us. To succeed in business, you have to surround yourself with a team of people who are all aligned and focused on what you're trying to achieve. Ken failed miserably there. His office was a playground of half-baked ideas, some of which he could monetize enough to keep his small operation afloat. The first time I saw the TV show *Hoarders*, I immediately thought of his office. He had a lot of great ideas, but he mainly created things with no strategy or goals in mind.

Here's a perfect example: in the mid-1990s, he spent countless hours working on something he called a Millie Lock (named after his mother), designed to keep kids from opening a liquor bottle. He was inspired by the idea and agonized over getting the device made to his exacting specifications. Then that was it—no business plan, rollout strategy, or marketing approach. At the time, Ken had moved from the Flatiron District into a dingy basement office below a steakhouse under the shadow of the Brooklyn Bridge in Lower Manhattan. Whereas for me, the basement became the place where I would take my biggest dreams and devise plans to turn them into reality, for Ken, the basement was a place to hide. He spent countless hours in his basement office devising the Millie Lock, only for it to become just another addition to the piles of his dusty relics. You can find lots of these devices for sale nowadays, but none of them are called the Millie Lock because others ran with his great idea and did the critical strategic work to bring their versions to market.

Candice Amato (sister):

In the early 1990s, my dad asked me to come work for him. His company was in the coolest area of the city, and I loved walking around Manhattan with him to visit clients. He was a wild child—definitely a character. He looked like Jerry Garcia and Kenny Rogers all rolled into one. And when we went to visit his clients, the top-shelf liquor companies, everybody knew who he was.

I was a jack-of-all-trades for him, trying to help keep his office running while I learned about the industry and how to deal with clients and vendors. Sometimes he would employ a full-time assistant or secretary, but for the most part, he was a one-man show. His office was crazy. On any given day, it might have been filled with freelancers and vendors working on different projects, models in bikinis walking around the office for casting calls for clients like Blue Nun or Galliano, or other women or friends hanging around for God-knows-what reasons.

If my father had a specific assignment to do for a client, he got it done. Left to his own devices, he spent his time coming up with all kinds of creative ideas—but he was terrible with follow-through. He was a tinkerer, not a businessman. He did all of his work in pencil and marker on sketch pads or the backs of napkins. When the industry moved to computer-aided design, he refused to conform.

Working there was a great learning experience—I wouldn't trade it for anything in the world. But it was hard. He had difficult relationships with everyone, and we fought a lot. And he kept secrets. I worked there for three years and had to scramble down the fire escape like Spider-Girl every time his wife would come into the office because she never knew that I worked there. He said she wouldn't have liked me working in his office, so he just never told her.

But Ben does have to thank that crazy man because the creative blood that runs through his veins comes from our father.

It's certainly true that I inherited a creative side from Ken (as did Candice, whose ingenuity I saw firsthand when she came to work with me at Bai). But I see myself more as a creator who is inspired to build ideas into something concrete. With my Basementality, I've relied on my vision to see what is lacking or missing entirely in the marketplace, and then I've fought to turn concepts into realities to fulfill people's needs and desires.

It's clear to me that my mother, much more than Ken, is the source of the traits that helped me advance in business. In her work in real estate (and later, working for Bai), she had an innate ability to communicate and inspire people, to connect her business with people's emotions, and to bring them happiness and satisfaction. She treated her career like a journey, constantly growing each step of the way. And she was a hard, hard worker.

My mother, Pat, has always been my role model (2017)

Ken, on the other hand, spent a lot of time at work—often coming into the office around noon and staying until midnight or later—but I wouldn't call him a hard worker in the same sense as my mother. To me, he was this kooky "entrepreneurial" guy who didn't seem to care about sustaining a functional business. He just wanted to create stuff. I think that's irresponsible. It's a waste of people's time and money if you don't have a plan and if you aren't prepared for the fights that will inevitably ensue in business. Watching how Ken conducted himself in business has motivated me to go further with my own ideas. I'd rather have fewer ideas and take them further along, even if they die.

As much as Ken frustrated and disappointed me, I know he was a good man at heart. Though I mostly saw his unpredictable and emotionally troubled side, sometimes a different Ken would appear, seemingly at random. After I went off to college at Boston University, my mom and Ray moved to Laguna Niguel, California. One summer while I was home from college, I was living with them and working in a retail shop when Ken called me out of the blue, saying he was going to fly out to see me that day. No real explanation, no checking in ahead of time to make sure I'd be around—he was just doing it. Typical impulsive Ken behavior. Not knowing what to expect but feeling happy that he wanted to fly across the country just to see me, I drove to the airport in Los Angeles to pick him up.

We decided to head over to Venice Beach to take a stroll on the boardwalk. It was a normal Southern California summer day—ninety-plus degrees with sunny skies. And there was Ken clad in black, as usual, with long sleeves and long pants, shuffling along as we passed the throngs of bodybuilders, surfers, and women in bikinis. We came upon a circle of people gathered around a guy who was blaring music from his boom box and doing a funny dance routine. The dancer began scanning the crowd to find someone to join him in the middle of the circle to make everyone laugh. I knew instantly he would zero in on the big, sweaty, bushy-haired New Yorker who was dressed like Johnny Cash and looked like he was about to pass out from the heat. I was right. As the guy pointed to Ken and invited him into the circle, I cringed. I grabbed Ken's hand to lead him away from the crowd, but to my surprise, he let go.

He looked at me, tipped his Elvis-style blue sunglasses down his nose and winked. "This one's for you," he said. Then he joined the guy in the middle of the circle and showed off some of his best Brooklyn disco moves.

The crowd roared.

I couldn't tell if those onlookers were surprised and impressed by Ken's dancing skills or if they were laughing at him as I had initially feared they would. Ultimately, it didn't matter. In that moment, I didn't see the same guy who often lashed out at those closest to him because of his insecurities. Rather, I saw a good sport who was letting his guard down and having fun, even if it was at his own expense. That may seem like a small thing, but to me, it was one of the few times that Ken resembled a hero in my eyes. He was more relatable, more human—a father sacrificing his own ego to create a memorable moment for his son. Watching him out there doing his *Saturday Night Fever* routine brought a genuine smile to my face. It was so memorable that nearly thirty years later, I find myself telling the story of that day to my kids—the grandchildren he never got to know—when I talk to them about the importance of simple acts of kindness. Sadly, 99 percent of the time, Ken seemed too wrapped up in his own angst to focus on lifting up others, even the ones he loved. But I will always remember that day he flew three thousand miles just to visit me and share some laughs on the boardwalk in Venice Beach. I wish we'd had more days like that.

***

After college, Ken allowed me to use space in his office and gave me creative guidance when I went into business for myself. Although I certainly appreciated those efforts he made, by my mid-twenties, I was becoming more and more frustrated being around him. I simply couldn't stand the negative energy that surrounded him. The tipping point came one day in 1996, when he started screaming and insulting Candice at work, which unfortunately happened often. Candice, as usual, fought back. The office was in a small building, and I'm sure you could hear them yelling on all six floors.

Ken kept a Louisville Slugger amidst all the mess in his office, and fed up with hearing the way he was talking to my sister, I grabbed it. I just wanted to shut him up. My veins pulsated madly as I tightened my grip on the bat and stared at him. I didn't hate Ken—I never did and I don't now—but I was so disgusted, angry, and embarrassed in that moment. Holding that bat in my hand, I was looking into the window of my future

At that point, Danna and I had been dating for about a year, and it was getting serious. I could already see that she was the perfect partner for me. Danna was thoughtful, hardworking, and practical, but she also embraced the dreamer in me because she was a stargazer herself. I dreamed about having a different kind of life and being a different kind of man than Ken. I wanted to have a family that I could enjoy, to live in a warm, beautiful home and be successful in business. Ken was, in my eyes, so broken and so unhealthy—there was no way I was going to let Danna, and ultimately my kids, be dragged into his chaotic world. His problems started way before me, and they weren't going to change—so I had to be the one to make the change.

In that moment, I was so close to storming over and swinging that bat at him to make the noise stop. But I couldn't do it. Instead, I told him off, walked out, and vowed never to come back. While I still had occasional contact with him in the years following our last blowup, our relationship was effectively over from that day on. Fifteen years later, in 2011, Ken died at age sixty-five after years of poor health.

As I left his building and walked out onto East Twenty-Second Street the day of our blowup, I glanced back up at the narrow floor-to-ceiling window on the second floor that looked into his office. From the outside, it always looked like a jungle—with fake trees, dilapidated liquor-store displays, and other junk piled up. Ken was standing in front of the mess, quietly looking outside. I was all too familiar with that scene—after his many blowups with Candice or me or anyone else, he would stare out the window for what seemed like hours, sometimes crying, sometimes stone silent. I believed that he was trying to say he was sorry but just couldn't get the words out. At least that's what I wanted to believe.

Even with all of the dysfunction and melodrama that accompanied Ken, it was difficult for me to turn away from him. But I had to do it. I couldn't allow that lonely, dark figure in the window to block the view of my own future. I needed a fresh start so I could chase my dreams.

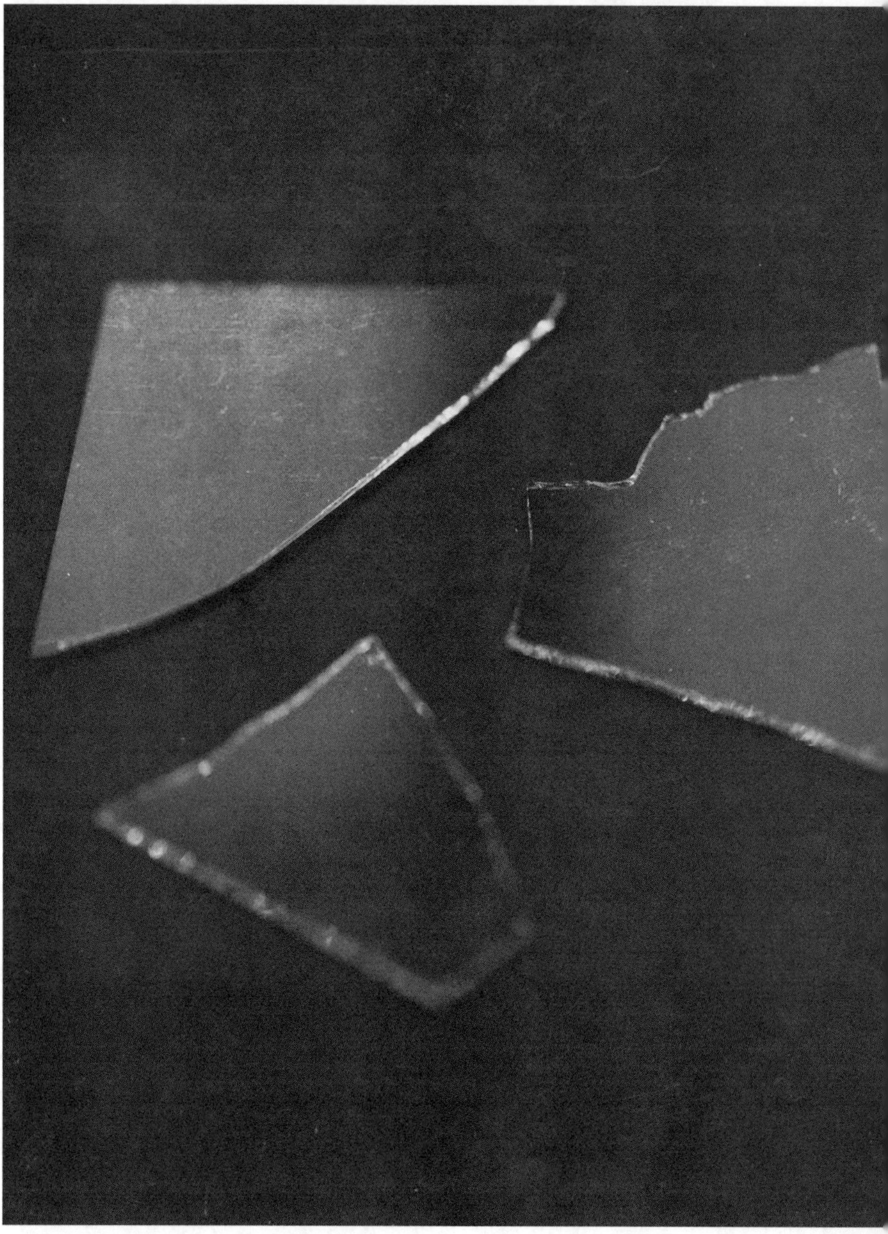

BASEMENTALITY

AGITATE YOURSELF

Agitation is good. It's about disturbing your thoughts and feelings. Sometimes that happens by simply staring out the window—seeing something or nothing. Your greatest moments of inspiration may come from dreaming and observing. Too many people are obsessed with being "busy." That's wasted energy. The edge is born out of instinctive looking, not frantic doing. In those times of contemplation, you'll develop your Basementality and your resolve to charge forward on your journey.

CHAPTER 3
TWO TICKETS FOR THE ROLLER COASTER

When Danna stared out the windows of her childhood home imagining life with her future husband, I'm sure she never pictured the roller-coaster ride that we would wind up taking together.

Danna and I actually met and became friends as students at Boston University, but we lost touch after I graduated and moved back to the New York area. We eventually ran into each other in Manhattan, where I was living at the time, and discovered we were living about ten blocks apart on the Upper East Side. I was so obsessed with trying to start my own business that I wasn't focused on looking for a girlfriend, but that changed when I reconnected with Danna.

One of the first times we ran into each other at a local gym, she mentioned that her VCR was broken, and I confidently offered to fix it for her. She accepted, and we settled on a time for me to come by her place later that night. I immediately called my stepfather, Ray, and had him give me a crash course over the phone on how to fix a VCR.

Danna Weiss (wife):
It was a dark evening in December of 1995. I ran into Ben as I was coming home from a day of holiday shopping with my sister, Jill. I don't know how he recognized me because I didn't recognize him at first.

We chatted for a while, and he said he would call me. Jill kept telling me how cute he was and checked in for a couple of days to see if he called. A week went by, and I didn't hear from him, so I figured, "Forget it."

For the New Year, I made a resolution to start going to the gym. I was on the treadmill the first day I went to work out, and who walks in? Ben. He apologized and told me that he had forgotten to mention that he was going to visit his parents in California, which is why he hadn't called. Jill was right—he was cute. So I accepted his apology.

We started meeting up at the gym on a regular basis and then began dating. I guess it was meant to be. I don't think I've been to the gym since.

Danna was—and still is—intelligent, beautiful, funny (with an infectious laugh), and exceptionally creative. After studying graphic design and photography at Boston University, she worked for Calvin Klein Jeans' marketing department in Manhattan as the director of visual imaging when we were dating and through the early years of our marriage. When I think of all the roles Danna plays—wife, mother to our kids, confidant, advisor, best friend—I know that I could not have found a better partner with whom to share my life. Danna has always encouraged me to pursue my ideas and given me honest feedback, positive and negative. She's supported me through every endeavor and stuck by me through times when it surely would have been more comforting to have a husband with a nine-to-five job, a 401(k), and a plan for our family's financial future instead of a starry-eyed entrepreneur who couldn't stomach the notion of working for someone else. Danna and I have fought and stressed and yelled—and we've comforted and laughed and dreamed. When I've failed, she's been there to pick me up and inspire me to start over. And when I've succeeded, I knew that there was no way in hell it could have happened without her. If you decide you're going to ride the proverbial roller coaster in life, my best advice is to latch on to and strap in with an amazing partner and seatmate.

Not long after Danna and I started dating, I moved into her 650-square-foot studio apartment. We wound up staying there for another decade—adding a dog, an infant son, and a handful of business ventures along the way. Those coffee-infused goodnight kisses from my mom truly sunk in because coffee became the launching point for the entrepreneurial ups and downs that Danna and I wound up riding out together.

***

Three years before I reconnected with Danna, I graduated from Boston University with a degree in finance in spring 1992, just as the US economy was starting to emerge from a recession. I knew that I eventually wanted to strike out on my own in business, but given that my folks had just shelled out tens of thousands of dollars for me to get a college degree, I initially thought I should play it safe, like my fellow business school graduates who were jumping into careers in the corporate sector. A few weeks after earning my diploma, I started my first adult gig as an entry-level analyst in the jumbo mortgage finance department of the Boston Safe Deposit & Trust Co.

That lasted about six months, and I never even learned how to properly tie a necktie (which I still don't know how to do). From day one, I couldn't get inspired by the idea of climbing the corporate ladder instead of the path to my own dream. Every day, I hunched over reams of home-loan data in my dimly lit cubicle, returning every night to my tiny studio apartment with that same yearning in the pit of my stomach that I felt as a kid on Staten Island. I was miserable. I needed out. So I gave my two weeks' notice to begin following my own path.

My ambitions at that time were modest. I wanted to open a coffee bar, which felt like a good way to gain experience running a business and to do something I would enjoy. This was right at the cusp of the specialty coffee boom in the United States, and the timing seemed ideal. While working at the bank, I had already started talking with potential investors about the idea of opening my own shop, and their enthusiasm encouraged me to go for it.

Knowing that I needed to learn more about the business before I made the leap, I drove up to Montreal at my mother's recommendation to check out some cafés on Rue St. Denis, a bustling street full of great restaurants, nightlife, art, and culture. In the first shop I visited in Montreal, I was captivated by the intoxicating aroma of fresh roasted beans and the welcoming, intimate ambience. Time had slowed as customers savored the premium taste of their coffee while reading, chatting, or falling deep into their thoughts.

To immerse myself in classic coffee culture, I set off for Europe on a backpacking trip. I spent a few weeks sleeping on trains and staying in youth hostels and cheap hotels while traveling through London, Paris, Amsterdam, Rome, Florence, Vienna, Munich, and Zurich. As in Montreal, the environment of the cafés in those European cities was so inspiring—such beautiful and comfortable surroundings, with customers of all ages taking their time to enjoy great coffee and pastries over relaxed conversation. These experiences were so different from my own growing up in New York and attending college in Boston, where I would rush in and out of a Dunkin' Donuts if I wanted to splurge on something a little better than the watery "cuppa joe" at my corner deli or diner. There were some higher-end cafés in the United States modeled after the European style, but they weren't as common then as they are today.

When I returned from Europe, I took a short trip out to Seattle, home of a fast-growing coffeehouse operator called Starbucks. At that time, Starbucks was a newly publicly traded company and had around two hundred locations in the West and Midwest. It was about a year away from opening its first New York City location. Visiting a Starbucks for the first time—seeing firsthand how it paid homage to the European coffee culture and how Americans were embracing the experience—made me fall even deeper in love with the idea of opening my own café. Now I was certain I had the drive, but I still needed hands-on knowledge.

I moved in with my parents, who had relocated back east from California to a town in central New Jersey called Matawan. I got a job at a bustling coffee shop called Café Newz nearby in New Brunswick, right off the campus of Rutgers University. A few months later, wanting to work in the city instead of the suburbs, I found a job at Eureka Joe's, a trendy café near Ken's Silverado office in the Flatiron section of Manhattan, where lots of budding internet moguls hung out. I did everything I could to learn how to run a coffee bar: handing out flyers, sweeping floors, waiting on customers, making drinks, opening and closing the shop. You name it and I did it.

By day, I was a busy barista. At night, I worked on developing my business plan. Starbucks's rapid growth proved that strong demand existed for premium coffee, but although I was gaining valuable experience working in the coffee business, I was not getting any closer to my goal of opening my own shop. The potential investors I had lined up a year earlier had lost interest or were no longer in a position to provide funding.

My optimism was waning, but I never stopped dreaming. And soon enough, I found my first successful business venture—not in a café but through the window of my ninety-minute daily bus ride from Matawan to Manhattan.

***

One morning, I was staring out the window of a New Jersey Transit bus as it rolled past the Amboy Multiplex Cinemas, a sprawling fourteen-screen movie theater on Route 9, about twenty minutes from my parents' house. As I took a sip from my cheap cup of coffee, a thought popped into my head. Hundreds of people came in and out of the multiplex every day, just like the hundreds of people I saw coming in and out of Eureka Joe's, but the theater didn't sell coffee. In fact, I couldn't think of any movie theater I'd seen that sold coffee. Why not? It seemed like a huge missed opportunity not to sell coffee to people who were already willing to pay a premium for popcorn, soda, and candy.

In an instant, I pivoted to a new idea. I knew nothing about the movie theater business, but I didn't let that stop me from fleshing out what I saw as an exciting opportunity to put my newfound knowledge about the coffee industry to work in a different way.

Experience is undeniably important in building a business venture, but I've learned over the years that tenacity, obsession, and flexibility (and luck, of course) are even more critical. You can always gain experience, but you can't succeed without resolve and intense focus to keep fighting past the inevitable challenges that arise in building a business. At the same time, you have to be willing to consider new ideas and be nimble if a better approach or opportunity presents itself. In this case, my coffee bar idea had to wait while I focused all my energy on this new concept of marrying coffee and movies.

I felt myself being pushed toward the idea by what I later came to call the "invisible hand," a steadying force that guides me toward a future that I can't always see clearly but that I know I have to chase. If you've studied business or economics, you may recognize the invisible hand as the term coined by Adam Smith (the pioneer of modern economics) to advocate for free markets—meaning that individuals who pursue their self-interests will ultimately benefit the economy and society more broadly. I didn't make the connection with Smith's philosophy when I started trying to describe the intangible force that I felt guiding me forward. But as a businessman, I certainly agree with his concept—and it dovetails with my own sense of what has helped push me forward when others might get stymied by doubts, uncertainties, or fear.

In my case, the invisible hand is my instincts. I have a feel and vision for the direction I want to go, and I've been consistent about following my instincts, even if, at the outset, I can't fully articulate where my end goal is. Of course, those instincts haven't always led to success, but that approach ultimately led me to founding Bai and building it into a remarkable brand. And I've been able to take the momentum gained from that invisible hand and use it to push others along the journey.

Guided by this invisible hand and my Basementality, I made my first attempt to disrupt a market by bringing coffee into movie theaters. Today, you can have dinner with beer or cocktails in many movie theaters, but in the early 1990s, the only available options were the same old popcorn, candy, and soda—and I wanted to change that. I envisioned every movie theater in the country selling premium coffee to create a new experience for customers. So, while still working shifts at Eureka Joe's, I incorporated a company called Brewed Awakening and started developing my concept. Coffee carts and kiosks had been popping up in office buildings around New York, and I thought the same idea would work well in theaters. This venture kicked off before I broke away from Ken, so he let me use space in his office and helped me build a prototype of my own coffee cart for theaters. I called it Café Cinema.

Because I was working a lot of late nights at Eureka Joe's, I moved into an extra room in my college buddy Darren Moskowitz's fifth-floor-walk-up apartment in midtown Manhattan. (This was before I reconnected with Danna.) Not only did Darren let me move in with him, he also agreed to pose as the model for my new Café Cinema brochures. After those were done, I hit the road.

The black sheep in me ignored the fact that I was simply a kid with an idea and little else. I pitched my idea to several big theater operators, including Regal Cinemas in Knoxville, Tennessee, United Artists in Denver, Colorado, and Cinemark in Dallas, Texas. I was thankful the executives at those big companies would take a meeting with a twenty-three-year-old guy who had nothing but a brochure and a concept. But everyone I talked to said essentially the same thing: "Great idea, kid, but what is Café Cinema? I have Coke, Hershey, and Mars in the waiting room. Good luck. See ya later."

Then I went to National Amusements, a Boston-based theater operator owned by the media magnate Sumner Redstone. The head of National Amusements' concessions business listened to my pitch and gave me my first ray of hope. "Great idea, kid," he started, just like the others, before adding, "but you need to go out and get a brand. Then we can talk."

That was the perfect idea. I just had no clue how to execute it. How do you get a big-name brand to sign on to an idea you came up with staring out a bus window?

As I came to learn over two decades, this moment was the most fun part of the entrepreneurial process—the period when you've shared your idea with a few people, it has gained a little bit of traction, and you get enough confidence to start running full speed ahead to turn it into a real business. It's the time when I've always felt the most alive in business, when the seed of an idea has started to grow, and the possibilities seem limitless.

While I continued to stew over National Amusements' advice to land a major brand, I was sitting in Ken's office and saw an unattended pile of mail spilling off a small side table. My neurotic neatness kicked in, so I started to straighten the stack of brochures and other papers. One of the mailings leapt out at me. It was an advertisement for Café Godiva, the chocolate company's new coffee line, with a glossy photo of the brand's signature golden logo embossed on a pair of coffee bags and a mug. Then I turned to my left and saw a display that Ken had recently created for Godiva Liquor. The light bulb went off. Godiva was Ken's client. And as an established chocolate brand looking to break in to the coffee market, it was a perfect fit for Café Cinema. Ken made a call on my behalf to his contact at Godiva, who hooked me up with a meeting with Michael Simon, a marketing executive who oversaw the company's product innovations.

That turned out to be one of the most important phone calls of my life. Michael became one of my most valued mentors, colleagues, and friends over the next two decades—eventually serving as Bai's chief marketing officer and playing a critical role in accelerating our national growth. In many ways, Michael and I are opposites. He's an Ivy League guy, with a bachelor's degree from Dartmouth, an MBA from the University of Chicago, and formal training in marketing. He is deliberate and data-driven, patient, and professorial—unlike me, he's very comfortable with focus groups and meticulous marketing planning processes. Michael has thrived and earned tremendous respect from his peers, working in large corporate environments like Ralston Purina, Godiva, and Panera Bread—places where I could never survive because I wouldn't be able to follow the rules. But he and I have always been in sync when we've worked together because he thinks like an entrepreneur even though he built his career in big companies. Michael gets excited by the prospect of building an idea into something big, and he supports dreamers who are scrappy and committed to putting in the work to back up their visions.

When Michael and I were introduced at a meeting in Ken's office, I was an upstart with no business track record asking seasoned executives of a multinational, multimillion-dollar company to take a chance on my idea. I had one shot to make a good first impression.

Michael came to the meeting with Gene Dunkin, then Godiva's vice president of sales and marketing, who later became the company's president. In preparation, I spent hours (with Ken's help) turning my Café Cinema cart into a professional-looking mini replica of a Godiva store. The cart had a cherrywood finish, two Café Godiva–branded thermoses, and a display of the company's new line of "impulse" chocolates, which were single-serve pieces in various flavors. Disruption wasn't the popular term then that it is today, but it was the theme I stressed in pitching my vision for a new experience at the movie theater. I emphasized that Godiva would benefit by getting customers to sample its new products outside of its retail stores, while moviegoers would surely be enticed by enjoying a good cup of coffee or a better snack than Goobers or Twizzlers. The movie concession business had tremendous untapped potential, and theater operators would welcome opportunities to build their revenue streams.

I really believed that this idea was a winner. Fortunately, Michael and Gene agreed. They gave me a three-year contract and an opportunity to build out the Café Cinema concept.

Michael Simon (former chief marketing officer of Bai):
I've dealt with a lot of budding entrepreneurs in my career, and I think what made Ben stand out from the start was his persistence and his enthusiasm. He has an ability to engage you in the potential of the idea. He can see what others can't. It's hard to describe, but it's palpable when you're talking with him—he can make the most mundane or the most complicated idea feel like it's the greatest thing since sliced bread. He has a unique ability to capture other people's imagination with his ideas and really sell the vision.

Just as important, he has the work ethic to do whatever it takes to make an idea succeed. One thing that's true for any entrepreneur is that you must roll up your sleeves and do a lot of the grunt work yourself, especially in the early stages of a company. And Ben has always been so relentlessly focused on the endgame that he would do whatever it would take to give his ideas the best chance of success.

Under my agreement with Godiva, I changed the displays from carts to countertop fixtures and tweaked the name to Godiva Theater Café. I was charged with selling the displays to theater operators, who would purchase the coffee and chocolates directly from Godiva. I reconnected with National Amusements, this time with a strong brand in tow—and now the company was interested in buying. To start, they authorized a test run of the Godiva Theater Café at one of the company's IMAX theaters on the Upper West Side of Manhattan. I set up my display with Café Godiva–branded coffee thermoses and cups and achieved my first proof of concept with strong sales at that theater. (I also came with an entourage. Danna and I had started dating by then, and she joined my parents and other family members and friends to help me set up and cheer on my big opening night. She was on board for the roller-coaster ride.)

In those early days, I noticed that Danna's father, Natie Muchnick, who was in the clothing business, always carried around a wad of cash. When I would go to an ATM, I'd punch the buttons to withdraw twenty dollars and hope I had enough in my account to cover it. When I dreamed about succeeding in business, I thought that if I could one day carry two hundred dollars in my pocket, folded into a small wad, like Natie did, then I would know that I had made it. I remember sitting at my little desk in our apartment and opening my first check from National Amusements—$2,400 for the sale of two Godiva Theater Café displays. I felt such satisfaction and pride knowing that check grew from the seed of an idea I had many months earlier while staring out a bus window on Route 9 in New Jersey. I was on my way.

Over the next three years, I sold Godiva Theater Café displays to roughly eighty National Amusements theaters in the Northeast and Mid-Atlantic regions. I was very hands on, installing two or three displays in each theater and training their staff members. Motivating a bunch of teenage part-timers to steer customers toward Godiva's premium items was definitely frustrating at times, but it was a key lesson for me to realize how important it is for an entrepreneur to find ways to inspire employees, to get them to believe in your idea, and to care as much as you do. Overall, Godiva Theater Café was moderately successful—it didn't sweep through the country as I had envisioned, but the concept was solid, and I proved that it had traction. To dramatically expand the business, however, would have required Godiva to make a bigger financial investment, which the company wasn't prepared to do at that time. So when our three-year contract expired, we amicably parted ways, and I walked away with Godiva's trust, a strong relationship with Michael, and my first experience growing an idea into an actual business.

Michael's willingness to take a chance on a young guy with an ambitious idea was absolutely the springboard for the rest of my career.

Every entrepreneur needs a massive dose of luck to succeed, and I will be forever grateful that a proven executive like Michael took a chance on me. After Godiva Theater Café ran its course, he and I stayed in frequent touch to brainstorm ideas. When Michael worked for Godiva's Pepperidge Farm bakery division, for example, we spent many weekend mornings meeting for breakfast at a diner in Rye, New York, about an hour north of the city, to talk about a project I was trying to launch called Dewey Bakem & Goode. This endeavor started as a line of cookies but eventually morphed into flavored pita chips. I was working with a partner who had a connection with a homeless shelter in downtown Manhattan, where we baked the pita chips in an industrial-sized oven. Dewey Bakem & Goode ultimately fizzled, but Michael was always there to patiently advise and encourage me as I tried to bring it to life. Thankfully, I would have more opportunities to partner with Michael in the years to come.

The three years I spent working on the Godiva Theater Café venture gave me a small financial cushion and the confidence that I could turn an idea into a real business. As my contract with Godiva wound down, I wanted to stay in the coffee industry. I pitched to Michael the concept of launching Café Godiva–branded specialty coffee shops to rival Starbucks. He liked the idea, and together, we pitched it to Godiva's senior management, but the company didn't want to invest in a retail concept. So I went back on my own and found the inspiration for my next venture in an unusual place—a firehouse.

***

If you've never been inside a firehouse, imagine a college fraternity house with packs of guys living and eating together. But instead of rowdy college dudes, these places are home to some of the world's bravest people. Firehouses are full of courage, camaraderie, and coffee. Lots of coffee.

Over the years, I've had the pleasure of spending some time in New York firehouses. During one visit after my time with Godiva Theater Café ended, a new business idea was born.

I've always admired firefighters' dedication to helping others. Although New York City's firefighters are paid for their work, nearly 70 percent of firefighters in the United States are volunteers. My idea was to sell high-quality coffee to residents of communities with volunteer fire departments, with part of the proceeds going to those departments. I took some firefighters to a roaster in Queens and came up with a blend of beans that they liked so we could say that our coffee was designed by firefighters for firefighters. I called it Five Alarm Brew.

I drew up a business plan and shared it with Danna, who loved the idea and agreed to road test it with me. We found out about a trade show for volunteer fire associations in Upstate New York, so we packed our Isuzu Trooper with cases of Five Alarm Brew and set up a small booth at the Nevele Grande Hotel, an aging, shag-carpeted hotel in the Catskill Mountains about two hours north of Manhattan. We tried to drum up interest for our new venture with Danna calling out "Fiiiiiiiive Alarm Brew! Coffee for firefighters!" Fire chiefs from a bunch of small towns, many of whom did double duty as mayors and officials of their communities, gave us their cards and welcomed us to come visit. Danna and I then spent months driving upstate to meet with the leaders of volunteer departments and their ladies' auxiliaries to explain our unique approach—we didn't want to sell Five Alarm Brew to their firehouses; we wanted to sell it through them.

Volunteer firefighters typically are well-known members of their communities and universally respected for their bravery, and we thought that would make them ideal ambassadors for our brand. We envisioned them selling Five Alarm Brew to their friends and neighbors, who would gladly buy a pound of freshly roasted coffee if that purchase made a much-needed contribution to their local volunteer firehouse at the same time.

Our motto was a takeoff of the classic Maxwell House slogan of "Good to the Last Drop"—our coffee was "Good Well Past the Last Drop." Firefighters loved the idea, and we left many of these meetings with dozens of attendees pledging to sell Five Alarm Brew. Each of these departments had their own history and tradition represented in colorful patches, and we set up a website where people could click on their local department's patch to make a purchase online. Danna and I had so much fun driving around and talking with kind, civic-minded people in suburbs and rural communities away from the clamor of New York City, getting them excited about our idea. Based on the early reception, we were convinced that Five Alarm Brew would take off and one day replace every can of Folgers and Maxwell House in every firehouse and home kitchen in America.

With Five Alarm Brew, we were chasing a big, audacious idea, running toward our edge. And as I did when I was trying to introduce coffee into movie theaters, I had to keep two perspectives in mind—the dream and the work—while building this new business. This has been a recurring part of my journey—the need to look up and out over the horizon to see what others can't, while also looking directly in front of me to manage the details of what had to get done to accomplish my goals.

In my mind, I had to view Five Alarm Brew through a set of bifocals. When I gazed through the top half of those lenses, I envisioned a future where Five Alarm Brew would be the best-known brand in the coffee industry and our business would support volunteer firefighters serving their communities across America. When I looked down through the bottom half of the lenses, I saw all the work needed to make that vision a reality. Hours, days, weeks, months, and years of tireless effort to keep all the facets of the business running: production, distribution, marketing, sales, finance. Tipping my vision downward kept me grounded and reminded me that the only way to achieve our ultimate goals was to put in the day-to-day work. At the same time, to find my inspiration, I could lift my eyes upward and see our dreams come into focus.

Unfortunately, there was one big problem with Five Alarm Brew that I didn't foresee: volunteer firefighters were not ideal salespeople. For all their genuine enthusiasm about our business, these were busy people who had full-time jobs and families on top of their volunteer duties. Designing our business model to rely upon on a sales force of volunteers with limited time was a mistake. The firefighters could not put in the work needed to grow the business, and they simply didn't generate enough revenue. Even as I think back on it now, I still believe Five Alarm Brew was a great concept that could have been profitable and benefited a lot of communities. But we failed in the execution.

This was our first low point on the roller coaster.

Danna Weiss (wife):

I've always loved the fact that Ben was a dreamer, that he wasn't one of the guys in a suit and tie taking the train to an office job every day. Of course, living with an entrepreneur has been nerve-wracking, but I love that he has the ability to stare off in the distance, imagine something, and bring you in so you can visualize it with him. And I was working before Jack was born, so we had my paycheck to rely on while Ben was trying to build his next big thing.

After Five Alarm Brew's demise, I needed a new direction. My desire to bring great coffee to the masses remained strong, so I sought to launch a distribution business to provide high-quality brewing equipment and coffee to restaurants and cafés. Using the Brewed Awakening name that I had incorporated years earlier, I began to establish relationships with equipment manufacturers, roasters, and potential retail customers. I initially wanted Brewed Awakening to focus on supplying higher-end establishments, but I wound up pursuing opportunities to supply the small twenty-four-hour delis (better known as bodegas) that dotted New York City's landscape. The bodegas enabled me to tap into a market that wasn't being served by

Starbucks and pricier specialty coffee outlets. I purchased push-button cappuccino machines that produced French vanilla and mocha flavors as well as hot chocolate, and I gave them to bodegas in exchange for selling them the powdered ingredients for those drinks.

Over the next four years, Brewed Awakening accumulated more than three hundred accounts across the five boroughs. But not long after I started the business, it dawned on me that I had made a critical misstep by focusing on the bodegas. I was making some money, but I was on call 24/7, and most of my customers were in dicey neighborhoods. After Jack was born, there were times when I would get a call to make a late-night delivery to a bodega in a rough neighborhood in the Bronx or Brooklyn, and I'd pile everyone in our car to drop off six cases of powdered cappuccino for $200. We needed the money, and I didn't want to sacrifice more time away from my family, so I'd bring them along without thinking about what a terrible idea it was.

For the first time since I worked at the bank, I didn't love what I was doing. Even though I had been frustrated trying to turn firefighters into a sales force with Five Alarm Brew, I loved that experience because I was going after a big idea. As the Brewed Awakening distribution business developed, I realized that I was just selling coffee. And, honestly, it wasn't even good coffee. I liked to fancy myself a coffee purist, and here I was selling powdered, watery junk to make a buck. I had no bifocals on—there was no grand vision in the distance. I was lost, blinded by the reality of a barely functioning business.

For the first time in business, I felt stuck. All I could see was the same thing everyone else saw.

***

While I was building the Brewed Awakening business, Danna and I married in 1998 on Long Island, where she was raised. Her mother, Jan, whom Danna adored (as did I and everyone in my family), had been battling breast cancer and passed away about a year and a half after we were married. I remember how happy it made Jan to see Danna in her beautiful wedding dress, and I'm so thankful that we were able to share that special day with her. Danna and I still miss Jan terribly, and I wish our kids would have had the opportunity to know her, as I know she would have been an amazing grandmother to Jack and Shayna.

Danna Weiss (wife):
My mother passed shortly after Ben and I were married. She was diagnosed with breast cancer at forty-six and she fought for eleven years. I still miss her every day. When she died, I realized that life is too short. Money doesn't matter if you don't have the people you love around you. I knew that Ben and I would make our life work if we loved each other, even if he didn't make it big in business.

My mother adored Ben. He called her Millie—a nickname for M.I.L., or mother-in-law. (It was also his grandmother's name.) One day, not long before she passed, I thought Ben had gone missing. I was calling him all day, and he never answered—even though he always had his little flip phone clipped onto his belt. It turned out he was at my mother's bedside at Mount Sinai Hospital talking with her. She knew she was dying, and she called Ben that day to ask if he would write her eulogy. He worked so hard to write the eulogy and capture her spirit. Then he stood up at her funeral and delivered it in front of two hundred people—I'll never forget it. At the end he wrote, "Jan taught me a story of maternal love and extraordinary courage. She taught me a way of walking through life, not with a sense of urgency but, rather, with an appreciation for living. She taught me that without courage, you cannot love, believe, forgive, or be charitable."

I was working out of our apartment, but it was barely big enough for the two of us and our new dog, a white Labrador that Danna's father named

With Danna and Candice, welcoming Brewster to the family (1997)

Brewster in homage to our coffee business. I needed to find a new office space. Years earlier, my mother bought a town house on Staten Island as a rental property investment. (I actually helped build the town houses in that development when I was a teenager working summer construction gigs.) Unfortunately, the neighborhood had gotten worse in the years since my mom bought the place, and her most recent renter—my sister, Candice—bolted after a small mouse infestation prompted her to move closer to her job in New Jersey. I swooped in, ready to accept a mouse or two as the cost of doing business and took over the space. Soon the three-hundred-square-foot living room was filled with a couple of desks, a few pallets of coffee, and my first employees: a driver, who delivered product to our customers, and an administrative assistant, who kept track of our orders and helped reconcile our books.

It didn't take long for us to outgrow the town house on Staten Island, so I started looking for more space and found a modest warehouse in a middle-class neighborhood of Queens called Glendale. The warehouse, which I used for my coffee distribution business, was attached to a small retail space—an ideal location to finally open the coffee bar I'd been dreaming of since I graduated from college several years earlier. This was the spark I needed so I could feel like I was building toward something other than just adding a few new accounts to the distribution business. Crafting the plans to start the coffee bar—and thinking back to the thrill of experiencing the coffee culture of Europe—reinvigorated me. Situated on Myrtle Avenue—the neighborhood's main drag—near a number of businesses and two nice parks, the new location seemed like the perfect spot to attract customers throughout the day. But to pull off this expansion of the business, I needed more manpower—and I knew just the guy.

At that time, Candice was working at a marketing agency in East Rutherford, New Jersey, near Giants Stadium, and she was dating her future husband, Nic Amato, who was the FedEx delivery man for her office. Nic is an affable, salt-of-the-earth guy who was raised by Italian immigrants. He became a part of our family well before he asked Candice to marry him. He also has a phenomenal work ethic, an analytical mind, and a magic set of hands that can fix anything you put in front of him. Nic had started working for FedEx in college and had advanced into the company's management track when I approached him with a crazy idea—how about leaving FedEx and opening up the coffee bar with me instead? It didn't matter that he had no experience. I knew that Nic was the type of person who would work his hardest to tackle any challenge. Plus, we still had to install and service all of the cappuccino machines that I placed in the bodegas, and Nic's skills were perfect for handling the ghosts that were always creeping up in those machines.

Nic Amato (brother-in-law):
Candice and I had just gotten engaged, and Ben asked me to consider leaving FedEx. He said, "I know you're in management there now, but I could really use the help." The stars were in his eyes. I couldn't help but get excited about being part of his plans. As a kid from Jersey, going to Queens every day was a bear. But I was young at the time, and after eight years at FedEx, I felt like it was time for me to move on and take a chance.

At our height, we had about ten people working in the coffee bar. Ben always loved the idea of making it a true café experience. We'd have different foods on the menu, with great music playing in the background. We started a jazz night once a week. It was an ideal setting. But the retail business is hard and expensive. We were open 6 a.m. to 6 p.m. Monday through Saturday, staying open until 10 p.m. or 11 p.m. on special late nights. We started hitting some troubles moneywise, so we tried opening on Sundays, stretching our hours, expanding our menu. We had so much fun, but at times, it was definitely a struggle.

Opening the coffee bar represented a realization of my dream but also a new reality. Keeping that shop afloat was difficult, and I was stretching myself thin between the café, the distribution business, and our newest addition, our baby boy, Jack. We did our best to fit our bustling life into the confines of our Manhattan studio. Ray and Nic had previously helped me build a wall in the alcove of our apartment to divide the room in half and create a bedroom for Danna and me. When Jack was born, we moved him into that room. Then we built another wall to create a new bedroom for the two of us, which included a bed that occupied most of the space, a dresser, and a closet jammed with clothes, a stroller, and a bouncy seat. Our living room had just enough room for a couch and a TV, and we squeezed a table for two into our eat-in kitchen. Anyone who's ever lived in New York can surely relate to feeling jammed like a pack of fucking sardines in your own home. Danna and I worked hard together to manage life with a business going through ups and downs and caring for a new baby. She spent countless hours with me at Brewed Awakening, both of us taking turns carrying Jack on our hip, in a carrier, or in a stroller, all the while, helping customers out front in the coffee bar or dealing with the distribution operation out of the warehouse space in the back.

Danna Weiss (wife):
  After Jack was born, I left my job at Calvin Klein to stay home with him. But I wound up driving with the baby out to Queens a lot, especially on weekends when the café was busier. Being in the retail business was definitely not my favorite experience. I remember one day when we were in the back office, and someone left the door to the coffee bar open. Brewster was with us, and he darted right into the kitchen, grabbed an entire roast beef off the counter, and started engulfing the thing. Ben had to wrestle this big slab of meat away from our hundred-pound dog. It sounds funny now, but at that time, it was a lot of money for us. And that was the last time Brewster came to the office with us.

  I loved the experience of opening my own coffee bar, but I also felt trapped by the long hours. Plus, it was losing money. It became clear that this shop was not going to be my launching pad to creating the next Starbucks. And at the same time, I had grown to resent the distribution business—I didn't have any vision or love for it anymore, and I was working seven days a week just to stay afloat. I needed a reason to dream and wear those bifocals again, so out of desperation, I turned to my previous brainchild: Five Alarm Brew.
  I rebranded our generic-looking cappuccino machines as Five Alarm Brew machines, with an image of a firefighter rescuing a child on the front. I

devised a new plan to partner with firefighters by splitting the cost of buying the machines and having them hit the streets to get new accounts in their neighborhoods. Unfortunately, my enthusiasm clouded my memory—the firefighters simply were not great salespeople. My second shot at Five Alarm Brew taught me a critical lesson. In any successful business, everyone involved has to be fully committed—as an entrepreneur and a leader, you have the responsibility to inspire others to care as much as you do. Relying on salespeople who couldn't devote their full attention to building the brand, no matter how good their intentions, was the wrong approach.

The failed resurrection of Five Alarm Brew was not the only painful experience I had to endure around this time.

**

Central Park was our family's favorite spot to unwind and dream. Danna and I often took Jack and Brewster into the park to play and sit on a big rock where we would imagine our family's future. I did some of my most intense thinking while running or walking through the park, as there's something about the feeling of moving forward, whether on foot or in a car, that stimulates my imagination. I frequently took Brewster with me, and that's how I met Sam Metzger.

Sam was a co-founder of Chipwich, an ice cream sandwich first sold from street carts in New York that became a sensation in the early 1980s and grew into a national brand. Sam and I bumped into each other one day as I was headed to the park with Brewster. We started chatting because we both had Labradors and lived in the same neighborhood, then we made the connection that we were both entrepreneurs. Sam was about thirty years older than me and had been through the peaks and valleys of the business world. We got together occasionally so I could mine some of his wisdom—we got along well because I think he saw a little bit of his younger self in me. When I told him about my idea to resurrect Five Alarm

Brew, Sam got very excited. He saw the same potential in the brand that I did and expressed interest in becoming a partner in Brewed Awakening. We made plans for him to come visit us in Queens the following Friday at the coffee bar.

This was a huge opportunity for me not only to get an infusion of capital from Sam but to benefit from his experience. I scheduled our meeting for the busiest time at the coffee shop to set the right tone. Nic and I both arrived early to ensure everything looked flawless in the coffee bar and in our warehouse. As wafts of fresh coffee passed over our growing line of customers, I realized we were low on milk, so I hopped in my car to pick up a couple of gallons at a market down the street.

On my way back, I drove over a bump as I pulled up to a red light a couple of blocks away from the coffee shop. Jack was about two years old then, and any time we drove over a bump when he was in the car, he would yell "Bumpsies!" with a huge smile on his face. I was excited about the upcoming meeting with Sam and in a good mood, so I called home and asked Danna to put Jack on the phone so I could tell him that I just went over a bump. I was yelling "Bumpsies! Bumpsies!" into my phone as the light turned green, and I proceeded through the intersection. Then I noticed the red and blue lights of a police car behind me.

"Oh shit!" I told Danna, "I'm going to get a ticket for being on the phone." I didn't have a hands-free speakerphone option in my car at the time, so I was holding the phone to my ear. I knew I was getting busted.

"I hope I know this guy," I thought as the cop approached my window.

We had lots of police officers come in to the coffee bar every day, but I didn't recognize this one. He confirmed that he pulled me over for using my phone. As he took my license and registration back to his car, I could see the line of customers out the door at Brewed Awakening down the street.

"Hurry up!" I screamed at him in my head as he sat in his cruiser looking over my information.

After what seemed like an hour, he walked back to my window. I expected him to hand me a ticket. Instead, I heard him say, "Get out of the car and put your hands on the vehicle."

He said I was under arrest for driving with a suspended license. I had absolutely no idea what he was talking about!

As he handcuffed me and put me into the back of his cruiser, the cop explained that it was because of my parking tickets. My stomach sank. I knew that our Brewed Awakening delivery vans, which were registered under my name, had racked up dozens of tickets, and I figured some of them must have slipped through the cracks.

He brought me to the local station, where the other cops—my regular customers—were surprised to see me and asked me what was going on. Luckily, after I was put in a holding cell, one of the officers slipped a cell phone through the bars so I could call Nic. I told Nic what happened and asked him to go pick up my car that was now parked up the street.

"The most important thing," I told Nic, "is to make Sam comfortable when he gets there. Let him know I'm just running a bit late."

I figured I would pay the tickets and be out of there in no time. But there was more bad news. The cops told me I would need to go through the whole booking process, including being fingerprinted and taken to the much larger Queens Detention Complex. New York City was still reeling from the effects of 9/11, and law enforcement was on high alert when dealing with any kind of crime.

"This can't be fucking happening," I thought.

Two of the cops I knew put me in the back of their car to take me downtown—I pleaded with them that I had the meeting of my life that morning and needed to get back to work. "There's no way you're making that meeting," one of them said. Taking pity on me, they pulled in to one of Glendale's many cemeteries, took my handcuffs off, handed me a cell phone, and gave me a chance to call Sam and reschedule. Wandering nervously through the tombstones, I called Sam more than an hour after we were supposed to meet. I made up a lame excuse that my friend was sick and asked if he wouldn't mind rescheduling.

"Nope," Sam said, clearly annoyed. "Sorry, that was your chance."

When I got back into the police car, I was a different person. I was angry. "You can book me now," I told the cops. "Send me to the electric chair for all I care."

They took me to the jail, where I was allowed to call Danna to explain the situation. She said she would find someone to get me out of there. Then the cops had me remove my shoelaces and belt, and they put me in a cell full of some badass-looking dudes who didn't seem at all fazed to be behind bars. And there I was, in my tucked-in polo shirt and khaki pants, looking like I was late for a round of golf instead of an arraignment.

A few minutes later, the door opened, and another dozen or so hardened guys piled into the cell after the cops made a sweep for illegal activity on Jamaica Avenue. That's when it really started to dawn on me that I was in jail. My anger drained. I sat with my head down and my heart pounding so hard it made my knees quiver. I tried not to look scared sitting next to these guys, who seemed so casual about being locked up. A couple of them tried to talk to me, but I said nothing and just stared at the floor. With my slicked hair and pressed clothes, I looked like Christian Bale's preppy murderer from *American Psycho*—these guys probably thought I had killed my wife over some insurance policy or stock holdings.

Hours passed as I sat there trying to hold myself together. If I didn't get to see a judge by 5 p.m., I would be locked up for the weekend. Finally, as the end-of-day deadline grew nearer, I was taken out of the main cell and met with an attorney, who told me to simply plead guilty to driving with a suspended license and pay a fine. I agreed.

When I walked into the courtroom, my parents were there, and I saw my mother crying. I must have looked like a murderer because I was so mad that I had to go through all of this because of some parking tickets.

"How do you plead?" the judge asked.

"Guilty, your honor," I said.

Then I paid a sixty-five-dollar fine, and my parents drove me home. Two jail cells, eight hours, one critical meeting lost—all for a sixty-five-dollar offense.

It turned out, in fact, that I had paid the parking tickets—but I hadn't paid the surcharges attached to them. I was managing the Brewed Awakening cash flow down to the penny, and my mentality was, "I'm out here hustling, trying to stay in business. I'll pay the tickets—but if the city wants to hit me with surcharges, they're going to have to wait for those." So I learned a hard lesson that the city expects every last penny on time.

I've often wondered how my path would have changed if that day had gone as originally planned. I still think that Five Alarm Brew was a good idea—perhaps with Sam's partnership and guidance, it would have become a big business. Would that have become the focus of my career? Does that mean Bai never would have happened? Would my whole life have turned out differently if I hadn't yelled "Bumpsies!" into the phone to my baby boy?

That day from hell became a turning point in my life. I needed to make a change. After years of trying to sustain Brewed Awakening, the business was in a financial hole that was only going to get bigger. Danna's father, Natie, had co-signed for a bank loan to help me get Brewed Awakening off the ground, and after years of struggling, I was able to pay it back in full. But toward the end of the company's run, I had to borrow $45,000 from my parents just to cover some pressing bills. When I talked with Natie about co-signing that initial loan, I was chasing a dream, and he was inspired to help kick-start my journey. But when I had to borrow that money from my parents, I was simply trying to plug my financial holes. At a time when they were scraping by themselves, they gave me that money even though I didn't know how I was going to pay them back. I deeply appreciated their sacrifice and hated that I had to ask them to make it.

The coffee bar had a decent base of regular customers but not enough to turn a profit. Shifting the distribution business to focus on the Five Alarm Brew brand and create partnerships with firefighters turned out to be a bust, especially after I lost my opportunity to partner with Sam. I received an unsolicited offer to buy the Brewed Awakening distribution routes, so I took it. The time had come to move on from this venture.

Nic, my loyal deputy at the Brewed Awakening café (2000)

Nic Amato (brother-in-law):
The bills became too hard to manage. The café relied on perishables, so when we had slow days, we wound up throwing away a lot of stuff at a loss. We also had a lot of bodega customers in downtown Manhattan

affected by 9/11 — some had to shut down; others were hurting. The writing was on the wall.

The day we decided to close down was probably one of the hardest days in Ben's life. He had grown that business for years and invested so much time that it felt kind of like the death of a child to him. It was tough for both of us. Candice and I had gotten married and bought a town house in New Jersey. Our son was a few days from being born. When we were in the delivery room, I remember thinking, "Surprise! Welcome to the world, Max — your dad doesn't have a job."

At the end of the last day, Ben and I were sitting at the bar. Everything was shut off. We had spent the day getting ready to auction off all the equipment to help cover some of the bills. So there we were, two guys who, a few years earlier, were going to take over the world, and now we were looking at each other thinking, "What now?" Ben didn't know what direction he was going to go. I said to him, "Listen, you don't need to work for a bank or another coffee business or anybody else. Do what you do best. You're a natural salesman and marketer. Bet on yourself. Go — be great."

Nic's encouragement meant the world to me and inspired me to keep following my own path. He's such a loyal, hardworking guy, and he put so much time and sweat into Brewed Awakening — I felt terrible that I had failed him. Nic walked away from a management career at FedEx and upended his own life to help me chase my dream. He was my most trusted ally, and I let him down. After Brewed Awakening, Nic bounced back and found a new job right away. And I told him that someday I would come back for him to bring him along on another journey.

Every dreamer like me needs people like Nic, the ones who will listen to your craziest ideas, see the fire in your eyes, and agree to run alongside you even when you're not entirely sure where you're going. It's all part of chasing your edge.

***

After we shut down the Brewed Awakening café, I came home to Danna that night, and we sat together, shedding some tears on our old brown couch. I told her that I was sorry the business hadn't worked out, but she wouldn't allow me to sink into a state of regret. In this moment when I felt like I had let her down, she simply encouraged me to get back up and take another swing. Danna has always been the biggest supporter of my dreams in business, so much so that she later talked me into trying out for *The Apprentice*, Donald Trump's business competition show on NBC that became a megahit in the mid-2000s. Danna thought I would be a perfect fit for the show, but after a full day of sitting around tables with dozens of other aspiring apprentices, I didn't make the cut—which, in retrospect, was a blessing. I had my own path to follow.

During the late stages of the Brewed Awakening business, Danna stopped working after Jack was born. We had taken the risk of giving up her paycheck because she wanted to stay home with our son. We were now living off a little bit of savings that I had tucked away, so I didn't have much time before I needed to start generating more income. Fortunately, a new idea came to me fairly quickly.

I went jogging routinely in Central Park to try to spark my creativity and come up with new concepts. On the way to the park, I always noticed the Godiva store near my apartment. In a way, it was like seeing a childhood sweetheart—I would instantly flash back to the good old days. I would think about my first venture working with Michael Simon, the Godiva Theater Café, and relive the excitement of getting that idea off the ground and turning it into a viable business. Michael always kept his door open for me to pitch new ideas, so as I brainstormed on the jogging paths, I often thought about ways to connect the Godiva brand to a fresh concept.

One particularly hot afternoon, I put Jack down for a nap and took my usual running route across Fifth Avenue into the east side of the park, passing the rock where Danna and I so often sat and daydreamed about our future. As I ran what seemed like my thousandth loop around the Central Park Reservoir, with sweat drenching my hair and clothes, it hit me. I thought about how nice it would be to have one of our Cold Brews, our most popular drink at the coffee bar in Queens. They were similar to Starbucks Frappuccinos but were more decadent because they were made with ice cream. Many of our customers told us that they passed by the nearby Starbucks and came to Brewed Awakening specifically for the Cold Brews. I began to imagine a new concoction similar to those Cold Brews but even colder—a frozen blended beverage made with Godiva chocolate.

I ran home as quickly as I could to flesh out the idea. I had learned from Michael that Godiva stores did the vast majority of their business from November to mid-February—the Christmas and Valentine's Day seasons—and it was an ongoing challenge for Godiva to find ways to draw retail customers during other times of the year. Earlier that week, I had noticed a new display of full-size chocolate bars in my neighborhood store's window, part of Godiva's efforts to expand its product line beyond its signature gift boxes and baskets. On a hot summer day like this one, a frozen drink could be the perfect innovation to lure customers into a Godiva store.

I called Blendtec, a company that made high-end blenders used by Starbucks, and was put in touch with a salesperson named Eric Kellems (who, like Michael and Nic, would become a fixture in my life from this point on). I told Eric about my idea, and he sent me a machine that would suit my needs. Then I got busy. I ordered a variety of flavored syrups and frappe powders, went to the Godiva store to load up on chocolate bars, and got to work mixing different concoctions in my kitchen.

Danna and some of her friends from our building served as my tasters and critics. After weeks of trial and error, I settled on three flavor combinations that seemed to have the most promise: White Chocolate Raspberry, Dark Chocolate Decadence, and Milk Chocolate Caramel. Then I called

Michael to tell him about my idea, and we made an appointment for me to come in to his office to deliver a formal pitch.

By this time, in 2003, my parents had moved to the Princeton area, and we often drove out to their house on weekends to get out of the city, give Jack and Brewster more room to run around, and do our laundry without needing a sack of quarters for the washer and dryer. On the Friday before I was set to make my pitch at Godiva, my phone rang just as I exited the Lincoln Tunnel into New Jersey. I saw the 212 area code, and my stomach churned as I feared Michael was calling to cancel our meeting. Sure enough, it was Michael on the line—he needed to postpone our meeting because of a last-minute overseas business trip.

"Don't worry," he said, "we'll reschedule for next month."

I calmly said, "Sure, Michael, we can reschedule." But inside I was thinking, "Fuck! How am I going to pay rent this month?"

Michael was true to his word and set up a meeting a few weeks later. I put on a suit (thanks to Danna for tying my necktie) and walked about twenty minutes to Godiva's office on Lexington Avenue, schlepping a rolling cooler filled with ice and all of my ingredients, along with a blender. I had worked up a good sweat by the time I reached Godiva's headquarters. I was still trying to cool off in the waiting area when Michael called me into his office. Taking a deep breath, I dragged all of my stuff behind me into the room where Michael was waiting with Shelly Kramer, Godiva's head of merchandising.

I jumped right into my pitch about how this drink would give customers something to crave on hot summer days like this one, drawing traffic into Godiva stores outside of their holiday busy seasons. I pointed out the success of Starbucks Frappuccinos and how this new drink would be an even more indulgent and tempting option. As I spoke, I set up my blender and ingredients. When I reached the point where I felt I had really built up Michael and Shelly's thirst for this decadent new treat, I hit the blend button. But I had overlooked one key thing: the lid. When I hit the button, the blender's noise engulfed the room and chewed-up ice, syrup, powder, and chocolate splattered all over the front of my suit. What a fucking mess! I quickly put the lid on and resumed blending the drink as I wiped off my clothes, hoping I didn't seem too frantic.

Amazingly, forgetting the lid turned out to be one of the best mistakes I ever made. That initial blast of noise attracted the attention of several of Michael and Shelly's colleagues in adjacent offices, who came over to see what all the racket was about.

So I said, "We're making drinks—come on in!"

I handed samples to everyone, and they loved them. Then Gene Dunkin, the head of marketing whom I had first met on the Godiva Theater Café project, joined the group, and I offered him a taste. I watched Gene intently as he took a sip and then started chewing. My mind was racing. Did he hate it? Had I left chunks of ice in his sample? That would surely be the death knell for what was supposed to be a smooth, luscious frozen beverage.

Gene continued chewing for what seemed like forever and finally said, "Mmmm, that's really good. I just got this big piece of chocolate—it's like the hidden treasure in the drink."

"Exactly!" I blurted out, seizing the moment. "That's exactly what I was going for!"

Gene, Michael, and Shelly all loved the drink—especially my happy accident of a bonus, chewable chocolate piece that would give Godiva customers the experience they were familiar with. On the spot, Michael offered me a trial run in seven Godiva stores and guaranteed me $20,000 per month for three months, which was a fortune to me. After the past few years of struggling to keep Brewed Awakening afloat, Michael's contract offer allowed me to feel like I could breathe again. Together, we decided to call the drink Godiva Frappe during the test phase.

With Michael's kick start, I had the chance to build a new idea into another business with a lot of potential. Godiva had nearly three hundred stores around the world at that time, and I started to have visions of Godiva Frappe machines in every one of them. Keep in mind, I didn't actually know anything about producing a drink in retail stores on a large scale. But that's where my Basementality kicked in. I didn't see lack of experience or expertise as an impediment—to me, it's always about the strength of the idea and the willingness to put in the work to bring it to life. I was able to put my bifocals on again. I saw that if I essentially lived in those seven stores and proved that this drink was a real difference-maker for Godiva, this idea could grow into a global phenomenon.

Michael identified the seven stores—from New York City down to Columbia, Maryland—where I would get my test run. I spent every waking moment of the next three months in those stores. My first call was to Eric Kellems at Blendtec to order blenders and ask him to help me figure out how to install them in each location and train the Godiva store staff on how to use them.

The New York stores were street locations, and the stores outside the city were in malls, so they all enjoyed a good amount of foot traffic. My challenge was to divert some of the folks who would normally pass by a Godiva store on a nice day and entice them to come inside. Godiva provided some window posters and counter displays to help call attention to the drink. I spent my time trying to inspire the stores' employees to talk to customers about the new product and encourage them to taste the drinks—this often meant teaching by example, standing outside a store for hours myself, handing out samples, and talking to passersby about the wonders of this decadent treat.

Luckily, it quickly proved to be a winner. The drink accounted for 48 percent of sales volume in the seven stores over those three months—far beyond Godiva's expectations. That sensational test run led Godiva's senior management to plan a global rollout. The company's marketing team came up with a new name, Chocolixir, to emphasize the drink's indulgent quality. And just a few months after I had been sitting in my coffee bar wondering if I could rescue my floundering business, I was in an entirely new venture that was taking off like a rocket.

Michael signed me to a new six-month consulting contract to manage the Chocolixir rollout. Godiva never gave me a contract longer than six months, but I signed several of those deals over the next four-plus years that we stayed in business together. Chocolixir was the first major brand of my career—it's still in the market today, and it was a legitimate competitor to established brands like Starbucks Frappuccino. Even though Bai would become a disruptive powerhouse in the beverage industry, I consider Chocolixir my biggest personal success because it came on the heels of Brewed Awakening's failure. With Chocolixir, I was able to pay off all the debts that I had incurred through Brewed Awakening and move our family out of our cramped Manhattan apartment into a town house in Princeton—the home where, in 2005, our daughter, Shayna, was born and where, a few years later, Bai was born too.

Eric and I wound up traveling together all over the United States and to Japan, installing Chocolixir blenders and training staff in Godiva stores. Every location presented a different challenge—cutting through a wall here, installing new pipes there—to get the machines up and running. Eric and I worked hard and had a lot of fun during this time. As with Michael, Eric's background is much different than mine—he's an earnest, devoutly religious Mormon from Utah who has cursed fewer times in his life than I do in any given morning. But we share an entrepreneurial spirit and a strong work ethic. He became one of my good friends and one of my closest colleagues over the next decade as he helped me build Bai nearly from the beginning.

Japan was a very successful market for Chocolixir, and it was also where we had some of our best times. Eric was a particularly great asset on those trips, as he speaks fluent Japanese from spending two years there doing missionary work for the Church of Jesus Christ of Latter-day Saints. On one of our first trips, we were walking in a mall in Tokyo toward a Godiva outlet when I saw a young boy, maybe six or seven years old, grab his mother's hand and drag her toward the store while pointing at the Chocolixir poster in the window. Eric and I stood in the concourse about thirty yards away and watched them go into the store, exiting a few minutes later with the boy sipping a Chocolixir and his mom carrying a box of chocolates. I noted to Eric that we traveled six thousand-plus miles to see Chocolixir come to life, and it was totally worth the effort. Watching that little kid pull his mom into the store gave me such confidence that this product would become a real game changer by drawing in a younger demographic to shop at Godiva.

On that same trip, I was able to bring my stepfather, Ray, who had always wanted to visit Japan. After all that Ray had done for me since I was a kid, I wanted to treat him to a memorable experience. We upgraded to business class, which he enjoyed, and stayed in the Mandarin Oriental hotel in Tokyo and the Four Seasons in Osaka like a couple of big shots. (For legal reasons, I can neither confirm nor deny whether Ray made off with the shampoos, robes, and slippers from the hotels.) And we were treated to a traditional dinner by former neighbors of ours from Princeton who had moved back to Japan. Ray is a fairly picky eater, and raw fish is not his favorite. I had to laugh when I saw his eyes bug out at some dishes that were so fresh they might still have been moving on his plate. Over the course of two weeks, while Eric and I were working at Godiva stores, Ray took the opportunity to explore Tokyo and Osaka on his own for the first time.

In addition to the Japan trip with Ray, I had an opportunity to bring my brother-in-law, Nic, with me to Newport, Rhode Island, where we served Chocolixir samples over four days to attendees of the International Tennis Hall of Fame ceremony and tournament. Nic and I watched legends Pete Sampras and Jimmy Connors play in person, met a lot of nice people, and spread the word about Chocolixir. Being able to create memories with my family—which we did on a much grander scale with Bai—has been the most fulfilling result of any of my successes in business.

In 2005, Chocolixir was named Best New Product Innovation by the Campbell Soup Company, which was then Godiva's parent company. The drinks remain a major part of Godiva's retail product line. Jim Goldman, the former president of Godiva, visited me at Bai headquarters a few years ago and told me that Chocolixir was generating around $60 million of annual revenue for the company. Chocolixir was a fantastic launching pad for me in so many ways: enabling me to take better care of my family and move us to Princeton, strengthening my relationship with Michael, connecting me with Eric, enabling me to travel across the world, and giving me invaluable experience in learning how to scale an innovation. As Chocolixir became more firmly entrenched at Godiva in the years after it launched, I realized that they would have less incentive to keep me around as a consultant. It was time for me to start thinking about what I would do once those contracts and commissions dried up. When Godiva declined to renew my contract in 2007, we parted again on friendly terms.

***

When you are on the quest for your edge, you aren't simply providing a product that fills a need. You are creating something new, something exciting, something risky.

Unfortunately, I failed to keep that in mind with my next venture, Boosta Shot.

By this time, Red Bull and other energy drinks had become wildly popular, and the specialty coffee industry, led by Starbucks, continued to thrive. I began to brainstorm ways to create a business that reflected both of these trends but took them in a new direction. Through my experience running Brewed Awakening, I knew that most coffee shops wouldn't sell energy drinks like Red Bull because they would compete with made-to-order beverages, which are more profitable. My idea was to create a product that could be added to any beverage to give it a boost of energy. So in

2007, I launched Boosta Shot, an all-natural, vitamin-rich ingredient that we could market to operators of coffee shops, restaurants, convenience stores, and other locations that sold beverages. Shortly after founding the business, I convinced Eric Kellems to leave Blendtec to come aboard as our national sales director.

We saw ourselves as pioneers of a new market for healthy, handcrafted energy drinks. The idea was that Boosta Shot could give any beverage—hot, cold, or frozen—a botanical boost without changing its taste or color or adding any sugar or caffeine. We thought a customer at a café might order a specialty coffee drink or a smoothie with a "boost," or someone grabbing a coffee at a convenience store might hit it with a pump full of Boosta Shot for a little extra oomph. We encouraged café owners to create their own recipes for premium beverages with a boost of energy. We even hired an actor in a giant rooster costume to play the Boosta Roosta and screech "Wake up!" at attendees of the Specialty Coffee Association of America trade show (complete with cheesy video that, if you have nothing better to do with five minutes of your time, you can still find on YouTube).

From the outset, Boosta Shot was a challenging product to sell. It required a fair bit of explanation, and it was targeted to businesses, not individual consumers. For Boosta Shot to really take off, we needed retailers to incorporate it into their own sales and marketing efforts, and we needed baristas to promote it—a much different and more complex model compared with Red Bull, Five-Hour Energy, Monster, and other ascendant energy brands. Boosta Shot gained a bit of traction—particularly with Second Cup, a Canadian coffee shop operator, and AMPM, a US convenience store chain—but we burned through our capital as we tried to expand too quickly without a strong proof of concept.

Eric Kellems (former senior vice president of Bai):
Maybe, in some ways, Boosta Shot was a little before its time. When you're trying to blaze a trail for a new category that hasn't been established,

there are a lot of challenges. When we ran out of funds, Ben had to let me go. In some ways, I think that was a little harder on Ben than it was on me. I went back to Blendtec because I had to pay the rent, and Blendtec made me pay a bit of penance. I think I did three straight months of road shows—ten days on, two days off—when I came back. But I kept talking to Ben in the meantime because he was always coming up with new ideas.

Taking an honest look back, Boosta Shot is the one business where I was not truly on a quest for my edge—I was really just trying to create a product. I definitely worked hard at building Boosta Shot, but I never had a breakthrough vision for how to make Boosta Shot something distinctly special. Plus, I didn't use Boosta Shot myself—I was not a true believer in the product, which is a recipe for failure. Overall, I wasn't wearing my bifocals. I was looking at the present and simply doing the work to build a business without being tethered to an inspired vision for the future.

By the time we ended the Boosta Shot venture in 2008, I had been on a fifteen-year roller-coaster ride in the business world. I had no doubt that I was an entrepreneur at heart. I had tasted enough success to know that I could never go back to working for someone else, and I had a thick enough skin to withstand the bruises that inevitably come with being ambitiously independent. Most important, I had Danna, who encouraged me to keep searching for the next big thing, even as we had two young mouths to feed. Together, we were about to embark on the greatest adventure of our lives.

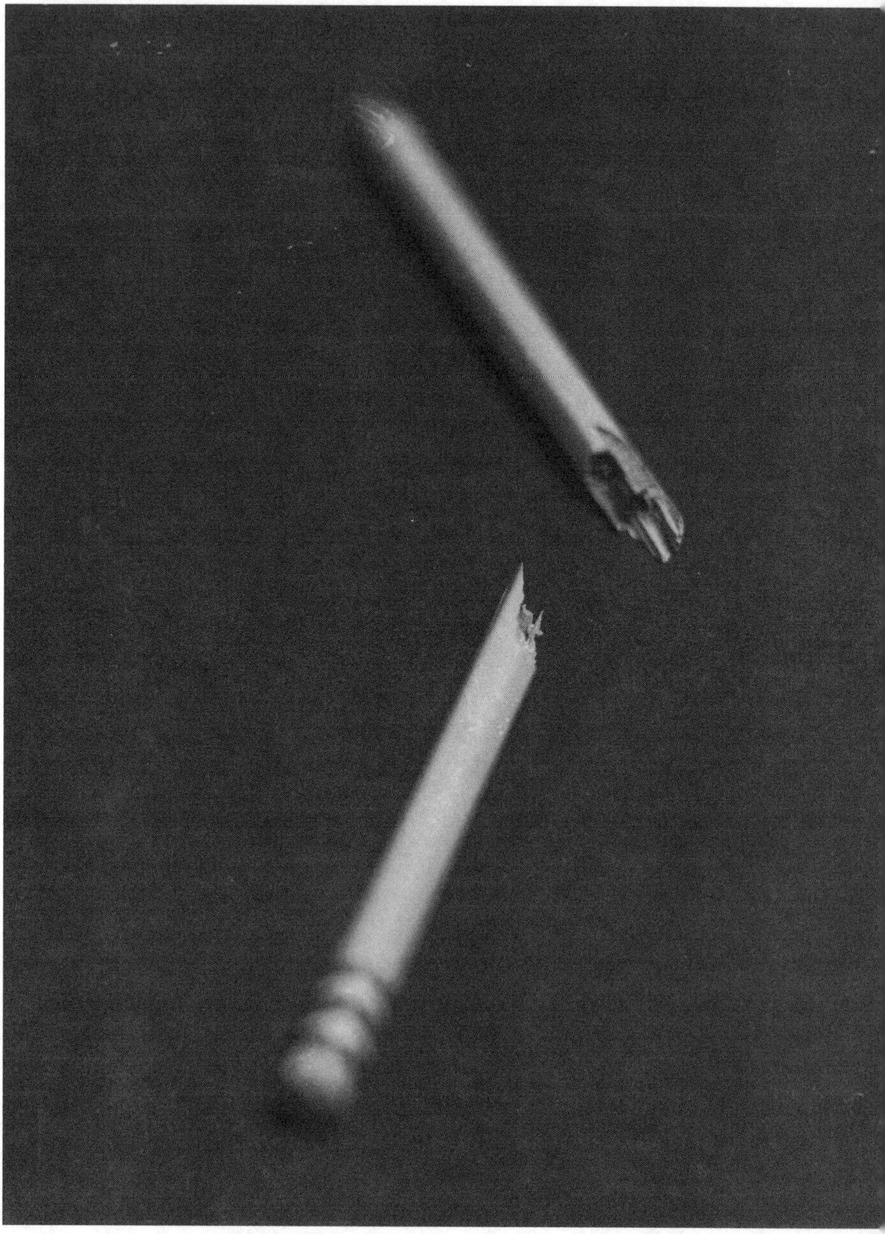

BASEMENTALITY

RISK THE FAILURE

A true black sheep must learn to live with setbacks.

Getting knocked down teaches you how to rise up.

Understanding and accepting failure is the essence of

Basementality. Success takes time. Don't be in a rush.

Be willing to pound the pavement. Through trial and

error, you learn that your vision must be matched by

your effort and your willingness to fail and try again.

CHAPTER 4
SEEING THE BEVOLUTION

After fifteen years on the roller coaster of business, I had learned some lessons the hard way and gained some rewards from being able to see what others did not. Through success, failure, coffee, chocolate, and Boosta Roostas, these experiences honed my ability to see more and to trust my instincts. When I didn't follow genuinely new visions, I ended up relegating myself to just selling stuff.

By the end of 2008, I was primed to find my edge.

My prior successes teaming with Godiva were built upon satisfying a taste for indulgence, whether that meant sipping premium coffee at the movies or enjoying a frozen Chocolixir on a summer day. But as I observed the state of the beverage industry in 2009, there was clearly a new consumer moving to the forefront—one who prioritized natural ingredients and a healthy lifestyle. In my heart, I was still a coffee guy. So I wanted to find a way to keep following my passion, coffee, while pursuing this new generation of health-conscious customers.

Through my forays in the coffee business, I had heard about something called the coffeefruit, which seemed to have untapped potential. The coffeefruit is the red berry that surrounds the coffee bean. Most people have never seen or heard of it because, typically, it's tossed aside by coffee growers as they pluck out the beans for harvesting and roasting. I learned that the coffeefruit is high in antioxidants and that workers in coffee fields would nibble on it to get a natural energy boost. It sounded

Declaring our mission at BaiQuarters (2016)

to me like an ideal ingredient to appeal to people who were increasingly seeking functional benefits from their foods and beverages, yet no one had found a way to make it widely available in a consumer product in the United States.

    The coffeefruit quickly became my new obsession. It was on my mind while I was driving the kids to school, while I was hanging out with friends—even while I was coaching Jack's Little League team and trying in vain to keep seven-year-olds from crying after every strikeout. And it was the number one topic of discussion at home: during the day, I worked out of my basement office, trying to build a new business concept around this unusual ingredient, and at night, Danna, Jack, Shayna, and I piled onto our beat-up living room couch to dream about the directions this idea could go.

The original concept for this new venture was borrowed from my Godiva days. One day, sitting at the desk in my office, I looked up at a small Chocolixir poster on the wall and wondered if I could recapture the magic of that product but, this time, with a blend incorporating the coffeefruit. I envisioned creating a line of frozen, blended fruit drinks that I could pitch to cafés, delis, and coffee shops as a better-for-you version of a smoothie or a Slurpee, with natural fruit flavors and an added bonus of antioxidants from the coffeefruit. The kids, Danna, and I spent weeks thinking about product names, researching words and terms that would convey the focus of this new drink and highlight our new signature ingredient. When we discovered that the word *bai* was Mandarin for "pure," we all agreed that it would be the perfect name for this new venture. Not only did it highlight the natural goodness of our core ingredient, Bai was also a play on the fact that the coffeefruit was a by-product of the harvesting. This was our first iteration of Bai, and we named our new frozen drink line Bai Berry Blends.

As the idea began to take shape, I called upon two guys—both of whom had consulted on Boosta Shot—to help me kick-start the essential process of making this new product taste good and look good. Paul Sapan, an experienced food and beverage product formulator based in California, began experimenting with some flavor combinations that would pair well with the coffeefruit. Chad Portas, a gifted designer and creative strategist from the Boston area, brainstormed with me about how to build a brand around the coffeefruit. Both Paul and Chad were immensely talented, and neither of them were afraid to follow my lead in fleshing out unusual ideas. Both of them wound up playing essential roles in Bai's development throughout the company's history, and their impact showed me that empowering the right people was just as important to the brand as the ingredients in the bottle.

Not long after we moved to Princeton, I met an Australian expat named Simon Richmond, whose wife Wendy had become friends with Danna. Simon was an entrepreneur himself and was working on a line of heated clothing when we met. The Richmonds' kids were similar in age to Jack and Shayna, so our families started seeing each other on the birthday-party circuit in town. Simon and I wound up talking a lot about business and becoming good mates, as he would say. When I began to develop the Bai Berry Blends idea, I asked Simon if he could help me put together a business model. We spent a few days sitting in the café of a local Borders bookstore hunched over a laptop, building out cashflow models and sales projections.

With Simon's help, I realized quickly the Bai Berry Blends idea needed to take on a new direction. Our projections showed that it would cost a small fortune to purchase and supply retailers with the commercial blenders needed to make the drink. Those expenses would only get steeper if Bai Berry Blends started to take off, making it difficult to project a financially viable path forward. I started having flashbacks to the dog days of my Brewed Awakening venture—hustling around New York City to install and service coffee machines, just trying to keep my head above water. I knew, of course, that any new business would require a 24/7 effort, but I didn't want to find myself in Brewed Awakening 2.0, grinding away for little or no return.

When I told Danna about the issues with the frozen drink idea, she offered some pointed advice: "Honey, it's time to get out from the behind the counter."

She encouraged me to reimagine Bai as a bottled drink. So, working with Paul and Chad, I pivoted and began to develop a ready-to-drink beverage—and shortened the name from Bai Berry Blends to simply Bai.

By 2009, the market for functional beverages (those with added vitamins, nutrients, or other better-for-you ingredients) was exploding—and Vitaminwater was its star. Two years earlier, Coca-Cola acquired

Vitaminwater for an astounding $4.1 billion, recognizing that demand for functional beverages was rewriting the future of its soda empire. Coke had previously spent hundreds of millions of dollars to purchase noncarbonated, functional brands such as Odwalla and Fuze, while its premier rival, Pepsi, had paid handsomely to add brands like SoBe and Izze to its product lineup. As I sat in my basement office planning my first leap into the soft drink business, I put on my trusty set of bifocals (or, now, my Bai-focals) and began to imagine a future where Bai would rise to the top of the ranks of this booming new category. I wanted to launch a brand that would ultimately make the Cokes and Pepsis of the beverage world take notice.

But I knew that future wouldn't arrive overnight, and my immediate focus was on the hard work required to get Bai off the ground. I spent countless hours on the phone with Paul and Chad to shape the product's taste and branding, and I plunged into conversations with bottle suppliers and contract packagers (also known as co-packers) to figure out how to get Bai ready to sell. Our town house had very spotty cell phone reception, particularly in the basement. As calls would drop, I would often dart outside with my phone glued to my ear, forgetting my shoes. Our neighbors came to know me as the guy in his socks who was always on his phone.

When Jack, Shayna, and their neighborhood friends would come home from school and play in our cul-de-sac, I learned to weave in and out of erratic scooter and bicycle traffic while I walked and talked, and I got pretty good at shooting baskets or quarterbacking touch football games with one hand as I tried to not drop my phone. Those were precious times that I'll never forget. But even as I enjoyed the spoils of working from home, I was pushing myself and others very hard to get Bai launched. I had not solicited any outside investment at that point, so I was keenly aware that every minute I wasn't out selling Bai was another minute that I was spending money instead of earning it.

Paul Sapan (former vice president of research and development for Bai):
Ben is a giant pain in the ass. And I mean that in the best way possible. He's probably the pushiest, most obnoxious client I've ever dealt with in the twenty-five-plus years I've been in this business. He wants what he wants when he wants it, and I did my best to fulfill that. On the plus side, his obsessiveness is why Bai became what it is and why the people who worked for him also shared that trait. He didn't teach people how to be obsessive—he led by demonstration.

I had never worked with coffeefruit before Ben came up with Bai. So there was a lot of trial and error as we got started. Coffeefruit on its own is kind of bitter—it took some work to mask that bitterness and find flavors that complemented it or, at least, didn't conflict with it as much.

The first Bai beverages were not the five-calorie versions that would fuel our later growth. Initially, Bai was a mid-calorie beverage (seventy per serving) sweetened with organic evaporated cane juice. Knowing that consumers were shying away from artificial ingredients, we avoided using sugar substitutes like aspartame or sucralose, which you find in diet sodas and other low-calorie drinks. The drinks also contained 35 mg of caffeine per serving, similar to the amount in a cup of green tea (the caffeine was derived from white tea extract and coffeefruit).

As Paul shipped each new sample from his office in California, I sought feedback from Danna and the kids, my parents, and other family and friends to help us hone the recipe. On any given day, you could find me outside in my driveway handing out tiny cups like a vendor in a supermarket trying to entice customers with free samples.

"Just try one more! What do you think of this one?"

When I wasn't outside passing out samples, I was in the basement on my phone and laptop as Chad and I collaborated on creative concepts for the brand. The bifocals were back on. I was perspiring in the moment while looking ahead to the future—chasing my edge.

By late summer, we decided on three flavors for our launch. We called them Jamaica Blueberry, Tanzania Strawberry, and Mango Kauai, starting Bai's tradition of naming each flavor for a coffee-growing region of the world to pay homage to the coffeefruit. Finally, I was ready to introduce consumers to this new line of beverages powered by our "secret superfruit."

Chad Portas (former chief creative officer of Bai):
I thought the coffeefruit was a really interesting ingredient—there was a lot of mystery around it. So we started working on some creative positioning for Bai Berry Blends. One early idea was a script for a TV spot with coffeefruit rising up out of the bushes and floating like hot air balloons. We never made the spot, but I designed a Bai logo to include on the document with that script—and that's the logo they're still using.

As the brand evolved into bottled drinks, we came up with the concept to play off the Bai name by calling them "Botanical Antioxidant Infusions." I also worked on the first labels and the first website. When I sent Ben the first label design, he printed it from his home computer and glued it to a bottle. He took a picture of it in his backyard and wanted me to use that shot for an ad.

I said, "Dude, I can see your grill in the reflection on the bottle!"

We always laughed about that. He was so excited he just couldn't wait to get the brand launched.

All of those early projects were really exciting for me. But honestly, I thought Bai was just going to be some relatively quick freelance work—I'd bill Ben for my time, and maybe I'd hear from him again when the next thing came up. I never thought it would get as big as it did.

With Paul and Chad's help, I felt confident that Bai was a high-quality product with amazing flavor and a value proposition that would resonate with health-conscious consumers. People were growing more aware of antioxidant-rich fruits and vegetables and how they could aid the body in combating cell damage caused by the oxidation process. Think about, for example, how an apple or pear turns brown if it's left out in the open too long—that's akin to what can happen to cells that interact with oxygen molecules. With Bai, we aimed to introduce people to the antioxidant properties of our exotic ingredient, the coffeefruit. We wanted to help consumers discover a new option to feel good about what they drink without having to sacrifice great taste.

But our messaging wouldn't matter if our drinks didn't stand out on store shelves and entice people to try them. Bai's initial design featured a crisp white label that contrasted beautifully with the deep colors of our drinks. At the top of the label was our simple yet distinctive logo—with

Bai's first birthday! (2010)

the brand name in lowercase black type and a green leaf dotting the i to signify Bai's natural goodness—perched above a vibrant fruit illustration for each flavor. Bai's label design has gone through modifications over the years, but it's largely the same as it was when we launched.

For our first real production run, I worked with a co-packer in Northern California to produce about 650 cases, or more than 15,000 bottles. That first batch was more than I could fit in my garage, so I rented a ten-foot-by-ten-foot shed in a self-storage facility across from a used-car lot in the neighboring town of Lawrenceville. On August 4, 2009, the first three pallets of Bai were delivered from the co-packer. I remember that day as vividly as my children's birthdays.

As I drove Danna's SUV to the storage shed on that roasting summer afternoon, one thought ran over and over in my mind: "It's taken me nine months to get to this day."

I arrived at the storage shed, and there was no delivery truck. I started pacing around the shed, convincing myself that the truck was lost or had broken down somewhere on the New Jersey Turnpike with my precious cargo trapped inside the dark, stifling trailer. After what seemed like ten hours, but was more likely about ten minutes, the truck appeared and backed into the lot toward my shed. I waved furiously to the driver to help guide him into the right spot.

The truck came to a stop, belching exhaust into my face, and the driver, Manny, slowly climbed down from the cab. We shook hands, and Manny told me, with a clear sigh of relief, that this was his final stop of the day. Then he rolled up the door. Inside I saw fifty-three feet of empty trailer, except for three pallets all the way up at the front. I stared at them in awe like a father staring at his newborn.

"Nine months—my babies are finally here!" I said to Manny, throwing my arm around his shoulder as if we hadn't just met thirty seconds earlier.

"Aren't they beautiful? Look at them!"

Manny nodded politely as he raised his eyebrows and looked at me out of the side of his eye, half-expecting me to hand him a celebratory cigar.

As I gazed lovingly at the pallets at the front of the truck, memories and lessons from my previous businesses flashed in and out of my mind, and I felt a rush of excitement as visions of Bai's future washed over those scenes from the past. Then, suddenly, I snapped out of my daydream.

"Manny," I said. "Where's your pallet jack?"

"I was just gonna ask you the same thing," he responded.

My eyes nearly popped out of my head. "You don't have one?"

Manny shook his head. His job was to drive the cases, not to move them.

"Well, how the fuck am I going to get those pallets in the back of the truck?" I asked him.

Manny shrugged and stepped to the side of the truck into the shade, his movements proving the old saying: "Your problem is not my emergency."

"Maybe there's something around here," he suggested, gesturing toward the rows of storage sheds surrounding mine.

I walked over to the office of the storage facility, but nobody answered the door or the phone. I scrolled furiously through the contacts on my iPhone, trying to think of anyone nearby who would have access to a pallet jack, but I couldn't come up with a name.

Desperate, I started rummaging around outside of the sheds and found a long chain near a pile of broken pallets. I dragged the chain back to Manny's truck. Fortunately, the chain was long enough to reach the rear of the trailer. So I tied one end around a pallet and the other around the hitch of the car. Then I slowly dragged that 1,600-pound pallet toward daylight.

Manny stood outside the truck and waved for me to stop when the first pallet reached the back edge of the trailer. Then we repeated the process twice more. Finally, with the bright afternoon sun reflecting off the plastic wrap surrounding the cases, I took a step back from the truck and repeated, "Look at how beautiful those babies are."

Manny, again, nodded politely.

Then my proud smile washed away. "Wait, how the fuck am I going to get them off the truck? I don't have a forklift."

Manny realized he wasn't getting away from me so easily.

Looking up at the three pallets, I said, "I guess I'll just have to break them down by hand."

Taking pity on me, Manny tossed his keys to the ground beside the truck and walked over to where I stood. He pulled his baseball cap down closer to his eyes, rolled his shoulders like a boxer waiting for the bell to ring, and said, "Okay, c'mon, let's go. I'll help you."

I climbed up into the trailer and tore the shrink-wrap off the first pallet. (Thankfully, Manny had a box cutter, so I didn't have to go on another frantic search.) I started handing cases down to Manny—324 in all—and he stacked them on the ground. We settled into a rhythm and a half hour passed quickly. My eyes stung from sweat, and my shirt was drenched. When all of the cases were finally off the truck, I pulled the three empty pallets down from the trailer. Then, with the heat radiating from the blacktop underneath us, Manny and I went in reverse—restacking every single case onto the pallets.

After we finished, I thanked Manny profusely and offered him a tip, which, to my surprise, he rejected. I know that Manny couldn't leave until I figured out how to get those pallets off his truck. But I also like to think he could tell how important that delivery was to me, and that's why he stepped in to help.

Manny climbed back into his truck, started it up and rumbled away, blasting a final puff of exhaust into my face. I waved goodbye and thought about how grateful I was for the help that he didn't have to give me. Then I looked at the three pallets in the middle of the parking lot, turned my head toward the empty storage shed ten feet away, and thought, "Why didn't we put the pallets inside the shed? How the fuck am I gonna get them over there?"

Manny's truck had disappeared into the distance—and I'm sure that he was not looking in his rearview mirror. So my only option was to unstack those 324 cases by myself, schlep them into the shed and restack the pallets for a second time. When I was done, my back and knees were barking at me and I was kicking myself for not being better prepared for the day. But as I pulled the shed door closed and locked it, I also felt satisfied. I said to myself, "Now I'm in business."

That day was an example of a moment that confronts every business owner in some form. With a seemingly impossible task in front of you, how do you respond? Focus on all the reasons you can't get something done? Get frustrated and look for someone to blame for your predicament? No, you must do whatever it takes to accomplish your goal—or, in this case, to get those fucking pallets from the front of the truck to the back, from the back of the truck to the ground, and from the ground to the shed. Then, in reality, you're only at the starting line. You need to continue to find the Mannys of the world who will put in extra time and effort to get the job done alongside you. And you must be willing to tackle any task of any size to move your business forward.

***

Just after we received that first delivery of Bai, our family went on vacation with Simon Richmond and his family down to Ocean City, Maryland, and we brought some of the drinks with us. Simon and Wendy's three kids—Madison, Eden, and Toby—joined with Jack and Shayna in catching their dads' entrepreneurial bug, and they set up a stand in front of our rental house to introduce local beachgoers to Bai. People naturally couldn't resist our cute salespeople, so we had a good response to our first impromptu sampling event. But when we got back to Princeton, I had to get down to answering the most important question: Would people actually buy Bai?

I decided to focus on launching the brand in two markets: in the Princeton area, where I could experience Bai's reception firsthand in my own community, and in New York City, where I had experience selling in a tough but potentially lucrative environment. But I couldn't handle two markets by myself. Fortunately, the perfect candidate for Bai's employee number one was easy to find.

My stepfather, Ray, had worked in tandem with my mom in the real estate business for many years. But in 2009, with the US economy in the throes of the Great Recession, the housing market was in tatters—particularly new home construction, their area of specialty. Ray had taken a position with a local real estate firm doing resales. Business was painfully slow, and he was unhappy.

On the same day I received the first shipment of Bai, I went to my parents' house for dinner afterward and found Ray scouring the help-wanted ads in the newspaper. He had been looking for sales jobs in different industries for a while, but every conversation with a prospective employer ended basically the same way: although they appreciated his forty years of work experience, their business was changing, and they needed to "go in a different direction." Ray was sixty-five years old with grey hair and two hearing aids. All around him, computers and smartphones were changing the way people shopped, worked, and interacted. Ray, who based his career on building relationships face-to-face with his clients, got the message employers were telling him: "You're no longer needed."

So, that night, I pulled a chair up next to him and said, "Hey, I appreciate that you have exactly zero years of experience in the beverage business and you've never sold a bottle of anything in your life. But a lot of things are changing in this industry, and I could use a fresh perspective. Why don't you come sell with me?" And he agreed. It was a great deal for me, because I couldn't afford to pay him a salary at the outset. But Ray didn't care. He wanted to help his son—and he wanted to feel needed again. What I got in return was a dynamite salesperson who went above and beyond every day to help Bai gain traction in the Princeton area by shaking hands, talking sports, remembering names, and forging relationships with managers of small markets, big grocery stores, bagel shops, pizza places, sandwich joints, and other retailers block by block, town by town.

While I was focused on trying to break into New York City, Ray worked to break open the Princeton market for Bai—and, oh, did he ever! Ray's sales numbers were astronomical and soon became the North Star that I pointed out to every salesperson who came along after him.

Ray Schlaefer (stepfather):

Our first account was a place called Blawenburg Market up the road from my house. I knew the owners—a mother and daughter—because I went in there all the time, so they agreed to give Bai a try. I remember going back out to my car and saying, "Yes!" It felt as good as selling a whole community of real estate at one time. I couldn't wait to tell Ben. Then I went into Olives, a popular deli in Princeton, and the owner, Adam, said, "Okay, I'll let you in, but if those bottles are still here on Friday, you're outta here." That was on a Monday—Bai has been in Olives ever since.

We did it all ourselves back then—selling, delivering, collecting money. It was fun because I was doing it for Ben and because I was working hard. When we started out, I put as many cases as I could in the back of my SUV. I dragged my rolling cooler around to any place that sold drinks and tried to get Bai in there.

Ben was so happy when I would come back saying that I opened new accounts. Eventually, he got me a small van with our logo on the side. If I was in a crowded area, I would pull over, put the radio on loud, open the doors to the van, and hand out samples. Ben would get upset that I was giving away so much product, but I think it worked to get the name out there.

Pretty soon, I had almost two hundred accounts, driving around in this little truck that held maybe one hundred cases if I was really pushing it. Because I packed as many cases I could in the back of that van, the front tires almost felt like they were off the ground while I was driving. When I got a new account, I always brought the cases in from the van right away—I didn't want to give them until the next day to change their mind. And I would talk with anybody in those stores who had something to do with selling Bai to customers to educate them about our product.

We really started to take off when we got some of the bigger supermarkets in the area. I remember one day at Wegmans, a district manager from Coke said to me, "Who the fuck do you know? You have more space in here than I do!"

I asked him, "Have you ever had Bai? Try it sometime—you'll see why we have all this real estate."

I would take space anywhere I could get it. I didn't care if it was under the counter, on top of the pizza counter, wherever.

When we got into Whole Foods, I asked the manager for an endcap—the space at the end of an aisle, which is prime real estate.

He said, "Give me one reason why I should."

I told him, "The reason is I come here every day—stacking shelves, fixing displays. Who else does that?"

"Okay," he said. "You got it."

I told him I could make his store the number one location for selling Bai in the whole region if he just gave me the space. He let me put a big display with a surfboard up at the front of the store. Eventually, it did become the top store in the region, and we wound up getting into Whole Foods in Philadelphia because we did so well in Princeton.

You had to have good relationships with everyone. Sometimes managers change, and you have to get to know the new ones. Maybe those new guys already have a relationship with another brand, so you have to make a connection with them. That's what it's all about. Sure, I used to get pissed off at people if they didn't want to give us what we wanted, but they never knew about it. You have to keep smiling.

Ray's attitude and work ethic set the bar for everyone who followed him on Team Bai. People around town started calling him the "Bai Guy" because you'd see him everywhere in his van, making sales calls and deliveries. Soon after he started, I was able to provide him with a modest salary that still wasn't commensurate with the impact that he had on the company. After we started to bring on other salespeople, Ray remained our top performer—and he became a mentor and role model to others. Over the years, I hired lots of people who commanded higher salaries than Ray because they had years of experience in the industry. They wound up chasing marks set by a guy who never sold a bottle of anything before he came to Bai but who became a legend simply because he cared more than anyone else.

Ray had deeper purposes than working to build a commercial product: he was determined to help his son realize a dream, and he didn't want to disappoint me. As a father, I can understand that motivation, but to this day, I'm humbled by Ray's dedication to Bai and to me.

The man nearly killed himself working for Bai. After a couple of years of chatting with store managers over blueberry muffins and egg-and-cheese sandwiches, trekking miles every day through store aisles and up and down stairways, Ray's inattention to his health caught up with him. He had opened a Bai account with a local tennis club, which most sales reps would have passed right by without seeing it as an opportunity. One day, as he was delivering cases up the sixty-five steps to the clubhouse, he started feeling unusually tired. My mother's insistence overpowered his stubbornness, and Ray went to the doctor, who informed him that he needed immediate triple bypass surgery because of blockages around his heart. Ray dismissed the procedure as a minor setback and returned to work shortly afterward, probably too soon. The incident reinforced for me how committed Ray was to building Bai's future, but it also scared me to see the physical toll it took on him and made me realize how incredibly hard we all were running.

At the same time, I was thrilled to see how much joy and pride Ray took in his work. His performance in our early days not only proved that

Ray, always proud to be the "Bai Guy" (2010)

Bai could sell well in a variety of retail settings, but it also showed him how much he was worth and helped him regain his confidence after a rough patch in his career. Ray was the first example of someone who needed Bai as much as Bai needed him—a formula that would apply to some of the most important people who became part of the company's journey in the years to come.

Fortunately, a few of them came along within Bai's first year, and their talents and drive were vital to our success.

**

Not only were Ray and I committed to getting Bai into as many accounts as possible after our launch, we also listened carefully to our customers' feedback. What we heard most often was, "This tastes great—but do you have one with fewer calories?"

Health-conscious consumers were attracted to the fresh look of Bai's packaging and our emphasis on antioxidants, but many were turned off by its seventy calories per serving, even though we used an organic sweetener instead of the artificial kind. I challenged Paul to come up with a lower-calorie version without compromising our commitment to high-quality ingredients—and he delivered.

Seven months after launching Bai, we introduced Sumatra Dragonfruit in March 2010. It was the first flavor of our Bai5 line, with just five calories per serving.

Paul crafted this flavor by finding the perfect combination of stevia and erythritol, two natural sweeteners that were not widely used in the United States at the time. Stevia leaf extract is an extremely intense plant-based sweetener, more than two hundred times sweeter than sugar. We balanced the stevia with erythritol, a sugar alcohol that is made from simple sugars derived from plant starches. Erythritol looks and tastes like common table sugar, but it's actually about 30 percent less sweet, providing an ideal counterpoint to stevia.

Bai5 was an immediate hit. Within our first year, we expanded our lineup to include four flavors of original Bai and four flavors of Bai5. As our product lineup evolved, so did our team.

***

New Yorkers generally don't stop for anything, even if it's free. So when I set out my sample table in front of a bodega near the corner of Ninth Street and Second Avenue in Manhattan's East Village, I knew I had my work cut out for me.

I smiled and waved to hundreds of people who zipped past my table, ignoring my calls of "Antioxidant infusions!" But then a young woman named Kat Haddon stopped to taste Bai and listen to my story about the coffeefruit and antioxidants.

Kat and I had a nice conversation—I was sure I had created a new "Bailiever." After our chat, she walked over to a nearby stoop, sat down, and made a phone call, looking over at me frequently while she talked. A few minutes later, she walked back to my table and told me that she was working with a team to open a cafe in New Haven, Connecticut, and she recommended that the owner, Chris, start selling Bai there. She put us in touch, and I sent Chris some product. He loved it and ordered a pallet. So Kat actually wound up selling the first full pallet of Bai, even though she didn't work for us—at least, not yet.

Kat Haddon (former director of shopper marketing for Bai):
I had just graduated from New York University and was working in real estate when I met Ben while I was waiting for a client. I was a Vitaminwater drinker and thought Bai was interesting—the coffeefruit story was really cool. I had spent the past several months building plans for a coffee shop, and I didn't even realize that coffee was a fruit. I immediately thought that Chris's café would be a great place for Bai. They started doing business together, and a couple of months later, Ben asked Chris what I was up to. Then he called and offered me a job. I didn't even have to think about it, even though it was basically for no money. I just wanted to be part of Bai.

Ben told me, "I know you want to be a marketer, but there's no point of doing marketing right now if people can't find the product on shelves."

"First, you need to be a salesperson," he said.

So my job became schlepping a cooler up and down the streets of New York trying to sell Bai to bodegas. It didn't help that our coolers weren't very good—almost every time they went over a bump in the sidewalk, all the ice and bottles would come crashing out.

Beverage sales was not intuitive to me—and it was not an easy job. Especially in a market like New York City, where bodegas have hundreds of essential products vying for shelf space and where every brand is hoping to find its big break. I found myself spending my days in dingy basements, pleading with guys who did not care about resetting a shelf to support a brand no one has heard of. I didn't want to be pushy or impolite, but I began to feel beaten down by the constant, resounding sound of "no."

One afternoon, at a companywide meeting (of eight people), Ben started by showing us a clock. As the seconds ticked on, the clock showed how much overhead we were accruing by having all our salaried employees sitting in a room. At the end of that meeting, he cornered me. He said, "I know you're giving it your all out there, but I need you to figure out how to crack the code and be successful at this."

I believed that the product deserved to be in those coolers. I just had to find a way to make others believe it, too.

From the beginning, Kat demonstrated that she cared deeply about building the brand and would put in any amount of time to help it succeed. Kat embodied the spirit of the type of people I wanted for our team. Ultimately, she became one of our most valuable all-purpose players, filling numerous roles across sales, logistics, marketing—wherever and whenever she was needed.

But first I had to teach Kat, and our other new salespeople, how to sell our product.

Bai wasn't a soda, a juice, or a sports drink—it needed more explanation. Our brand was categorized as an "enhanced water," which doesn't quite roll off the tongue, so we needed to unpack our key attributes. I developed a pretty simple selling tool from the bottle itself, and I started using the label to help our salespeople identify and express our points of difference, which we called the founder's story pitch:

1. **Name:** Found on the logo on the front of the bottle. Bai is Mandarin for "pure." It also stands for "Botanical Antioxidant Infusion." Finally, it connotes that the coffeefruit is a by-product of the coffee harvest.

2. **ORAC:** On the side label, ORAC stands for Oxygen Radical Absorbance Capacity, a scoring method used by the US Department of Agriculture to measure antioxidant power of foods and beverages. ORAC explained the function of antioxidants and how the coffeefruit compared with better-known fruits like pomegranate and acai.

3. **Coffeefruit:** On the other side label, we highlighted the story of our "secret superfruit."

4. **Natural sweeteners:** On the back of the bottle, we pointed to our ingredients panel featuring stevia and erythritol, our natural sweeteners.

We didn't intentionally design the label as a sales tool, but it worked well and became a big part of our early culture. In our first year, I took every new hire into a room with a bottle of Bai and coached them one-on-one for as long as it took to understand the four points.

To get their competitive juices going, we had all new salespeople deliver this pitch to everyone at the company. We celebrated the best presentations and jokingly bequeathed our infamous Golden Toilet Award, along with a roll of toilet paper, to the person with the worst presentation to encourage improvement. From the beginning, I tried to set a tone that everyone at Bai was expected to work extremely hard and perform at a high level, but I also wanted to create a fun environment that made people excited and energized to come to work. We had no idea how much energy we were going to need for the rest of our journey together, chasing our edge.

***

Our next key hire was the guy who wound up by my side through almost every moment of my Bai journey. At the beginning, I was able to fund Bai's launch myself, but once Ray and I started to succeed in opening accounts around Princeton and New York City, I had to seek outside investment so I could hire more employees and scale the business. I needed a formal business plan to present to prospective investors. Of course, I didn't have time to craft one because I was so busy out on the streets selling the product. A friend recommended I contact Ari Soroken, who earned his MBA from the renowned Wharton School and helped local entrepreneurs as an intern at the school's Small Business Development Center. By the time we met, Ari had worked in entrepreneurial environments in the technology and wine businesses, and his work had been featured in a business planning guide published by *Inc.* magazine. We clicked immediately. I was impressed with his acumen and appreciated his dedication to helping entrepreneurs develop their ideas into solid business plans.

Ari Soroken (former chief financial officer of Bai):

When I enrolled at Wharton, I intended to go into finance or banking, but halfway through my program, I realized that wasn't what I wanted. I majored instead in entrepreneurial studies and interned at the Small Business Development Center, where I had a caseload of about twenty businesses across all kinds of industries. When I met Ben to talk about Bai years later, I saw immediately that the product was so far ahead of where most early-stage businesses would be at that same point. After we talked about a business plan for Bai, I was thinking it would take a few months to get it done. But Ben already had a meeting scheduled with a big prospective investor.

He said, "You have a week."

So I drafted a quick business plan for Ben and then started working with him on a consulting basis for about three or four months until coming aboard full time in July 2010. I had another job while I was consulting for Bai, but I had been looking for the right opportunity to get involved with something more entrepreneurial. Look, everybody thinks they're giving 110 percent, but with Ben, I could tell he really believed in what he was doing. He was an evangelist for his idea—I knew he was going to go a long way. And it was fun. For me, coming to Bai was a no-brainer.

Ari quickly became my right-hand man. After a few months of consulting, he joined our team full time and served in leadership roles in sales and operations before becoming chief financial officer. Whether I was negotiating deals with distributors, retailers, or suppliers, or raising money, recruiting key hires, or handling any of the other millions of tasks involved with managing Bai's growth, I counted on Ari.

Ari and I both had to learn a lot on the fly about building the company because Bai's trajectory was unlike anything either of us had ever experienced. When he joined the company, he lived in Manhattan and spent many nights at our place in Princeton sleeping on a couch right next to my basement office, which was still Bai's corporate headquarters. We also spent a lot of time in New York City managing our small but growing sales team there and trying to build our distribution network. And we spent a ton of time on the road all over the country, overseeing production runs, meeting with prospective business partners and traveling to industry trade shows. I'm sure I spent way more time with Ari than I did with Danna during Bai's first few years.

Ari Soroken (former chief financial officer of Bai):

Those days were hugely energetic, and it was probably the most fun time for me. It requires so much commitment to engage people on a regular basis and still be excited about doing it. Every successful consumer brand is about passion. Why does a Louis Vuitton bag sell for so much more than a Coach bag? They're both leather bags. The difference is the passion and the emotion they've created around Louis Vuitton. Ben had so much passion for Bai, and it came through in every conversation he had. And he also saw that Bai was going to be huge when no one else did.

For me, the mission was about entrepreneurship—seeing a small business grow and overcoming all the obstacles that were in front of us.

We were going up against probably the most well-known trademark in the world, Coca-Cola, because we were trying to take shelf space from Vitaminwater. That's insanity.

There was so much to do in the early years, so we mostly worked out of the car. We'd pull up outside a Starbucks to catch a Wi-Fi signal, check our emails, send a contract, take a quick break, and then get back on the road. We were always scrambling. We were a cash-and-carry business to start—we weren't invoicing anyone. We had one person doing our accounting on QuickBooks. Our goal was to have enough money to pay for the next production run and then keep going from there. When we went to trade shows, we would buy stuff at IKEA for our booth, and when the show was over, we'd return it all.

Ben would say, "It's okay; they take stuff back."

Once, I was waiting in line at IKEA to return a whole set of bookshelves that we had used as displays, and the woman at customer service said to me, "Yeah, we take it back—but not after it's been assembled!" (We still returned it.)

Ari and I shared many long drives to Marion, Virginia, a small, remote town in the southwest corner of the state, just north of the Tennessee and North Carolina borders. First Fruits, a small co-packing company, had taken over a former Pepsi bottling plant in Marion, and that's where we produced Bai for the first couple of years after our initial production run in California.

Marion is just over five hundred miles from Princeton, so it was certainly not convenient, but at the time, it was the perfect location for us. Most independent beverages are produced at co-packing facilities that handle numerous brands, which can make it difficult to schedule precious line time. I didn't want our production time to be yanked away at the last minute and given to a bigger competitor. I needed to find a co-packer that would make Bai its priority, which First Fruits did, so I was okay with driving eight hours to get there. Actually, I enjoyed the drives. For me, driving has the same effect as running—it provides time for me to think and dream as I move forward. And there were fewer distractions while we were in the car, so Ari and I got a lot of work done on our way to and from Marion.

For each production run, Ari and I stayed for a week at the General Francis Marion Hotel, a century-old hotel named for a Revolutionary War hero. But we really lived at the First Fruits plant. If we weren't on the plant floor, we were working in an office or conference room elsewhere in the building. Typically we were on-site for twelve to sixteen hours each day.

Even now, when I crack open a bottle of Sumatra Dragonfruit, Ipanema Pomegranate, or one of our earlier flavors, the smell brings me back to Marion because we were so immersed in the production. We became intimately acquainted with the aromas because there was Bai on the floor, in the air, and on our clothes. Beverage production is like a well-choreographed ballet: everything has to go perfectly. But it rarely did, especially in our early days.

The first time Ari and I went down to Marion, we insisted on tasting the initial batch of Tanzania Strawberry before it was poured into the waiting lines of bottles. I needed them to know I was watching and that we cared more about the quality of our product than any of the other beverage producers they worked with. The guys at the plant rolled their eyes, looking at us like we were a couple of nervous rookies who didn't understand that they were professionals, but they gave in.

Whenever I tasted a batch of Bai, I had the consumer in mind. I had a strong instinct for what consumers were seeking and didn't feel that I needed formal testing and focus groups to deliver the best possible product. I imagined myself as someone taking his first sip of our beverage and asking himself, "Am I going for that second sip?"

I tasted that first Tanzania Strawberry batch and knew instantly that it wasn't quite right. I was happy with the strong strawberry flavor, but it was a bit too sweet—the balance just wasn't there. It was good, but not perfect, and I wasn't prepared to settle for anything less. This wasn't the taste that would make our consumer crave that second sip.

I looked at Ari and raised my eyebrows, silently asking him if he was thinking what I was thinking.

He nodded.

"Guys, we gotta dump it!" I shouted, lifting my voice above the din of the bottling lines. "Try again."

The head of the production team thought I was kidding, until he realized I wasn't smiling.

"We made it exactly to your specs," he said.

"Well, something went wrong, because it's not good enough," I responded.

"Unbelievable!" he said. "Don't you realize this will cost thousands of extra dollars and put everything behind schedule?"

Of course I did. But what he didn't realize was that when we said Bai had to be absolutely perfect, we meant it. In my head, I was already calculating the costs of the discarded product and the delayed production, hoping they would be manageable. Outwardly, I stood firm. This was Basementality in action.

"Run it again," I said.

As we waited for the next batch to be finished, Ari and I retreated to our office down the hall. A few hours passed as we made phone calls to employees, prospective distribution partners, and vendors to keep all of the parts of the business moving. After we got the call to return to the production area, we walked back down the hall like a couple of drill sergeants prepared to inspect a new class of recruits.

One of the production team members handed me a cup. The air tightened in the room as everyone awaited my response. Silently, I took a sip and put the cup down on a table. I looked down at my shoes for a moment, then lifted my gaze.

"Now that's fucking perfect," I said.

Ari and I shook hands with the foreman, and the team went off to move the product into the next step of the bottling process. I wish I could say that was the last time we had to dump any product, but that was not the case—it happened over and over again, not only with this co-packer but with every one of them we worked with over the years.

As frustrating as it was to lose time and money by discarding product, I refused to compromise our standards. That's why, during my tenure with Bai, we never put a product on the shelf that wasn't tasted and approved by one of our team members. In our earliest years, we often brought new employees with us to Marion so they could learn how to taste and assess the quality of the beverages on the production line. We expanded that effort and developed a program to formally train employees to become certified tasters and assume the authority of approving or rejecting batches for production.

Being a certified taster was demanding work, as it involved spending time around the clock in co-packing plants and dealing with frustrated partners who weren't used to companies taking such a zealous approach to their products. But each of our tasters understood that they were entrusted with a vital responsibility because quality was paramount. They needed to be sure that every batch was worthy of that second sip. I would always rather absorb a loss than allow anything less than our best to go into the bottle. Depending on your point of view, that level of obsession either makes me great or aggravating to work with—but it does deliver results.

Even with the exhausting travel and some fireworks that erupted between me and the First Fruits team when production problems arose, I look back fondly on those days in Marion. I felt so alive when I took part in actually making the product. If I'm not engaged with building something, then I feel like I'm in the world everyone else lives in, and that's kind of boring. I loved those early days when we didn't have a lot of employees, we weren't dealing with so many distributors, and our journey was really just getting started. When Ari and I would drive back after a week of production in Marion, I would immediately start thinking about how many cases we could produce next time and how many steps we would need to climb to reach our next goals. I loved the moments when it was clear there was so much runway in front of us.

***

As I quickly learned, distribution was going to be the biggest challenge in building the Bai brand. I had dreams of fighting Big Sugar and disrupting a market that the Big Three had cornered for so long. That wasn't going to happen with Ray, me, and other Bai salespeople lugging cases around in our cars or vans.

The beverage industry is built upon the direct store distribution (or DSD) model, in which suppliers like Bai partner with a full-service distributor, which delivers their products to retailers. Coming out of the gate, we were not going to capture the attention of the Big Three soda companies that dominated the beverage distribution landscape, so we had to forge deals with independent distributors as we started to move into additional markets. Although distributors were vital to helping our brand expand, our relationships with them were not easy to establish or maintain.

We started working with distributors in New York City at a time when we were looking for anyone to help us expand, which led to some adventurous relationships. One of our earliest partners was a natural foods distributor that mainly handled milk, yogurt, and other dairy products. Our salespeople rode along with the distributor on their refrigerated trucks and, upon making a sale to a retail account, delivered cold product on the spot. On a given night back then, you might find Kat riding around in a truck with a milkman at 3 a.m., trying to sell Bai. Luckily for us, New York City never sleeps, so we were able to open some new accounts. But that arrangement only lasted a few months.

Another early partner was a small distributor who specialized in dealing with Asian-owned groceries and delis around the city, which sell a lot of beverages because many of them have strong prepared-foods businesses.

This distributor helped us open around three hundred new accounts, but our relationship didn't last very long before we moved onto deals with bigger distributors that had more, shall we say, conventional business models.

Ari Soroken (former chief financial officer of Bai):
Somehow, we came across this young guy who did business out of a karaoke bar in Midtown Manhattan. In the early morning, his guys would arrive on bicycles, get their samples, and ride across the city to get orders.

When Ben and I went to meet with him for the first time, we arrived around 10:30 in the morning at the address he gave us. We walked into a dark hallway filled with garbage, with a freight elevator at the far end.

Ben said to me, "This can't be the place. Is he actually a distributor?"

We called his number—no answer. We took the elevator to the third floor and found ourselves in a nightclub that was pitch black and dead silent. All we could smell were cigarettes and stale booze, and the floor was sticky. There wasn't a soul around. Ben and I were thinking, "Are we gonna get tied up with duct tape and killed?"

The guy we were supposed to meet with was in a back room, and eventually he came out and found us. We had our meeting in a karaoke party room that he used as a conference space. We were sitting on these vinyl couches—God knows what took place on them the night before. Eventually we got a deal done with this guy, but that first meeting was one of the most hilarious experiences we had. And the guy did move some product for us.

Even from Bai's earliest days, I saw that the brand had real promise—even if we had to do business with some unusual partners to get it off the ground. I could see beyond the seedy surroundings of that karaoke bar and recognize that we needed to make that deal to help us take the critical first steps toward our envisioned future. I was used to haggling with owners of rundown shops and meeting with unusual characters to build businesses. But nothing about Ari's background suggested that he would be comfortable in those types of environments. For Ari, it was all new. But he understood that I was always thinking big, and he was the first person who truly embraced my idea that Bai could be a groundbreaking brand, even when we were so small that the idea seemed incredibly far-fetched. And he was willing to follow me through any unmarked door or any dank hallway to get where we needed to go.

***

With my Basementality, my mind was always somewhere in the future. The downside to that is I often struggled to stay in the present, which I know was frustrating for people—especially my family. I missed Danna and the kids while I was away, but even at home, Bai was always on my mind.

Recently, I watched a documentary about the famed investor Warren Buffett and was struck by how his daughter Susie described him:

He was there physically, but he was upstairs reading all the time. I always told my mother, "We have to talk in sound bites." I learned early on that if you start going into something long—unless you've explained to him ahead of time that it's going to be a long thing and you need him to hang in there—you lose him. You lose him to whatever giant thought he has in his head at the time that he was probably thinking about before you came in and really wants to get back to.

I saw myself in her comments, and unfortunately, I think my wife and kids could say the same. While launching and building Bai, I struggled with giving enough attention to my family. Even though Danna, Jack, and Shayna were part of the process of starting and growing the company—and I'll forever treasure those moments of dreaming together—I sacrificed a lot of time with them, even when we were together, because of my singular focus on Bai.

One day, not long after I started Bai, the reality of my family's sacrifice reared its head on the fields of Princeton Little League. I was in the stands watching Jack, who was about ten, play a Saturday doubleheader. Jack was pitching in the first game. I could tell that he just wasn't into the game—something about him felt off. During a break between innings, I took him aside and asked if everything was okay.

He was honest with me. He said, "No."

I said, "Okay, let's go take a walk."

We left the game and wound up walking through town and sitting on a bench in the middle of Princeton, about a mile and a half away from his baseball field. I pushed him to tell me what was wrong, and through tears, Jack finally said, "I miss you. Bai is taking you away from me."

When I realized that Jack had come to resent the business we had all built together, it rattled me to the core. I wondered, had I become less of a dad than I always wanted to be? Had I allowed this company to take me away from my family? Had I created a reality that he resented now and that I would resent ten years from now? I also recognized that Jack was speaking for Danna and Shayna, too, even though they had not expressed their frustrations as plainly as he did in that moment.

At that point, we were both crying. I realized that, in addition to trying to find ways to give more time to my family, I needed permission to keep building Bai. And I needed it from this beautiful kid in his baseball uniform who really wanted his dad around.

So I asked him, "Jack, can we figure this out together? Can we do this as a team?"

We talked about ways that I could make sure I was paying enough attention to our family at home, and how we could try to make sure that he, his sister, and his mom would always feel like the business was part of our family, too.

At that point, Jack gave me the permission I needed to keep building Bai and launch what we would later come to call our "bevolution." And I was able to rededicate myself to charting Bai's future with a renewed focus on my family—and with my family fully on board with our company's mission.

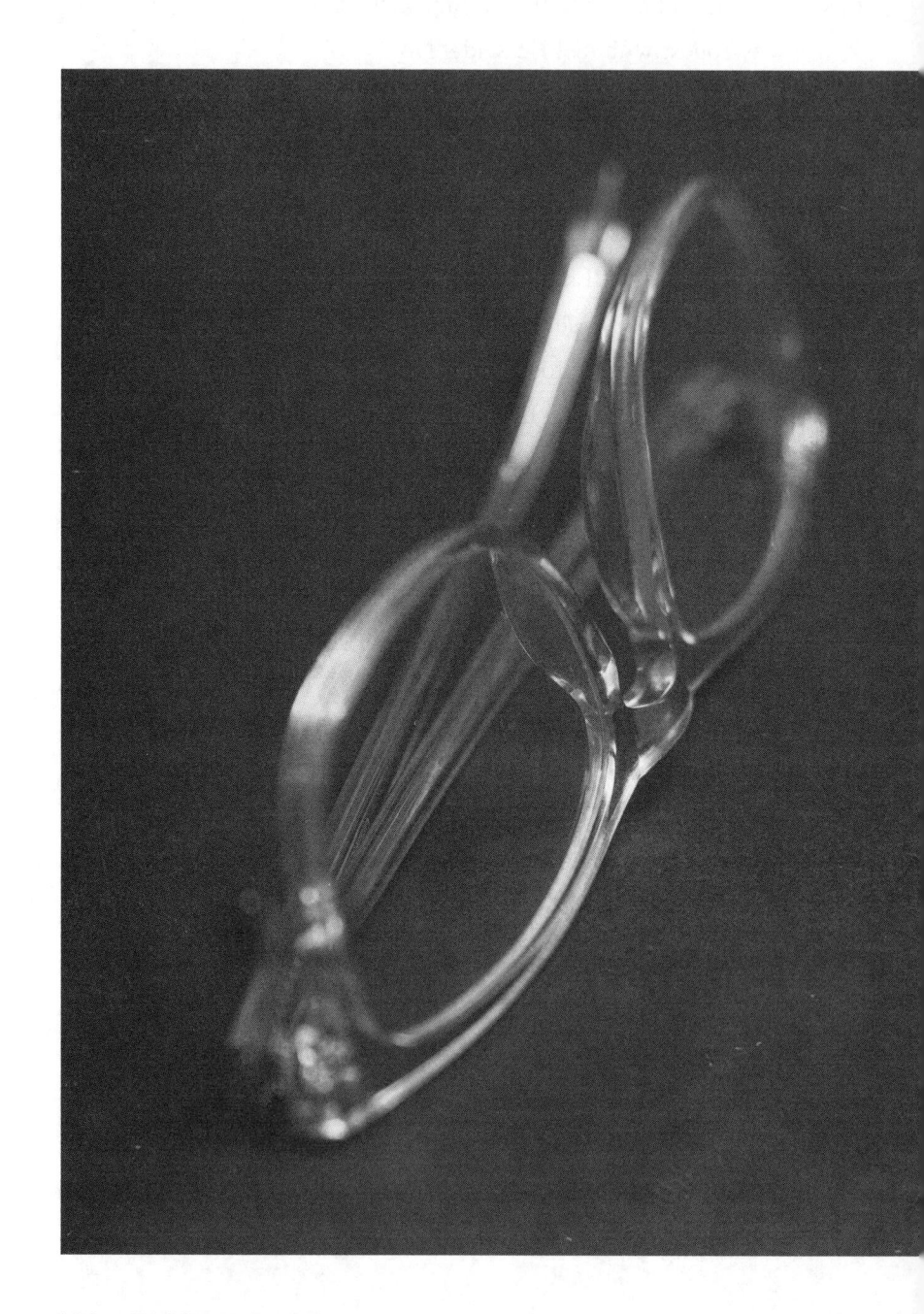

120 - BASEMENTALITY

BASEMENTALITY

KNOW THE ENDGAME

People will follow the vision of a new reality. A picture of success that is so vivid, even if it's unproven. A conviction so strong it can actually bring the endgame to life before someone's eyes. The endgame is not a place. It's not a number. It's a feeling. An understanding that you can see further into the future than others. As you inspire people to embark on the journey alongside you, fill them with a passionate belief to share what you see and do what needs to be done.

CHAPTER 5
$60 MILLION SHOULDERS

"This is the office of Senator Bill Bradley calling. He would like to speak with Ben Weiss."

"This is Ben Weiss," I said hesitantly, taking another look at the unfamiliar number on my iPhone screen and wondering if this was a prank call.

"Bill Bradley?" I thought. "Why would he be calling me?"

The woman on the other end sensed my confusion. "Don't worry, it's not anything government-related," she said. Then she whispered, "I think he really likes your drink."

A few seconds later, a big, burly voice came on the line and announced, "This is Bill Bradley. Ben, tell me about this drink Bai. What is this Jamaica Blueberry? And who thought of using the fruit of the coffee bean in a beverage?"

Bill explained that he had been in a deli on the Upper East Side of Manhattan looking for something to drink, and Bai caught his eye. He bought a bottle of Jamaica Blueberry and loved the taste. But this wasn't simply a congratulatory call. After he retired from politics, Bill became a managing director of the elite investment bank Allen & Co. and a member of Starbucks's board of directors, so he knew a lot about the beverage industry—but he'd never heard of Bai. So he had his assistant look us up.

"Why don't you come in, and we can talk?" he asked me.

BASEMENTALITY - 123

I readily agreed, and we arranged for a meeting at his Midtown Manhattan office for the next week. I thanked him for calling, hung up, and bolted upstairs to tell Danna what just happened.

We couldn't believe that our business—still in its infancy, operating out of our basement, car trunks, and a self-storage shed—was on the radar of someone like Bill Bradley. I had been preaching to Ray and Kat, as they were out in the field trying to make sales, that we just needed to get people to taste the product and good things would happen.

Well, Bai's taste was good enough to inspire a three-term US senator, former presidential candidate, and basketball Hall of Famer to call me out of the blue. That sure seemed like a sign of good things to come.

When the time for the meeting came, I presumed the setting would be formal and made an exception to my "no ties" rule. (Danna, again, had to tie it for me.) My instinct was correct.

I arrived at Allen & Co.'s office on Fifth Avenue with a cooler full of Bai and was led into a small but stately conference room with elegant, dark wooden furniture. When Bill entered the room, we shook hands and sat down across from one another at the conference table. I took a business card out of my breast pocket and intended to casually slide it over to him, but in my eagerness, I gave the card too much of a push and it zoomed across the shiny mahogany table. In the blink of an eye, Bill snatched the runaway card and tucked it into his pocket.

He smiled at me and said, "I was never the biggest guy or the fastest guy, but I always had the quickest hands in the NBA."

Bill's friendly manner put me at ease, and we had a great conversation about what I hoped to achieve with Bai. That meeting kick-started a wonderful relationship that continues to this day. Bill became an investor in Bai and a trusted adviser who was available whenever I sought counsel on strategic business decisions. I'm honored to call him a personal friend as well—he's even traveled down to Princeton to take my son out on the basketball court and show Jack some of the moves that made him a legend.

Through his wisdom, his connections, and his stamp of approval, Bill helped Bai open a lot of eyes and doors in the beverage industry. He also provided me with one of my fondest memories when he arranged for me to visit with then-Starbucks-CEO Howard Schultz.

Fifteen years earlier, I stared out of a bus window on my commute from New Jersey into Manhattan, dreaming of running a business like Starbucks. Now, as I was chasing my edge with Bai, I had the opportunity to spend time with the visionary whose approach to reinventing the coffee business helped inspire me to set off on my own path.

I felt a bond with Howard as he walked me through Starbucks headquarters and expressed his drive to continue innovating. I was honored to share my dreams for Bai with one of my business idols—and to see how energizing it was for Howard to talk about the journey of growing a brand with great potential. In some moments during our conversation, I sensed that he would have been just as happy to be in my position even though he was running a global, multibillion-dollar corporation because he was an entrepreneur and an innovator at heart.

Bill Bradley (early Bai investor):
The key for a young company is to have an idea of where you want to be, then lay out a plan that you have to meet. So many of them fail in terms of execution. I always told Ben, "You have to execute." It doesn't matter whether so-and-so company is interested in you or so-and-so press person is interested in you. That's all fluff. I would often call Ben on weekends and talk about whatever was on his mind. I felt very positive about not only his ability, his vision, and his ambition but also his execution. He didn't get discouraged. He kept driving it forward and kept adding products, and his vision kept getting bigger. And he assembled a really good team.

The attribute of great entrepreneurs and great politicians, frankly, is that you're always open to somebody else who has another idea that might be better. Ben was constantly out scanning the horizon for thoughts and ideas. He has a very active entrepreneurial mind and a very clear desire to learn. That capacity to grow is really important, not simply in running a company, but in life. And I think that's the one characteristic that I would say typified Ben—he grew.

Several months after I connected with Bill, he suggested that I meet with Rohan Oza, a former Vitaminwater executive who was interested in emerging brands. Rohan had spearheaded the marketing campaigns for Vitaminwater and Smartwater that fueled the brands' rise and led to their parent company Glaceau's landmark acquisition by Coca-Cola in 2007. Rohan was well known for putting together deals for celebrities and athletes, such as 50 Cent, Jennifer Aniston, and Kobe Bryant to endorse Vitaminwater and Smartwater in exchange for equity in the company—pioneering a trend that continues to shape entertainment marketing today. Before Glaceau, he worked for Coke as the head of marketing for Sprite and Powerade, and by the time we met, he was an investor in and adviser to a number of startup consumer brands, including Vita Coco and Popchips.

Rohan is a smooth, polished character with a lot of experience in the beverage industry. He has fantastic connections and a Hollywood dealmaker's swagger. When we first met in Bill's office, he told me that he loved the brand and wanted to make a major investment. And he wasn't shy about sharing other opinions in our first conversation—or in any of the hundreds of conversations that would follow.

Rohan Oza (early Bai investor):
I took the meeting as a favor to a friend of mine who was friendly with Senator Bradley. He knew I had a decent track record in beverages and wanted me to meet with this company that Senator Bradley had invested in. I immediately liked Ben—I thought he had tenacity and confidence. And I loved Bai5. I told him right there, "This is the holy grail." I wanted to be a part of it.

I also told Ben I didn't give two shits about the antioxidants in the beverage. I knew that Coke was always looking for a nonbubbly version of a diet drink, and I felt that Bai5 absolutely nailed it. I felt that the antioxidants were great, but they were an added benefit—the icing on the cake.

Rohan was not only an investor throughout the Bai journey, he was a confidant. He and I have different personalities and approaches to business, but that's what made us a great team. Rohan understood that my top priority in the company's early years was building distribution capacity, which sometimes came at the expense of nurturing Bai's branding. He consistently urged me to focus on branding and introduced me to talented marketing professionals who helped us improve Bai's messaging and look. Rohan and I had complementary skills and perspectives, and we knew that we (and Bai) were better with each other than without.

Rohan Oza (early Bai investor):
We were kind of like brothers—we fought and butted heads a lot. But I think we knew that in the end, our journey was together, so we listened to each other. In terms of the vision for where we should grow and how we should grow, we were very aligned a lot of the way. But we had healthy debates. Ben clearly is a much better operator than I am. He ran the company. I'm an idea guy. I provided the coaching, and I helped support the vision. Even when we battled, we would always hug it out and come to a better place for the company.

Rohan was indeed like family to me, as were others who invested their hard-earned money in the company and were willing to give me their time and insights when I was chewing over important issues or just needed to vent when the pressure was high. When you're trying to build an idea into a company and drive that company to transform an industry, you need people like these to help you get where you're going. They did more than just write checks and give good advice—they inspired me. Each of them followed their own paths to wind up on Bai's doorstep and had their own reasons for being part of Bai. But individually and together, they were all willing to dream alongside me.

Every night, I went to bed knowing that I had $60 million of other people's money resting on my shoulders—people I respected and cared for, people with spouses and children. Every day, they motivated me to fight for Bai's future. Over seven years, we shared an emotional journey that was often thrilling, sometimes frustrating, and always filled with purpose. They also taught me about trust. They trusted my vision and were reassured by my obsession. I couldn't have made Bai what it became—and I would not have loved the experience as much as I did—if it wasn't for them.

***

Sharing my Bai journey with friends who entrusted me with their investments was one of the most rewarding experiences of my career. I think back often to the moment my buddy Haim Blecher took his first sip from a bottle of Kenya Peach Bai, and I knew that it changed both of our lives.

Haim and his family are among our oldest friends in Princeton. We met them not long after we moved to town, about four years before I started Bai. Haim and I bonded over our love of (and frustrations with) the New York Jets and our shared experiences as fathers of young kids. Haim's wife, Shari, quickly became very close with Danna. The Blecher kids—Edan, Max, and Rachel—played with Jack and Shayna so often that it felt, at times, like we had adopted three more children.

Despite how tight our families had become, Haim and I didn't see much of each other in the months when I was starting Bai. He was immersed in building his spinal surgery practice, which came, naturally, with a demanding schedule, and I had gone underground with my head buried in all of the details involved with launching my company. Even after Ray and I started opening some retail accounts around Princeton, I realized I hadn't even told Haim about my new venture. That changed after Danna told Shari that we were looking for investors in Bai and gave her a bottle of Kenya Peach to bring home for Haim to try.

Haim, a die-hard Peach Snapple drinker, was floored by Bai's flavor. As a doctor, he also was intrigued by the antioxidant content of the coffeefruit. Having recently started to invest in startup companies, he reached out to me to learn more about Bai.

Haim Blecher (early Bai investor):
I didn't know anything about the beverage industry, and launching a new brand seemed to be a Herculean task. But the message of the product was very clear to me. I was a huge fan of Peach Snapple for years and tried to convert to Diet Snapple, but I just didn't like the taste. Then Ben brought along this vision of a new class of drink that's both good for you and has this incredibly cool message of using a coffee by-product.

I didn't necessarily want to invest in a beverage company because I thought it was going to do some sales and make some money—for me, it was about the disruptive message. And the most important thing was the messenger. I was 99.9 percent investing in Ben, knowing his entrepreneurial spirit, his vision, and the fact that he was a guy like me with a family in Princeton who was throwing his entire future behind this thing.

Haim and Shari agreed to become Bai's first investors. They gave us the much-needed funds to get Bai started on expanding beyond our initial foray into Princeton and New York City, and set the model for the type of people I would look for when raising money for the company over the next several years. Haim was enthusiastic about the product and my ability to grow the brand. He was an intelligent, thoughtful person

I could call upon for advice on any number of fronts. He was a fervent advocate for Bai who encouraged his own friends and colleagues to consider investing in the brand. And he was inspired to help Bai meet its long-term objective of pioneering a new beverage category and putting pressure on the industry's soda giants. I'll always be grateful that he believed in Bai and in me.

From a practical standpoint, Haim was an ideal investor because he did not demand a short-term return on his investment, nor did he insist on having operational oversight that would complicate my efforts to build the company. Many startups fall into the trap of giving away too much control—in terms of both equity and decision-making—in exchange for early investment from venture capitalists or private equity firms to help them get off the ground. It's easy to understand why. You want to believe that all you need is that first blast of fuel to ignite your rocket. It's hard to be patient. It's difficult to reject any investment offer, even one with onerous terms, when you have little or no revenue coming in and you want to grow your business. There's a good reason that the popular TV show about entrepreneurship is called *Shark Tank*—the startup waters are filled with potential predators circling vulnerable embryonic businesses.

At the stage of my career when Bai was starting out, I had enough experience dealing with investors from my previous ventures to be wary of the potential pitfalls involved with raising money. I also was extremely fortunate that I had enough resources to fund Bai's initial development and production phases and that I was in an environment where I could raise capital from investors like Haim rather than having to turn to venture capitalists.

Princeton turned out to be a great source for investors—it's a community with an affluent, professional population, and it's small enough that word travels quickly when a good business opportunity comes around. And, thankfully, enough people believed in me—people who said they were investing in the jockey as much as the horse—to support my dream of making Bai a success.

Haim Blecher (early Bai investor):
I'm involved with several companies, and my relationship with them is to serve as a sounding board. In the beginning of Bai, there weren't too many people to act as sounding boards, so Ben and I were on the phone quite often. I remember sitting in the parking lot before going into surgery one day and talking on the phone with Ben about a distributor in Albany, New York, that thought health insurance could cover Bai because of its antioxidants. We actually had serious conversations about the pros and cons of that idea.

The whole journey was amazing for me. Early on, I helped get Bai into the cafeteria of a hospital where I operated. It was the most expensive drink in the refrigerator, and within the first week, everybody was drinking it. There was no marketing behind it, but it was flying off the shelf! Every win felt so big in the beginning.

Bai caught on fire in Princeton and was very visible around town, so the excitement around it was contagious. But if anyone who invested says they knew it would become as successful as it did, they're full of it. This was one of those very, very rare rides that few investors get to experience. I'm generally an extremely cautious person, so I never really counted on any of this stuff to happen. About three years or so before Ben sold Bai to Dr Pepper, I started to see that it was still growing like crazy and that very talented people were leaving significant positions in other companies to come to Bai. They had the same trust in Ben and vision for Bai that investors had. And that's when it started to click for me that something very special was happening.

Just as my wife, Danna, was instrumental in bringing the Blechers into the fold as Bai investors, she also introduced the brand to another

Princeton physician, Tony Chiurco, who became one of our most important investors and recruited a significant number of other investors to follow his lead. Tony is a neurosurgeon who has lived in Princeton for more than forty years. He has traveled in high-society circles and sailed the seas as a champion yachtsman, but he never lost his attitude and street smarts from his hardscrabble South Philadelphia upbringing. Danna met Tony in the Princeton Little League bleachers in the summer of 2009, when I was coaching the team Jack played on with Tony's son Coleman. Several months later, she ran into Tony at his favorite lunch spot in Princeton, Nino's Pizza Star, and his connection with Bai was born.

Tony Chiurco (early Bai investor):
In the hot summer days, I would look for a place to sit down during Coleman's baseball games, and there were mostly moms in the stands. One of them was Danna. So I would sit next to her, and we would laugh our asses off, talking during the games. She was great fun. But I hardly knew Ben at all.

The following spring, I went into Pizza Star during a break while I was operating at Princeton Hospital. And Danna was sitting there with Jack having lunch. We started talking, and she told me that Ben had this new drink, he and his father were going around town selling it, and he was looking for investors.

I said, "Sure, I'll take a look at it," putting myself out there like I was a big fucking deal. She called Ben, and he showed up with his drinks ten minutes later.

He set up the bottles on the table and I tried the peach, blueberry, and dragonfruit flavors. I looked at the label of the Sumatra Dragonfruit Bai5 bottle and saw that it was five calories and naturally sweetened. I thought, "Well, that answers my dilemma when I go into a restaurant for lunch because usually I'm stuck drinking water or Diet Coke." And then I thought, "If it answers my problem, it's going to do the same for a million other people." When I saw the antioxidant language on the label, I knew that would attract people who were looking for healthy options.

I said to Ben, "This has a shot to be a winner."

We had just come through the collapse of the US financial markets in 2008, and I knew that two types of stocks that historically do well in a recession are beer and cigarette stocks. With that in mind, I thought it was reasonably safe to invest in another type of consumer product like Bai. And I thought the product had a great message. But I did think Ben was overvaluing the stock price. At the time, he was selling $2,000 to $3,000 of product per month, but he was valuing the company at $10 million. When I balked at the valuation, Ben pushed right back—he said it was a fair price and I could walk away if I didn't agree. I thought he was dreaming, but at the same time, I wanted to make the investment because I thought Bai was a great product. My rationale was that if he continued to price the stock high and it sold for that price, that would limit the number of shares being sold and keep my stake from getting diluted too much. So my wife, Kim, my brother-in-law, and I all wound up investing.

I was in my late sixties and said to myself, "You know, I never really made a big score in my life. Time is running out—my runway is getting shorter. And it looks like this could be it."

I told Kim, "I'm going in with both fists."

What I didn't know at the time was the fact that only 1 percent of beverages get past $10 million a year in sales. But in this case, ignorance was bliss.

Tony and I hit it off quickly, and our families started spending a lot of time together. Tony came to my house often on weekend mornings to drink coffee and talk business, and our family had many Sunday dinners at the Chiurcos' home. Bai was a consistent topic of conversation, of course, but we also shared many laughs talking about our kids and hearing Tony's millions of R-rated stories about his adventures growing up in post–World War II South Philly and working his way up in the field of neurosurgery.

As Bai grew over the next several years, Tony became a fixture around the office, coming to be known to everyone as "the Doc." There's a scene in the movie *Goodfellas* in which nightclub owner Sonny Bunz says of the main character, Henry Hill, "He's in the joint twenty-four hours a day. I mean, another fuckin' few minutes, he could be a stool, that's how often he's in here." It's always reminded me of Tony. That's not just because I could easily hear him say the same thing about someone, but because when he wasn't in surgery or seeing patients, you could usually find him sitting on the couch in my office, talking with me, Ari, or other members of our team about the company's direction. He was just a few conversations away from becoming Bai's barstool.

Tony did not consider himself a seasoned businessman, even though he ran his own medical practice for decades, but he was intensely curious about the beverage industry, and he thought deeply about how Bai might be affected by broader economic and societal trends. And he was our most enthusiastic fundraiser—bringing in investments from many friends and associates from the local medical and business communities. Tony's impact in building our investor base was so critical that I always give credit to "Chiurcovia Financial" for making Bai's growth possible.

Tony Chiurco (early Bai investor):

I love the tactics of business. I realized later in life that successfully managing the tactics of business is more complicated than managing a sick patient in the intensive care unit. You have so many more variables involved, such as managing people, recognizing talent, dealing with banks, convincing people that your product is good, and so on. Each one of them is equally important. If you fall short in picking the wrong talent, or negotiating with lenders, you will fail.

As my surgical career was winding down, I was glad to be involved in something that was brand-new and growing, where I could exercise other talents like fundraising. As an investor, a big part of my strategic thinking was that I couldn't let this company go under for lack of capital. In addition to wanting to help Ben succeed, I was protecting my own investment. So I pitched a lot of people to come in. A big point that I emphasized in my pitch was that the Western world was coming down on sugar. You could see the effect on soda sales in the United States. And in France, for example, President Nicolas Sarkozy imposed a national "soda tax" in 2011 to get people to cut back on sugary drinks. Bai was perfectly positioned.

Ben was confident in Bai, so he was always aggressive with his valuations. I brought in eighteen investors, including a lot of my doctor friends, and raised more than $10 million. A lot of investors who knew me trusted my judgment and came in. But others shit on me, especially bankers and people in finance. In fact, I counted them—twenty-two people shit on me. One guy, who I knew personally, laughed in my face.

In the end, those who came in made a lot of money. Ben has acknowledged that if I wasn't able to raise as much money as I did, he might have had to go to venture capitalists, and they would have imposed their will on the decision-making of the company. Business, just like life, is a matter of luck. I was very lucky to encounter Ben, and I think he was equally as lucky to encounter me. Now, if he didn't have a cute wife—and we still laugh about this—none of this would have happened for me and maybe not for Ben either.

Tony is 100 percent correct on two fronts. His tireless efforts to attract investors made my job much easier and generated capital we needed to manage Bai's growth. And as he noted, luck was absolutely on our side. I believe that I would have found a way to raise money if Danna had not connected with Tony and told him about Bai. But I can't imagine that we would have had a group of investors as fantastic as the ones Tony brought in—and I know we wouldn't have had as much fun along the way without the Doc.

***

Like Tony, many Bai investors battled naysayers among their friends and business associates who believed that backing a startup beverage company was foolish given the industry's graveyard of promising brands. From the beginning, I established aggressive valuations for Bai because I was supremely confident in my vision for the brand. The picture I painted of Bai's future was much brighter and more vibrant than any accountant or investment banker would ever conjure, which is why some prospective investors were taken aback by our valuations. The fact that some were willing to express their confidence in me by investing in Bai created daily pressure in the form of millions of dollars and immeasurable trust that I carried on my shoulders. That's why I take great pride in the fact that, for many Bai investors, their association with my company was life-changing. My friend Simon Richmond—who was there at the beginning of my Bai journey, hammering out financial projections with me in a bookstore coffee shop—is one who immediately comes to mind.

Simon was always enthusiastic about talking through any issues or problems that came up as the company was getting off its feet. He was a supportive friend and the closest entrepreneurial kindred spirit I encountered in my Bai years, someone who is exceedingly comfortable in the early stages of ideation and creation that I enjoy so much. But at the same time, I worried about Simon. He was a one-man show for his own venture selling heated clothing, and though he traveled to China several times a year, he was generally sequestered in his basement, working hard to grow his business.

I understand basement life. Basements can be amazing launching pads for businesses, but they can also start to feel like a cell if you're trapped in there for too long without working alongside others on a common mission.

Simon believed in Bai enough to make a personal financial investment in the company, which meant a lot to me, and I wanted to find ways for him to become more involved with the business. I was convinced that his insatiable curiosity and dogged problem-solving skills would benefit Bai, even though I initially didn't know where he would fit in the organization. But Simon was wary, at first, of mixing friendship and business at a deeper level because he didn't want to risk our relationship if working for Bai didn't pan out for him. Eventually, in 2015, I convinced him to join Bai on a part-time basis to help enhance our business processes

The Richmond and Weiss kids launch the first Bai stand (2009)

and intellectual property. He agreed to take on the project in exchange for additional shares in the company, to which I happily agreed. After completing that project, he agreed to take on another—and the pattern continued until he joined Bai full time as a vice president for corporate development, focusing on intellectual property, regulatory, and product development issues.

Bringing Simon aboard was one of the best moves I made at Bai, not only because he created tremendous value for the business but because the experience helped enrich him financially and personally. Simon was willing to put his own business dream on hold to help me realize mine, and I am deeply grateful that he placed such faith in me. I pulled Simon from his basement into the journey that started in my own basement, and despite his initial trepidation, our friendship blossomed as we became closer business colleagues.

When we sold Bai in 2017, I was so thrilled to be able to reward people like Simon, who invested their futures in my dream. And I know that, to this day, neither of us will forget that weekend on the Ocean City, Maryland, shore when our little children set up the first-ever Bai roadside stand and helped kick off an adventure that would bring both of our families such joy.

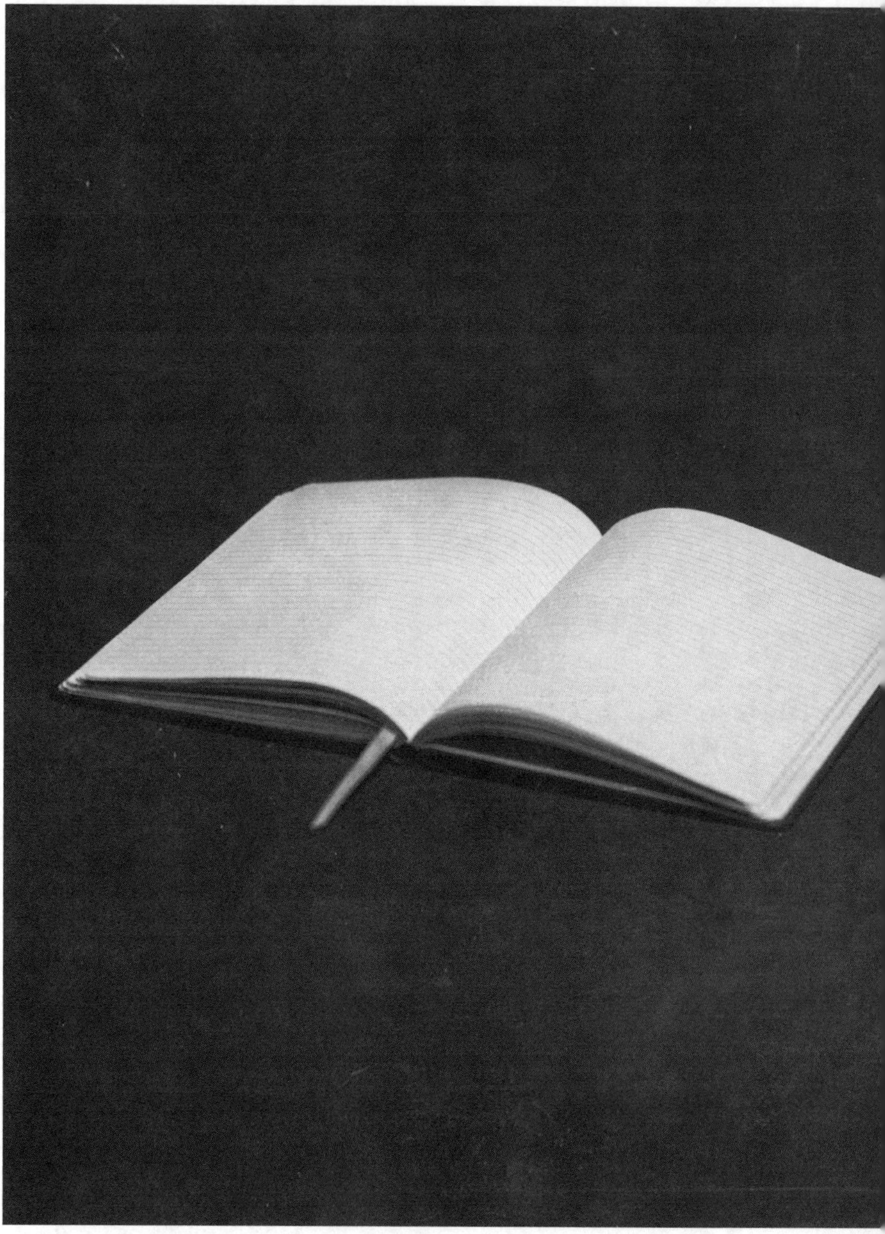

BASEMENTALITY

ENTHRALL, NOT ENSLAVE

Build a tribe of true believers who are inspired to join the black sheep's adventure. Enthrall them with a story of possibility and an invitation to share in success. But also take responsibility and accountability for their journey—their families, their futures, their hopes. Form a true family, guided by Basementality. Collectively carry the weight of your audacious goals instead of feeling enslaved to an unrealistic dream.

CHAPTER 6
TARGETING THE ENEMY

In the spring of 2012, I walked into the McCaffrey's supermarket in the Princeton Shopping Center around lunchtime and made my usual rounds through the beverage aisle and into the prepared foods area, where Bai vied for attention with dozens of brands in a large open cooler.

I spoke to the store manager, lobbying him to give us more space in the cooler and more prime end-cap real estate. I was pressing our case even though I was sure my hardworking stepfather, Ray, likely had a similar conversation with him earlier that day.

As I was making my pitch, I saw a shopper come in and browse the beverage options. She appeared to match Bai's ideal customer profile—a fit millennial mother in workout clothes, with her newborn in a carrier—so I was curious to see what she would select.

I watched her scan the cooler and pick up a bottle of Bai Kenya Peach. She spun the bottle, looked at the label, and quickly put it back on the shelf. Then she grabbed a Peach Diet Snapple and headed to the cash register.

She was clearly looking for a lower-calorie peach-flavored drink, and when she saw that Bai's Kenya Peach was seventy calories, she opted instead for the ten-calorie Diet Snapple. At first, I wished she had just kept scanning the Bai options a few more bottles to her right, because she would have found our five-calorie Bai5 Panama Peach. But then I recognized the flaw in my thinking. Seeing her walk away from the cooler with

BASEMENTALITY - 143

a competitor's product in hand, the realization hit me like a thunderbolt: we were confusing our customers.

And that was likely because we were slightly confused ourselves. We didn't know who our true enemy was.

***

Before we could get to the point of attacking our true nemesis, Bai still had a lot of growing to do. In 2011, we took a major step forward on that path by straying from the conventional industry playbook.

On a brisk, windy autumn Saturday, with Danna beside me and the kids in the backseat, I was driving home from a Bai sampling at a Costco in Northern New Jersey. My mind, as usual, was racing with sales figures and marketing ideas when I noticed the kids giggling and Danna holding back a smile. That's when I caught a glimpse of myself in the rearview mirror and realized I had been driving for at least a half hour while still sporting the hairnet the Costco manager required me to wear.

I snatched the hairnet off my head, balled it up, and whipped it over my shoulder at the kids. Their giggles turned into howls.

That day I found myself driving with the ever-fashionable accessory on my head was several months before the customer at McCaffrey's opened my eyes to Bai's problem of seeing our enemy. It was the fall of 2011, two years into our Bai journey, and we were laser focused on introducing our brand to as many consumers as possible. On many weekends like that one, our family drove all over the New Jersey and New York area for Bai "roadshows" at Costco stores. These sampling events at the warehouse club chain allowed the Bai team to meet consumers at what we call the "point of thirst" in stores.

Whenever Bai scheduled roadshows within a few hours of Princeton, Danna and I brought the kids along so they could see how people were reacting to the drinks and get a better understanding of how hard our team was working. And more than a few times, we put them to work opening cases, putting bottles on ice, and setting up sample cups—child labor laws be damned!

Costco was our first, and our most impactful, national account in Bai's early days. We were raised on Costco's notoriously difficult standards, and the aisles of those giant warehouse stores are where we strengthened our ability to compete with more established national brands.

Costco events were grueling, with long hours standing and talking to customers, but they were also extremely energizing. Not only did the Costco roadshows represent an occasional source of amusement for my kids when I forgot to take off my hairnet, they were a pivotal growth opportunity and a prime example of how Bai defied prevailing wisdom.

Typically, success in club stores like Costco and Sam's Club were the final frontier for emerging beverage brands, coming only after years of brand-building in grocery, convenience, and drug stores. Beverage insiders believed new brands could not thrive in club stores because shoppers in those environments were only interested in familiar products that they wanted to buy in bulk. Convenience and drug stores (known in the industry as small-format stores) were the more traditional testing grounds because consumers could sample unfamiliar brands one bottle or can at a time.

But I saw things differently.

In early 2011, I had a conversation with a Costco buyer who organized roadshows around the Northeast to feature brands that were not already on their shelves. Even though it was largely unprecedented for a new brand like Bai to focus heavily on club-store sales, I was quickly convinced that this would be a powerful springboard for us and that we needed to go all-in. Bolstered by how Bai was selling in grocery and small-format outlets in the New Jersey and New York areas, I was confident that people who tried our brand would want to purchase it in any kind of store. To me, there was no reason to hesitate about moving aggressively into the club-store environment.

Costco gave us a limited roadshow run that summer, and we made the most of it. We had a strong showing that summer, and Costco agreed to let Bai run multiple four-day roadshows from New England down into Virginia weekly. This put us face-to-face with thousands of customers, and their direct feedback on our flavors and messaging helped inform our decision-making as we continued to build the brand. Critically, Costco allowed us to sell cases on the spot if shoppers liked what they sampled, so we recouped costs and turned the roadshows into a sustained marketing effort that paid for itself. Plus, the roadshows let Bai establish a significant footprint at one of the nation's largest retailers at a time when we were still cobbling together regional distribution partnerships to grow our presence in the market. Costco store managers saw the strong demand for Bai at our samplings, and they gave us permanent floor space in premium locations. Other retailers took notice, which helped us expand into other national chains.

The Costco roadshows immediately became the centerpiece of Bai's emerging culture. The seeds of our scrappy, obsessive approach to building the Bai brand were sown in those giant warehouse stores. On any given Thursday through Sunday, we had four to six Bai representatives at each Costco location engaging with customers and selling cases for ten hours from open to close.

From the beginning, the roadshows were all-hands-on-deck events. During their earliest days, I, Danna, Ari Soroken, Kat Haddon, and our small team of salespeople, field marketers, and other employees regularly staffed the roadshows. I gave Kat the responsibility of overseeing the launch of this effort. She did a fantastic job, setting the tone by working relentlessly to execute killer roadshows and training other staff to follow her lead.

Kat Haddon (former director of shopper marketing for Bai):
The Costco roadshows became these epic team-building and sales

events. When we were in high-traffic stores, where everything was buzzing and cranking, no one would have time to breathe. The day would go by in the blink of an eye.

Ben believed you had to be more assertive than just sitting behind a table asking people to try a drink. So we always had one person stand in the aisle to wrangle people to the table. Then we had people at the table pouring samples and educating customers about the product. And we had people behind the table making sure everything was neat and tidy, opening cases for the samples and packing cases when someone wanted to make a purchase. Initially, we created custom mix-and-match twelve-packs based on the flavors each shopper wanted to take home. We kept tallies so we could see patterns in what people liked to mix together. When Costco later gave us the opportunity to sell variety packs on their store shelves, we knew what people liked because we had all of those handwritten notes from the roadshows. It was real guerrilla-style market research.

Bai was the highest-selling beverage roadshow of the summer in 2011, so Costco gave us the opportunity to expand the program. At that time, we had about twenty full-time staff in the company—mostly salespeople in the Northeast and Mid-Atlantic, with a few in Southern California. We scaled from one roadshow a week to two, then four, very quickly, so we had to hire hourly employees—we called them brand ambassadors—to work the roadshows. A lot of them were college kids; some were career brand ambassadors, who represented different brands on different days. The people piece was always the hardest part of the job—finding quality brand ambassadors, getting everyone trained, making sure they were present at every show, keeping their energy up and making them feel the same sense of ownership in Bai that we felt.

We always went above and beyond to pull off the roadshows. There were many times when we found ourselves running out of inventory on site after the first day or two—and there was no room for missed opportunity.

So I would call our distributor in the area in the middle of the night to get more product. They would come to the warehouse with keys to open up, let me borrow one of their trucks, and I would drive it to the Costco to unload. One time, when I was near my home in Connecticut, my dad came with me. Bai was always a family affair.

As the roadshow schedule expanded, Kat needed more support to manage them, so I assigned our ace salesperson—my stepfather, Ray—and a new employee—my mom, Pat—to work with her. With the real estate market still in the doldrums, my mom needed a fresh start, and I was thrilled to provide her with a growth opportunity after everything she had done for me. Plus, I knew she was one hell of a worker who would be tireless in pursuit of her goals, exactly the kind of person we sought for the Bai team.

Eventually, my mom took charge of hiring the brand ambassadors who staffed the Costco roadshows and other sampling events around the country. As with everything we did in Bai's early years, she approached recruiting with tenacity and frugality, relying mainly on free Craigslist job ads and her innate people skills. If she went to Chipotle for lunch and got great service, she would immediately start trying to recruit the person behind the counter—and, boom, we'd have a new brand ambassador. She proved to have a great eye for talent, bringing in a number of people who rose through the ranks and became key players at Bai for years. And, really, who's better to identify like-minded ambassadors for your business than your mommy?

Like she did whenever I needed her over the years, my mom made every effort to support and encourage me as I built Bai, and she made a true impact on the business. After we installed a formal human resources team, my mom moved out of recruiting and became our community liaison, forging relationships and finding opportunities for Bai to support children and families in the area, from Little League baseball to charitable organizations. And she remained a loving and supportive presence around our office—not just for me but for the many people she brought into the company. I will always be grateful for the boundless love and commitment she gave to me, the examples about tenacity and integrity that she showed me, the beautiful moments we have shared with our family, and the coffee-scented bedtime kisses she gave me as a kid, which set me off on my journey into business later in life. (I think there's a lesson in that for all parents—always kiss your kids goodnight because you never know what might inspire them.)

My folks weren't the only familiar faces who joined Bai around that time. My sister, Candice, and Eric Kellems, my former Chocolixir and Boosta Shot collaborator, also came aboard. They both took on roles that would evolve over time. Candice and Eric, like Ari, Kat, Ray, and some others, were the ideal kinds of people to build a business with—smart enough to figure out solutions to problems they've never faced before, selfless enough to move in and out of different roles without bruised egos or squabbles over titles or territory, and so committed and hardworking that they became the examples to follow as our team continued to grow.

Candice spent her first year focused on logistics, learning on the fly how to get our products shipped around the country on time and at reasonable costs. She then moved into ingredient purchasing and production roles before ultimately taking charge of sourcing and producing our point-of-sale marketing materials, using the experience she gained from years in the industry. Every eye-catching Bai display that went up in a retail store or at a promotional event had Candice's fingerprints on it. One minute, she was haggling with a local vendor to get the best price on decals for beverage coolers; the next, she was tracking down a manufacturer in China to make eight hundred bicycles with wheels that looked like giant slices of fruit. Candice excelled in managing the often-chaotic demands of our sales, marketing, and creative teams to make our brand look as premium as possible in the public eye. She personified one of the mantras heard frequently around Bai: "No is not an option."

Eric, meanwhile, wore numerous hats in our production operation. Eric started out working closely with Paul Sapan as he developed new flavors, which Eric would then move into production. He spent countless hours on our co-packers' plant floors, enforcing our quality standards and training other staff members to become certified tasters to ensure that every batch of Bai received our stamp of approval before going out for sale. Eric also took on responsibility for sourcing ingredients, like our coffeefruit and sweeteners, securing better pricing as our purchasing volumes increased substantially. And he carried out all of these duties while sacrificing considerable time with his wife and children, who remained in his home state of Utah for the first several years of his tenure with Bai.

Eric Kellems (former senior vice president of Bai):

When I joined Bai, I would work at the production plant or in the office all week, then work Costco roadshows on most weekends. We had a lot of people who didn't think of Bai as just a job—for us, it was a lifestyle. We had some eight-to-five people we hired at different points in time during Bai's growth, but they didn't make it because Bai wasn't an eight-to-five organization. It was really a collective of people who worked very hard and were passionate about what they did—and it showed. We used to joke that we were living in dog years because everything was done at such an accelerated, hypergrowth pace.

Ben and Danna allowed me to stay at their house and took me in as part of their family. I tried to get home to my own family as much as I could. The only red-eye flight out of Salt Lake City into the greater New York area was into John F. Kennedy Airport at the time. When I left home, I would hop on a plane at midnight on a Sunday night to get back east. The flight into JFK in Queens would land about 6 a.m., then I would take the AirTrain to the Long Island Railroad to Penn Station in Manhattan, and finally get on a New Jersey Transit train to get to work by 8 a.m. And I would hit the ground running from there. It absolutely took a toll on me and my family, but fortunately, I have a wonderful wife who was willing to allow me to go chase some dreams. After a few years, the business grew enough that we moved the family to New Jersey, which allowed me to have a little bit better work-life balance.

***

In our early years, my street-pounding, handshaking, sales machine of a stepfather, Ray, wound up needing triple bypass surgery—but that wasn't his only brush with catastrophe at Bai.

Our first full year was 2010, and we managed to clear $600,000 in revenue. By the end of 2011, that figure jumped to $1.7 million, and along the way, our storage needs were being stretched to capacity.

In mid-2011, we were renting space at the local self-storage facility to house our product. When we received a full trailer of product, it would take almost an entire day to unload it. The entryway into the facility was quite narrow, so it could take a driver up to forty-five minutes to back in and line up the truck perfectly. Then the fun started—getting eighteen pallets, weighing about 1,600 pounds each, into storage. Ray and I usually handled that job. As we outgrew our original ten-foot-by-ten-foot shed, we started storing additional product in a windowless room that we were told had once been used by the FBI. The doorway to that room was roughly the same width as a pallet, so we'd have to nudge one case here and smack another case there to make sure everything lined up perfectly so we could get the pallet through the door. It probably took us ten minutes just to get one pallet into the room. The room was big enough to stack our product two pallets high, but we didn't have a forklift, so we had to unpack one pallet and then repack it by hand on top of another one. The pallets were so jam-packed into the room that if you needed a case of a certain flavor that wasn't near the door, you'd have to climb over the other pallets to get to it. And because the room had no windows, it was hot as hell in there. I bought four portable air conditioners and ran them 24/7 to keep the product from going bad—luckily, we didn't have to pay the electric bill!

One day, Ray and I barely avoided a tragedy while unloading a trailer. I was using a jack to pull one pallet off the trailer and maneuver it down the liftgate, which came off the truck at an angle. Ray was on the opposite side of the pallet, helping me guide it off the truck toward the shed a few feet behind him. As the pallet started to gain speed heading down the liftgate, Ray's foot got caught underneath. For one terrifying moment, I thought he was going to get crushed up against the wall by the nearly two-ton stack of cases. I yanked the handle of the pallet jack to one side as hard as I could, and thankfully, it swerved enough that he was able to free his foot and avoid getting squashed. I still get chills thinking about it.

Our DIY self-storage solution was not typically so dangerous, but it definitely was inefficient. And storage wasn't our only issue. We were still using my basement as Bai's headquarters. Eric Kellems stayed over at our house most weeknights, so in the mornings, he would have to close up the sleepaway sofa in the basement so my sister, Candice, could have desk space. I was spending a lot of time on the road with Ari, meeting with prospective distribution and retail partners, but when I was home, I worked from my desk a few feet from Candice's. If I needed to have a meeting, I had to find outside space, usually at the Princeton Public Library or at local coffee shops, especially at times when the kids were home running around.

The time had come to look for a real office and warehousing solution for Bai. But I wasn't interested in moving into a cubicle farm with oatmeal-colored walls and floors. I wanted something with a little more style.

Luckily, we had two real estate pros, Pat and Ray, working for Bai. They found space available in a renovated warehouse facility that was about fifteen minutes from my home in Princeton but in a totally different environment. The facility is in the blue-collar town of Hamilton, right on the border of New Jersey's capital of Trenton, a once-bustling manufacturing city that has been battered by poverty and crime for decades as jobs disappeared. It was certainly not a glamorous option, but it was exactly what I was looking for. These humble surroundings seemed like an appropriate setting for an underdog brand in a beverage industry dominated by three giant corporations. And the facility itself—an unfinished mixed-use space that we could design to reflect Bai's culture and meet our changing needs—was ideal for our growing company.

In October 2011, we moved into the space we dubbed BaiQuarters (or BQ). We initially rented a five-hundred-square-foot suite for offices but quickly outgrew it. Within a few years, we added thousands of square feet of office space in BQ, as well as multiple spaces within our building and three other buildings nearby for product storage. Ultimately, BQ grew to 45,000 square feet of offices, spaces for our team to meet and eat, and a lab for product research and development.

By 2015, we no longer had room for product storage at BQ as our sales, marketing, and administrative teams continued to expand. So we consolidated our storage and distribution operations into one new facility, a 480,000-square-foot former Ocean Spray plant in the nearby town of Bordentown that had closed after seventy-one years of operation.

Bai's physical expansion was literally a dream come true for me. For years, even before I started Bai, I had a recurring dream in which Danna and I were standing in front of a warehouse and holding each other while taking a photo. Around the time that we were preparing to open the Bordentown facility, Danna's sister, Jill, and her father, Natie, were visiting us in Princeton, so we took them over to see the warehouse. As we were leaving, I asked someone to take a photo. When I saw it, I blurted out, "Holy shit!"

It was the exact same picture that I had dreamed about—from the shirt I was wearing to the way the warehouse looked in the background. All these years later, I still can't believe how surreal that moment was.

With Danna at our new warehouse, just as I had imagined (2015)

***

Ray wasn't the only one who risked his life for Bai during our early growth. Ari and I tangled with Mother Nature while trying to seal our first distribution deal in New England, and we almost didn't make it back.

Bai captured the industry's attention soon after our launch, as we won Best New Functional Drink and Best New Beverage Ingredient accolades at the InterBev 2010 Beverage Innovation Awards, a major industry event. And we began making inroads with the distributor community. In Bai's first two-plus years, we signed distribution agreements with about twenty-five regional operators in what was known as the beverage industry's white network—independent distributors that were not part of the Coca-Cola (red) or Pepsi (blue) networks.

All of our early distribution negotiations were very tough. It was a daunting proposition trying to figure out which markets to focus on and which distributors would be our best partners. That time was a baptism by fire for me in terms of learning how to negotiate with distributors who ostensibly held the future of my brand in their hands.

I viewed distributors as a necessary evil. We needed them to gain access to more retail markets, but I was wary about how much effort they would put into building the Bai brand. After all, we would be one of many brands on their delivery trucks—how hard was a distributor rep going to fight to get Bai placed in a supermarket when the manager says, "No thanks," and just wants to reorder the same number of cases of the same sodas and juices he's been carrying for years? Distributors position themselves as the industry's brand builders, but I just didn't have the confidence that they would have the same drive, work ethic, and commitment to Bai that our own team would.

The Vitaminwater deal a few years earlier further complicated negotiations between distributors and beverage suppliers. Many distributors had earned a nice windfall when Coca-Cola acquired Vitaminwater and had to buy up the brand's existing distribution rights. I quickly learned that distributors wanted deals that would offer similar compensation for losing hard-earned business if the brand was sold in the future. I was confident about Bai's potential and wanted to establish relationships within the DSD system that would benefit both parties as we grew, but I was adamant that they would not take advantage of us just because we were new to the game. I was not willing to sign deals with onerous buyout clauses that I might one day come to regret. It was hard to turn away opportunities at an early stage of building a company, but I had to stay resolute in not sacrificing our future to get Bai off the ground in new markets. As always, I had to keep my bifocals on to keep both our short-term and long-term goals in focus.

In 2010, I negotiated for weeks with a small company called G. Housen, which covered Vermont and select markets in New Hampshire and Western Massachusetts. When the deal was finally ready to sign, Ari and I made plans to make the four-hour drive up to G. Housen's office in Brattleboro, Vermont.

The day before we were scheduled to come to his office, Kevin Watterson, G. Housen's president, called me and said, "There's a major snowstorm developing up here, Ben. Why don't we do this next week?"

I didn't even bother to ask Ari what he thought. "No worries, Kevin," I said. "We're on our way. We need to do this now. We'll see you tomorrow!"

I would have walked to Vermont to sign that deal if I had to. Waiting until the next week was not an option. Ari and I filled a Bai van with product and hit the road.

The weather was fine as we headed up the New Jersey Turnpike, then over the George Washington Bridge into the New York City area. We breezed up Interstate 91 into Connecticut and Massachusetts. But not long after we passed Springfield, Massachusetts, we understood why Kevin wanted to postpone the meeting.

We were in the belly of a white-out blizzard.

We slowed down, then slowed again, then slowed again. I had the wipers on max, but we had such low visibility that Ari asked if we should pull over, find a hotel, and wait out the storm. But at that point we were just fifty miles from our destination, and I was laser-focused on sealing that deal.

"It's not so bad," I responded, probably thinking that if I said it out loud, I could convince Ari and myself that I was telling the truth. "Let's keep going."

With snow smearing under our windshield wipers and bitter winds whipping the sides of the van, we crawled up the slick highway. The trip from Springfield to Brattleboro should have taken about an hour.

It took four hours.

Along the way, I snapped a picture of the winter-not-so-wonderland scene as a reminder that you can't let anything, even Mother Nature, stand between you and your edge.

We finally settled into our hotel in Brattleboro that night, and the next morning, we met with Kevin to begin our partnership. Then we gathered with G. Housen's sales team to introduce them to our brand and train them on how to sell Bai. I believe they respected the initiative we showed traveling through the awful weather. And we tried our hardest to inspire those salespeople and make them feel like they needed this new brand on their trucks even though they had never heard of it before that week.

This was a relatively small deal in Bai's history, but at that time, it was huge, and we needed to treat it like the most important thing we'd ever done. In those days, we approached every phone call, negotiation, and training the same way. After striking deals with smaller players like G. Housen, we started to move up the ladder into discussions with bigger DSD players. In 2011, we reached an agreement with the Honickman Group, one of the nation's largest independent distributors, to dramatically increase our availability throughout the Mid-Atlantic region, from Southern New Jersey down to Virginia. We expanded further into New England with the members of the Northeast Independent Distributors Association, and we later aligned with Polar Beverage to accelerate our growth in the Northeast. In 2013, we signed with Dr Pepper Snapple Group as our New York distributor, kick-starting a relationship that would lead to national distribution and Dr Pepper's eventual acquisition of Bai.

For many years, we had a framed photo of that snow-blanketed highway hanging in BQ. I always pointed it out to new employees and visitors to help explain how we built Bai in the early years. Though I loved the entirety of my time with Bai—and we had so many big achievements in our later years—moments like that snowy trek through New England are what I look back upon most fondly.

***

With our expansion in distribution came growth in our product line. After creating our first five-calorie flavor, Bai5 Sumatra Dragonfruit, a year earlier, we had a lineup of about ten flavors by 2011—evenly split between the original Bai formula and Bai5.

But we still hadn't answered the burning question, "What is our identity at Bai?"

That is, until that day at McCaffrey's when I saw the young mom select Diet Snapple over our product.

I knew she was looking for a low-calorie drink. I knew she wanted peach. Why didn't she just keep digging through our products until she landed on Bai5 Panama Peach, which had half the calories of Diet Snapple?

That's when I realized our many options weren't the solution—they were the problem.

We were asking the customer to do too much work to understand the difference between the original Bai and Bai5 lines. Yes, they had different cap colors (black for Bai and red for Bai5) and the Bai5 label subtly highlighted the five-calorie option. But anyone glancing at both bottles would simply see the Bai brand and not likely notice any distinctions. Shoppers' time and attention was so precious that if we made it hard for them to figure out what we were offering, they would simply keep moving down the aisle as that shopper did. For a new brand trying to break into a crowded market, confusion was a death sentence.

As I watched us lose that customer's business at McCaffrey's, I knew it couldn't have been an isolated incident. And I knew I couldn't let it happen again.

I abruptly ended my conversation with the McCaffrey's manager, hustled to my car, and sped back to BQ. As I white-knuckled the steering wheel while battling the frustrating midday traffic on Route 1, I replayed in my mind the moment when I watched that customer reject Bai in favor of a diet iced tea made with artificial sweeteners.

It became clear to me that she wasn't running toward any particular brand as she scanned that cooler shelf—instead, she was actually running away from sugar and calories.

At that moment, I knew that we needed to refocus on targeting our true enemy: sugar.

We had developed something unprecedented in our business—a great-tasting drink with five calories, one gram of sugar, and no artificial sweeteners—and we needed to marshal all of our efforts to make that difference clear to consumers.

This was not the time to simply redesign our labels to make a stronger differentiation between Bai and Bai5. The coffeefruit and antioxidants would always be part of Bai's story, but our mission was now clear—we had to lead the charge to fight against Big Sugar's hold on the beverage aisles of every store in America. We had to plant our flag with the five-calorie version, to go with our strength and distinguish Bai as the premier low-calorie, better-for-you beverage option. This was our time to take a stand.

When I got back to BQ, I assembled everyone in the office and told them what I had just witnessed at the McCaffrey's cooler. An ideal customer wanted what we offered, searched for it, and couldn't find it because she was confused.

"That's it," I told them. "I don't ever want to sell another Black Cap again!"

The team was stunned. They sat there looking at me, somewhat like the plant manager back at First Fruits when I told him we needed to dump thousands of dollars of product because it wasn't perfect. Only this time, it wasn't a vendor looking at me; it was my own team.

Every silent face said the same thing: "Isn't this a rash decision?"

But just as I had done at First Fruits, I explained my rationale. As we talked through the reasons we needed to focus solely on our five-calorie products, I grew more confident about following my instinct. I urged our team to see the importance of finding our mission and rallying behind a common cause.

Within a few minutes, their initial surprise and hesitation turned into action.

Make no mistake—this was a painful decision in the short term. Over the course of a few weeks, we had to pull existing Black Cap inventory off store shelves and out of distributors' warehouses around the country. We lost thousands of bottles and hundreds of thousands of dollars in unsold product. At the same time, we had to quickly develop five-calorie versions of some of our popular original Bai flavors, such as blueberry and mango, which required us to work formulation magic at an unprecedented speed. And we had to explain our shift in strategy to our wholesale and retail partners without undermining their confidence in our brand. Despite the short-term challenges it presented, this change was necessary, and we knew a gradual transition would only prolong the confusion. So we banded together and tackled the hard work necessary to realize our newly refined vision and tackle our new enemy: Big Sugar.

When you're running a business with big dreams, you can't be satisfied with any one idea. You have to be obsessed with obtaining feedback from your customers to know if you are truly meeting their needs and distinguishing yourself from the competition. In our case, this led Bai to find its fight and launch a full-scale war on sugar.

The switch to an all five-calorie lineup proved to be a momentous leap forward for the brand. Yes, the coffeefruit was still a unique ingredient, and antioxidants remained an important part of Bai's story, but the pivot to five calories crystallized our brand's identity. In the months that followed, we strengthened our product positioning to emphasize our distinctive combination of low calories and great taste. Consumers had struggled for so long with the diet dilemma—finding a lower-calorie beverage that didn't depend on sugar or artificial sweeteners to deliver the flavor they craved. Now we had firmly established that Bai was the solution—and we knew who we were fighting.

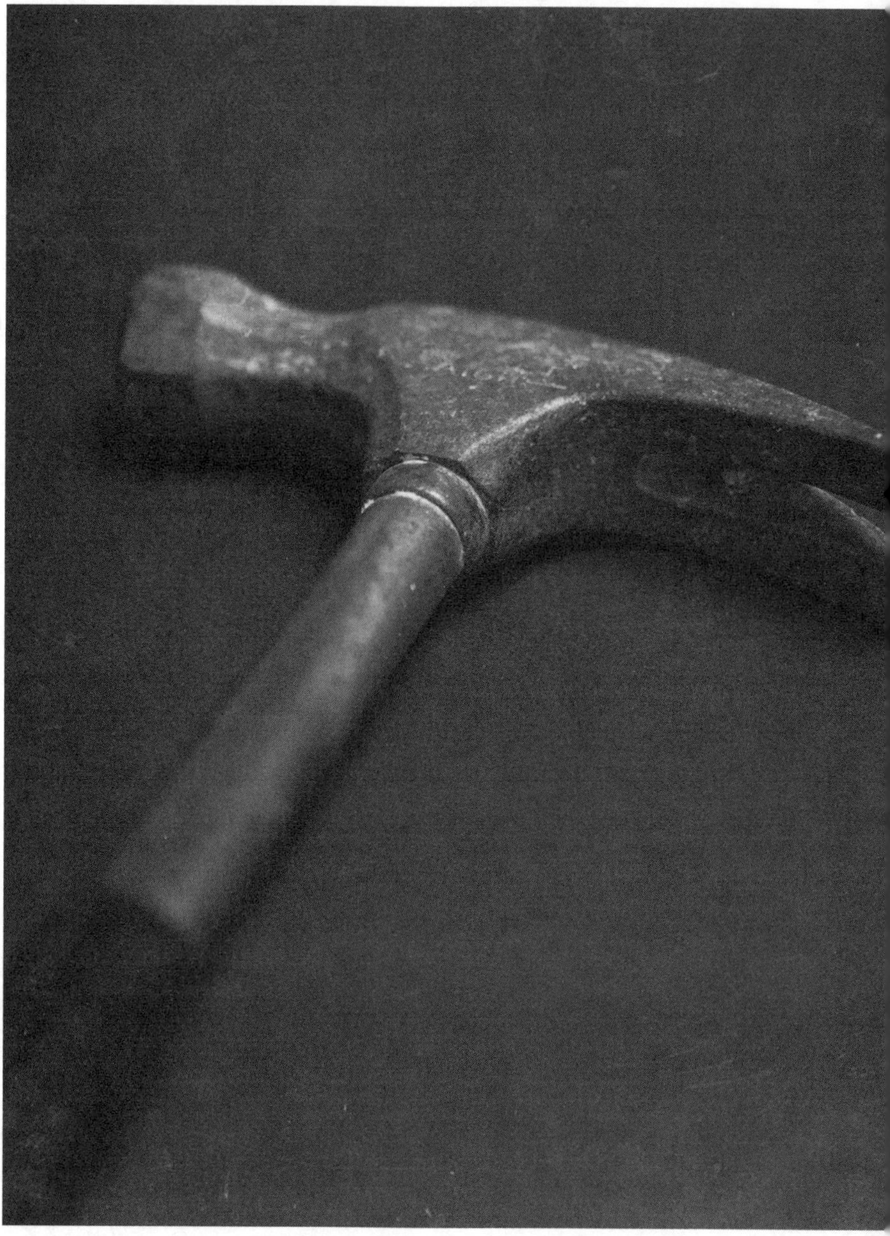

BASEMENTALITY

RIGHT THE WRONGS

Your mission must never waver—see a wrong and right it. That will focus you like nothing else. Know your enemy and call it out. Muster an old-fashioned hatred for shit that needs fixing. That's the fuel for the black sheep's fire. It's crucial to find your fight. Make sure that everyone around you knows what you're battling and that they're ready for war.

CHAPTER 7
ROYALS, REBELS, AND RANDOMS

In 2013, I was invited to fly down to Bentonville, Arkansas, to meet with a buyer at Walmart. At that point, Costco was our biggest account, the only national retailer carrying Bai. Walmart was more than four times Costco's size.

As I left the house for my trip, I gave Danna a longer hug than usual. "This one could be huge," I told her. "It could be a rocket ship."

Always optimistic but wary of getting overexcited, Danna wished me luck and told me to call her after the meeting. That evening, I flew into Northwest Arkansas Regional Airport, about twenty-five minutes away from Walmart headquarters. Beside me was Ken Kurtz, who had joined Bai in late 2011 to lead our sales team and quickly confirmed my instinct that he was the leader we needed to take our company to the next level.

Ken and I decided to grab dinner and a drink before settling into our hotel. Even though we both understood this was the biggest meeting in Bai's history up to that point, we had a very relaxed night. Ken and I had already developed a natural rhythm as a team, and I felt so confident with him by my side. I knew that with my evangelism for Bai and Ken's unrivaled experience with building beverage brands, we would wow the buyer with our vision for the future of Bai and Walmart together.

The next morning, we pulled up to Walmart's sprawling headquarters and made our way to the buyer's office. He was right on time and bounded into the meeting, smiling and carrying a bottle of Brasilia Blueberry.

"Guys," he said, "I gotta tell you, I love this stuff. My fiancée actually turned me onto it—she knows everything about the brand."

Before Ken or I could get more than a greeting out of our mouths and settle into our chairs, he got right down to business.

"Look, we see what you guys are doing on a regional basis. It's time for you to go national," he said, dropping down into his chair and thumping his bottle of Bai on the desk.

"I couldn't agree more," I said, as Ken smiled and nodded along with me.

"Great," the buyer said. "Here's the deal. We'll put Bai on the shelves right away at one dollar per bottle, and you'll ship directly to our warehouse. You'll be a $100 million brand before you know it."

The offer was a no-brainer. But not in the way he was thinking.

Bai's revenue had climbed from $1.7 million in 2011 to $5.4 million in 2012, and we were on pace to jump to $17.1 million in 2013. The idea of becoming a $100 million brand almost instantly was certainly enticing, but not with the strings that were attached to this offer.

We had worked hard to establish Bai as a premium brand in the enhanced water market—that was the foundation of our growth thus far and the key to our future. Consumers were demonstrating their willingness to pay two dollars per bottle for better ingredients without sacrificing great taste. I had no interest in suddenly dropping the price of Bai in half and undercutting its position as a premium brand for a short-term boost in volume and revenue. Plus, there was no way to produce Bai with our high-quality ingredients and sell it profitably for one dollar per bottle. Becoming a bargain beverage was not Bai's destiny.

In addition, the requirement to ship our product directly to Walmart's warehouses would cut out our wholesale partners in the direct store distribution (DSD) network, which in turn would make it impossible to grow Bai's availability outside of Walmart and severely limit our potential.

The speed and the terms of the Walmart buyer's offer put me back on my heels for a moment. But I quickly gathered my composure. I glanced over at Ken, who returned my look with confident resolution in his eyes. He gave me a quick nod, and I turned to the buyer, who was leaning back in his chair, expecting us to jump at his offer.

"Sorry," I said, "but Bai is a premium product that sells at two dollars per bottle. You don't get five calories to taste that good with just any ingredients. And," I added, "we're committed to going with DSD."

The buyer tilted his head to one side and slapped his hands on his desk. "Well, then, I guess that's it," he said.

"I guess so," I replied.

And just a few minutes after we walked into his office, Ken and I were headed back down the hall toward the exit of Walmart headquarters.

I could feel my blood pumping through my veins as we walked out into the parking lot. I had just told the world's largest retail chain that I wasn't interested in working together on their terms. I felt good about upholding my principles and refusing to undercut Bai's potential as a premium product. Still, going national with Walmart was a gigantic opportunity that most brands never get, and I couldn't help but wonder if that would be our only chance.

Ken and I walked in silence until we reached our rental car. Then, as I fished for my key in my jacket pocket, he threw his arm around me. He understood exactly what I was thinking.

"I know that was tough," Ken said. "But I'm proud of you for sticking to your guns and doing what you just did."

Ken had been through these battles before, and his reassurance was exactly what I needed. My gut told me that I had made the right call, but knowing Ken had my back dissolved any doubts that started to creep into my brain. That meeting may have only lasted a few minutes, but it had a longstanding impact on both of us, as it brought us closer together as brothers in arms, fighting for the same cause.

"Now," he said, as we climbed into our car to head to the airport, "we're just gonna have to go out and get Target instead."

I called Danna after Ken and I arrived at our gate for the flight home. She asked me how the meeting went and I told her that Walmart made a big offer, but I turned it down. Danna took it all in stride. She was, after all, intimately familiar with the roller-coaster ride at this point. And she knew I did things my own way, guided by my Basementality.

"Okay, well, onto the next, right?" she said.

"Right," I agreed. "And Ken says the next stop is Target."

Ken's words turned out to be prophetic. Staying the course we had set to grow Bai in the marketplace, we landed at Target on a regional basis later that year and nationally a year later, selling at full price and establishing an excellent merchandising presence. Bai eventually accounted for millions of dollars in sales going through Target's cash registers, and based on our success there, we wound up getting another call from Walmart. This time, we agreed to do business on our terms. In fact, Walmart ultimately became Bai's biggest retail partner—and we didn't have to sacrifice our brand's price integrity to make that happen.

Ken Kurtz (former president of Bai):

We called ourselves "The Ben & Ken Show" because we went everywhere together, especially on calls to big national accounts. We just had a natural chemistry. Whether Ben started the conversation or I started the conversation, whether he started the presentation or I started the presentation, we could end each other's sentences.

We had a lot of situations, like with Walmart, where we had to make decisions to walk away from business that would have driven a lot of revenue for the company but also would have upset a lot of the premium disciplines that we were building. But we had to keep our focus on fundamentals and building standards of excellence.

***

For Bai's first two years, we didn't have an executive team. Ari Soroken officially had the title of chief operating officer and served as my top deputy in all areas of the business.

Together, we hustled around the country, making deals with distributors and retailers, accelerating our production, and starting to build our sales team. We had several key players in different aspects of the business—including Eric Kellems, Kat Haddon, my stepfather, Ray, and my sister, Candice—and everyone was working nonstop. We scored a lot of wins in years one and two, but I knew that Bai could not continue to grow unless we filled out our senior executive team to guide our expansion.

By late 2011, Bai was on the verge of taking off, and the time had come to bring in additional firepower. The first step was to find a great sales leader to take the reins of that team and lead us into the future.

We needed someone who had experience with scaling a beverage brand from a regional to a national presence, who knew the major players in the distribution and retail communities and could help us kick open the right doors to expand. But just as important was finding someone with spirit and drive, who would care as much as I did about making Bai into a disruptive force in the market. We needed someone who would dream alongside me and fight just as hard for Bai as I would when anyone stood in our way.

After collecting recommendations from contacts in the industry, I reached out to a few potential candidates. Ari and I set up a first interview with a guy who seemed like he had an ideal background with a couple of well-known beverage brands. But once the three of us gathered in the conference room at BQ, I was immediately uninspired. He had no spark in his eyes. Instinctively, I knew he wasn't the right fit. Both he and Ari looked surprised as I stood and excused myself, leaving Ari to proceed with the interview. I'm sure that didn't make a good impression with this guy, but I wasn't worried about him. I needed a driver who would help me set the pace for the company—and he wasn't it.

I went back into my office and pulled up an email from one of our distributors, who had recommended two people for the role. While Ari was finishing the other interview in the conference room, I called the first name from the email and reached a guy who was running sales for an up-and-coming energy drink. We had a quick, pleasant conversation, and he told me he was happy where he was. So I moved on to the next name on the email—Ken Kurtz, who had been a sales leader at Fiji Water, Boston Beer Company (the maker of Sam Adams), and E & J Gallo Winery.

I called Ken's number and got his voicemail. He called back within minutes. When he did, it was the business equivalent of love at first sight.

Ken told me about getting his start at Gallo, which is renowned throughout the beverage industry for its training and the leadership skills it instills in employees. From there, he went on to play major roles in driving the growth of Boston Beer and Fiji, which were among the most successful brands of the previous two decades. I was impressed by Ken's background, of course, but I was even more encouraged by the tone of our conversation. He was a New York guy, like me, and I felt a fire behind his words. We talked about having a drive for bringing new ideas into the marketplace and how a commitment to steady, flawless execution was the key to making a new brand stand out in the crowded beverage space. We were speaking the same language.

After what seemed like just a couple of minutes, Ken said, "Ben, we've been talking for a half hour, and you haven't told me anything about Bai. How does it taste?"

I started laughing. "Oh, shit, I didn't tell you? That's the best part—it tastes amazing. You have to try it."

We agreed that he would come to BQ a few days later so we could talk in person. I hung up and rushed out of my office to find Ari and tell him about this great conversation. That's when I realized he was still in the conference room conducting the interview I had blown off. I came back in, apologized for my absence, and swiftly wrapped up the interview. My sights were set on Ken.

Ken Kurtz *(former president of Bai)*:
I grew up in the beverage industry, so I've seen both sides of it—a big corporation with Gallo Winery and entrepreneurial environments with Boston Beer and Fiji. What tied all those experiences together was the fact that those companies were not duplicating what was already out there. They were offering true variety at the premium end of their businesses, and they weren't just about good marketing—the products really delivered.

After Fiji, I took some time off and then started my own company to launch an electrolyte water brand, but I wound it down after a couple of years because I wasn't able to raise the money I needed to be competitive. I ended up having conversations with many brands and actually reached a verbal agreement with a new enhanced water company to run their sales team. But then I had a conversation with Ben Weiss that I'll never forget.

As Ben was talking to me about Bai, I could feel the passion in his voice. He also was educating me about coffeefruit, which I had never heard of, but most importantly, to me, he wasn't trying to do something else that had been done before. Even though I had already gone far down the path with the other enhanced water brand, I was so intrigued with Bai's unique story and product proposition that I agreed to get together with Ben to talk in person.

When Ken came to BQ later that week, it was like he exploded into the room. Dressed in a suit, with a big smile, perfectly coiffed hair, and a politician's firm handshake, he reminded me of a burlier and more gregarious version of Mitt Romney, who was then running for the Republican nomination for president. I remember thinking, "What the hell just walked through my door?" After he made the rounds meeting people in the office, we sat down with Ari and picked up right where our phone conversation had left off. Ken said all the right things about the effort needed to build a brand and made me feel confident that he was the person we needed to lead our sales team and take Bai to the next level. Ari agreed.

Ken Kurtz (former president of Bai):

My takeaway from my first meeting with Ben was that he was an incredible entrepreneur and that I could help him. I had a lot of the strengths that he hadn't necessarily learned yet about how to build a route to market and a "look of success" that would help a brand win at retail. Once we started to dig deeper into the business, I found it was good but not overly impressive—there wasn't a cohesive strategy that I could understand about how Ben was building the brand relative to the route to market, geography, or channel strategy. I sensed right away that if this brand had any legs to it, I could help get it out there in a strategic way and let the consumer decide its fate.

Honestly, after that first meeting, I wasn't 100 percent sure if I wanted to go with Bai. But Ben is a closer—he was relentless about calling me to try to get a deal done, and I really appreciated his intensity. I knew that we would be a really good fit for each other.

I sat down with my wife and kids to talk about the decision, and when I told my kids that I was seriously considering Bai, they started jumping up and down, saying, "Yeah! We love Bai!"

That pushed me over the line. I committed to Ben, and it was the best professional decision I've ever made.

Because of his background as a star with successful, extremely well-respected brands, I often referred to Ken as "beverage royalty." He typically commanded a much higher salary than we could afford, but we were able

The "Ben & Ken Show" with my business idol (2016)

to quickly negotiate compensation that satisfied both of us and made him the highest-paid employee at Bai. I was thrilled to have him aboard, and he was eager to get to work.

Once Ken signed on, he hit the ground running, literally. He was the architect of the sales strategies that helped launch us into hypergrowth. Ken came to Bai with strong relationships with some of our existing distributors and built new ones with others. He understood the importance of those relationships in the DSD system, but he knew we couldn't depend solely on our DSD partners to build the brand. Our own salespeople had to be the difference-makers. Ken spread the message companywide that Bai needed to establish and maintain a consistent look of success to earn our status as a premium brand. This meant making sure that we kept shelves filled and that we lined up every label perfectly, that we earned premium floor space from store managers, and that we created multiple points of interruption, with impactful displays throughout a store that would outshine the competition and make customers stop in their tracks as they pushed their carts down the aisles past brand after brand after brand. He demanded that our salespeople work doggedly, and he got their maximum effort in return because he earned their respect.

Ken was an unrivaled workhorse who spent countless hours in the field recruiting and training our sales force and leading by example. He didn't manage by email or conference call—he was in stores all over the country, side by side with his team members, showing them how to engage with store managers and how to create our look of success. I hung a photo of Ken on the wall at BQ as an example of the work ethic everyone at our company needed to embrace. The photo showed Ken in a dress shirt and slacks on his hands and knees, merchandising a six-foot Bai display at the end of a supermarket aisle. He was carefully aligning the labels of the bottles in the bottom row—what I called the most unshoppable part of the display given that it was at customers' ankles—to make sure every last inch of that display was perfect. That photo was emblematic of Ken's obsessiveness about making our brand stand out in the retail environment. My message in hanging the photo was clear: if our head of sales is out in the field doing this every day, all of our efforts need to match his.

Ken Kurtz *(former president of Bai)*:
On my first day, I met some of the team at a Whole Foods Market in New York City. That was an eye-opener for me. I got there an hour before everyone else and walked the store on my own, then had the team walk me through how they looked at the store. Their approach was pretty fundamental, and there wasn't much of a presence for the brand. But when

I looked at the sales velocity, it blew me away—I was really impressed that Bai had such good volume for the limited space they had. I saw the potential.

So I knew that, right away, we had to start thinking about our channel strategy—what were the types of stores where Bai should live and breathe? That would dictate our approach to building out our route to market with the right distributors. We also needed to focus on who we were going to compete against. Early on, we thought we might belong in the juice section at retail, where the healthy consumer was buying brands like Odwalla, Naked, and POM Wonderful. But we learned quickly that the enhanced water space was our sweet spot. Bai was a super premium brand in that space—50 to 100 percent more than the price of the market leader in Vitaminwater—but that consumer was willing to pay a premium for something they perceived to be better. We delivered on flavor, and we did it in a responsible way.

Our other big challenge was that Bai's sales team didn't have a lot of depth. Our salespeople all came from different backgrounds, which is one of the things I loved about our organization. You didn't have to have a beverage background to be successful. In fact, in a lot of ways, we preferred people who didn't come with a beverage background because a lot of times, that came with bad habits. As I built out the team, I felt that, first and foremost, you had to be passionate about what we were doing. Then the two things that would determine your success were your commitment and effort. It's not a complicated business. I believe Bai's core values—our relentless pursuit of excellence—enabled us to create greatness on a small scale with our sales team and then expand upon it over time.

Ken was someone I always could count on to carry the baton for Bai in a meeting with a prospective business partner or in a gathering of employees. And he challenged me to work even harder because I wasn't going to let him outwork me. As much as Ken believed in my audacious ideas that Bai could change the world in our own way, I believed in the path he charted to help us get there. We shared a warlike mentality about building the brand, and we understood that you can't be a true disruptor if you let others—distributors, retailers, or suppliers—win the battles.

Take retailers, for example. Obviously, they held the key to making our product available to consumers. But because we were confident that Bai met consumers' demand for a better product and retailers' need to overcome weakening soda sales, we operated from a position of strength. It was a ballsy attitude, especially in our earlier years, but that's how much we believed in Bai.

There were so many times when Ken and I left meetings with retail buyers without a deal because they were cautious about taking on a new brand, and they were only willing to give us minimal shelf space or allow us to sell a portion of our flavor lineup. Saying no to them was a risk, but we needed retailers to understand that if they wanted to carry our brand on their shelves, they needed to be as all-in on Bai as we were. And that was true even for the biggest retailer in the world, as we showed in our first meeting with Walmart.

Ken Kurtz (former president of Bai):

The early years of Bai were magical, but they weren't easy. When you're building a brand, there are so many days and nights when you think to yourself, "Do I really need to be doing this?" Like driving a van of product up to Massachusetts at 5:30 in the morning on a freezing day in January to show the team how to create a look of success. Or pulling cooler wagons with ice-cold Bai up and down the streets of Manhattan every day of the week, trying to break open that market.

I always said to Ben and our whole team, it's what you do when nobody's looking that really matters. When nobody's looking, are you still as passionate? Are you still willing to work as hard? If Ben or I come into a market, I get it—people will always give their best effort while we're there. But when we're not there, are you driving the business forward?

I do think we infused that culture into so many people—we used to call it "tipping markets" when we turned people into true Bailievers, and they realized success from our approach. I think what really made us successful was that, whether it was Ben or me, we walked the walk. We didn't just say, "This is how you do it." We went out and did it with you. It was very rewarding, but it was very humbling, too, because it was a lot of work. Ben and I knew what the vision for Bai was. We knew what the potential was. But it was tough to create it. You miss a lot of quality times with your family. You miss a ton of your kids' games. You miss birthdays. You have to live and breathe Bai every day.

I cannot overstate Ken's impact on Bai's success. He helped us mature quickly as a company. He was pivotal to the development of our culture internally and our reputation in the industry, establishing Bai as a disruptive force built upon a foundation of work ethic, strategic thinking, tenacity, and heart. And he and I were the perfect complements to one another, developing a balance that made both of us better leaders.

Ken is the son of a New York City cop, and he believes in order and discipline, yet he is as willing as I am to be disruptive in business and pick fights with bigger opponents when necessary. He is hesitant to allow people to get to know him on an intimate level, but he's extremely emotional and is easily brought to tears when he talks about the values of hard work, commitment, and loyalty. Ken is deeply devoted to his wife and children, but he never brought them around the business even though he loved working at Bai because he tried to keep his business and personal lives separate—exactly the opposite of my approach. To me, business is deeply personal because I'm inspired by my family to dream and create, and I want to involve them along every step of the way. In turn, those who play essential roles alongside me in business come to feel like an extension of my family—and no one more so than Ken.

During his first three-plus years at Bai, when Ken traveled for business, which was nearly every week, his father, Ken Sr., always picked him up at the airport when he returned. They were as close as a father and son could be—they lived in the same town, and Ken Sr. was a doting grandfather who proudly proclaimed himself president of the Kurtz Family Sports Fan Club. In 2015, Ken Sr. passed away, and Ken was understandably devastated at the loss of his best friend. Danna, Ray, and some of the Bai team joined me in driving up to Ken's hometown for the funeral, where we met his wife Kate for the first time. I'll never forget the powerful hug that Ken gave me when we arrived, as his grief mixed with deep appreciation that we had taken the time to come pay our respects to his beloved father.

Because of his intense love for his family and all that they had to tolerate because of his commitment to Bai's mission, Ken had created understandable distance between his personal and business life so his wife and children would get his full attention when he wasn't at work. But that day, the barrier came down for a few hours as we rallied to support Ken and his family in their time of need. I hoped in that moment—and I still hope to this day—that his family realized how much we at Bai appreciated their sacrifice of Ken's time and attention to help us realize our dream. Because, simply put, it never would have happened without him.

As our Bai journey continued, Ken and I shared so many laughs and occasional tears, so many plane and car trips, so many important meetings with distributors and retailers, and so many drinks toasting and reflecting on another hectic but exciting day. I can't imagine anyone better to have at my side through all the ups and downs of Bai's wild ride, both as a leader of the business and as a close friend. I truly think of Ken as a brother, and I love him dearly.

***

While Ken was the blue-chip pick with decades of beverage experience, my next executive hire was more of a gamble. I met Barak Bar-Cohen, a fellow resident of Princeton, a few years before I started Bai. Our kids attended the same nursery school, and we hit it off because we had mutual interests in business and entrepreneurship. Barak and his family temporarily relocated to Prague, and after they returned to Princeton in the fall of 2012, we ran into each other in town. I invited him to come by BQ to catch up.

Barak had served in a variety of senior roles—in marketing, finance, and administration—with companies in media, technology, and investment banking. His most recent gig had ended in a mess, and he wasn't sure about his next career move. His background intrigued me because we needed help on a number of fronts, and I thought that his assertive personality and his intellect might make him a fit for our scrappy young company. I thought Barak would be ideal to serve as our chief operating officer to oversee our production. I needed a bulldog who could fight for better ingredients and materials pricing and substantially increase our production capacity as Ken ramped up our sales. This would also allow me to move Ari into a new role as our chief financial officer, where I thought he would be an even better fit.

What I didn't think about was the impact that Barak's hiring would have on Ari and Ken. Neither of them was in favor of bringing Barak aboard, given his lack of beverage experience. I never considered that Ari also might feel offended or disrespected by my decision to move him into the chief financial officer role and give Barak the chief operating officer title he had held. To me, hiring Barak was a great move because it allowed Ari to be potentially successful in a different swimming lane. I was so excited to be growing our leadership team and getting people in their lanes that I didn't pay much attention to how it might be interpreted by others. Ari and I had been inseparable in dealing with every aspect of the company over Bai's first two years, but each addition to our executive team meant that his role became more specialized and that we spent less time together. Ari was always professional about it, but I know now that he sometimes felt alienated when I would focus my attention on new members of the executive team. Ari's importance to Bai and to me never wavered, but in retrospect, I could have done a better job in letting him know that.

Ari shows that we always strived for perfection at Bai (2015)

The truth is titles were never important to me because I had only ever worked for myself—I never had to climb a corporate ladder and think about what my job title meant to me or to others. When I decided to hire Barak, I thought, "He will be the chief operating officer, Ari will be the chief financial officer, I'm the chief executive officer—our C-suite is coming together." But Ken, whose title was executive vice president of sales, felt like he was left on the outside looking in, even though his role was arguably the most important in the company. I had fucked up!

From the minute I hired Ken, he was all about the work. We never talked about money or anything other than what needed to get done. In fact, there were several times I had to ask him to hand in his expenses to get reimbursed after he spent months on the road—that's how focused he was on constantly moving forward. So I was shocked that Ken expressed that he felt slighted after I told him that I decided to name Barak as our chief operating officer. That is, until I recalled a conversation we had over dinner one night.

Months before I hired Barak, Ken and I had spent a day selling in New York City—a typical nonstop Ken-style day with no break for lunch. That evening, I treated him to a nice steak dinner. As we were eating, I looked across the table and thought about how much I respected him, how flattered I was to have him on the Bai team, and how much he inspired me with his work ethic. (And I thought, "Damn, he really does look like Mitt Romney!")

With no real premeditation, I told him, "Ken, someday you're going to be the president of this company—and I'm going to be the proudest guy in the room when that happens."

You see, I always felt that serving as president is different than having a title with a C in front of it. To me, the president would ultimately be the person who was presiding over our organization, publicly appointed by me and entrusted with the direction of where we were collectively headed. Ken's industry experience and gravitas separated him from everyone else—including me—and I had no doubt that he could play the role. But I wanted to make sure that he was willing to stand alongside me, which wasn't always an easy place to be. I was once told that an entrepreneur has to be the most unrealistic person in the room, and on more than one occasion, things I've said have been met with sideways looks and eye rolls. I believed that Bai's president had to be someone who would stand next to me and say, "I'm with him," with such conviction that my audacity would become that much more believable. What made Ken great at his job is he did not have to fake that. He was as convinced as I was that this industry was broken and in desperate need of change and that we were the driving force for that change.

I felt good about telling Ken that I envisioned him as Bai's future president because I wanted to empower him and let him know that I truly believed in him. In typical Ken fashion, he never brought up that conversation again. And although I had every intention at the time of following through with that pledge—because I truly believed Ken was destined to become Bai's president—life got in the way, and I didn't push ahead with making it happen.

So when I announced that Barak would be our new chief operating officer, Ken understandably felt overlooked, and he told me so. That's when I realized I had dropped the ball on fulfilling my vow and inadvertently given him the impression that he was a rung below Barak and Ari. I needed to fix it. Quick!

"Ken," I said. "Remember that conversation we had, when I said this is going to be your show one day?"

"Of course I remember," he said.

"Look, Ken, I apologize that I'm saying this now after you've had to tap me on the shoulder like this. But I'm telling you right now that you are the president of this company."

I had thought that I would one day make a dramatic announcement about Ken becoming Bai's president, in a setting where he would be honored and applauded by everyone at the company. I didn't want to do it seemingly as a reaction to someone else's hiring. But I knew at that moment that I had created a sense of resentment by hiring Barak and not addressing Ken's status as a leader of our company.

We were both quiet for a few seconds, until Ken said, "I don't want it."

I was taken aback.

"What do you mean?" I asked him.

"I don't want the title just because you think it will make me happy," Ken responded.

"Man, that's not it at all," I said. "You deserve this! I intended to make you our president all along—and I'm sorry I didn't do it sooner."

After another long pause, Ken agreed. "Okay, Ben, I hear you, and I appreciate it," he said. "Now let's just get back to work."

I knew that Ken was still upset that he had to raise the issue, but at the same time, he was honored to assume the title of president. And I was honored to give it to him, even though neither the timing nor the setting was what I had envisioned.

Despite the fact that the conversation started with hard feelings, I was glad it happened. Making Ken the president of Bai was my way of letting the whole company know how important he was to the business and how much I admired him. And he embraced the title. As the years went on, there were times when he would get up and say, "My name is Ken Kurtz, and I'm the president of Bai," and a wave of pride would wash over me.

Barak, meanwhile, had a steep learning curve ahead of him. He had to learn the technical aspects of beverage production, but I felt his multi-faceted background and his natural salesmanship would serve him well in tackling what I saw as the most critical part of his job—keeping our costs of goods sold under control. We had to ensure that we didn't overspend on our ingredients, packaging, transportation, storage, and production line time, or we would risk crippling the business financially. I felt Barak had the right business and communications skills to accomplish our goal of improving our costs.

One of the biggest challenges for any young business is to avoid getting gouged by vendors, who will tell you that you haven't been around long enough or you're not ordering enough to get better pricing for whatever goods or services they provide. It's a classic Catch-22—it's difficult to grow a business when you're paying exorbitant rates to vendors, but you can't get better rates until you scale your business. My response? Sell the dream. Take the time to talk to vendors about what we were trying to accomplish and to present my vision for Bai's trajectory. Explain that we didn't view them simply as vendors—we wanted to think of them as partners. Encourage them to make an investment in Bai by giving us the same pricing they would give to a larger company and then sharing in our success as we grew and continued to order their goods and services in larger and larger quantities. The more our business thrived, the more theirs would as well. It would be a true partnership.

The key to these conversations was expressing enough drive and confidence—which I had in droves and which Barak acquired—to convince these companies to buy in to our vision. We had to be relentless in punching above our weight and driving home the message that just because we were small didn't mean we shouldn't get the same pricing as the big guys. This was critical to our success. Controlling our spending by getting better terms from vendors was another version of raising money for the company. Every dollar we saved on costs was a dollar that we could put back into the business without having to raise funds from an outside investor. And as a team, Barak and I were very good at it. We raised millions of dollars for Bai without having to issue an additional share in the company.

***

With Ken driving our sales operation, Ari assembling a more advanced financial and administrative infrastructure, and Barak getting more comfortable overseeing production and costs, Bai was on the rise. As our sales and production capabilities grew, I started thinking more seriously about expanding our creative and marketing teams.

Our early focus was on field marketing—making sure we had brand ambassadors in key locations who could run sampling events and get product in the hands of consumers. By late 2012, I felt the time had come to raise our marketing game. Through Barak, I met a vibrant young Australian guy named Daniel Goodfellow, who was starting his own marketing agency in New York. Goody, as I always called him, wanted Bai as a client of his agency. But after spending some time together, I was impressed enough by his creativity and spirit that I wanted him to be Bai's in-house head of marketing.

Daniel Goodfellow (former vice president of marketing for Bai):
My time at Bai felt like a year of unlearning everything I thought I knew. Although I was there in part to bring a bit of order to chaos, I quickly realized that the way to succeed was to get focused on initiatives that actually moved the business forward, often at the expense of other things which would have consumed my time in past roles. It was less about being on top of everything and more about making a difference. I think that cultural cue was a huge part of the company's ultimate success.

But with all that said, two things characterized the time I spent working at Bai. First, Ben and I established a partnership and a very irreverent banter that would endure for years and years. And second, I came to terms with the reality that at that moment in my life, I needed to return to Australia. My mom wasn't doing so well healthwise, but in a broader sense, neither was I. After six years away, I was homesick, and after much deliberation, it felt like I needed to head home.

So I took a deep breath, made the journey from New York City to Princeton, and told Ben the news. It was a tough conversation for both of us, and while he seemed to accept things, it was clearly on his mind in the weeks that followed as I prepared to leave.

The day of my departure, Ben, Danna, the kids, and I—plus a bunch of other friends—headed to the back lot of Lincoln Center in New York for an

Goody and Ken showing their stuff at Princeton Communiversity Day (2012)

afternoon performance of a circus under the big top. We were guests of the circus—most likely invited by someone hoping we'd buy advertising in their program—so we thought we'd make a day of it. I was leaving for Australia late that night, but as we settled into the after-party, Ben took me aside and produced an envelope from his jacket pocket. He gave it to me and said to read it on the plane and not before. "Think and ponder and dream as you read it," he said. Inside, as I discovered a few hours later, he implored me to stay, and included an incredibly generous offer of equity in Bai.

That was without question the most intense plane ride of my life. I sat clutching the letter, staring out the window for hours as we flew to LA and then over the Pacific Ocean to Melbourne. I knew for sure that the offer would ultimately be life-changing, but while it was the hardest thing I've ever done, I stuck with my convictions, and with a heavy heart I told Ben I had to make the move.

A few years later, I opened the newspaper one morning and saw what I knew I would one day read. That Bai had sold to Dr Pepper Snapple Group for $1.7 billion. My share, had I held on, would have been many millions of dollars. And truthfully, I was rattled. Really rattled. But after twenty-four hours, the fog lifted, and I picked up my phone and sent Ben and a few others a wholehearted message of congratulations. In the end, the time I spent in Australia was fruitful—I started a business, I met my husband, and I ultimately remained friends with a family in New Jersey that I would one day meet again.

In addition to creating a lasting bond with me and my family, Goody had an impact at Bai that far outlasted the single year he spent with our team. He brought organization to our marketing efforts and helped us refine our messaging to reflect what our brand ambassadors and salespeople were learning in the field. The coffeefruit and antioxidant messages we had emphasized from the beginning were not resonating—the reality was that people were drawn to Bai because our drinks were five calories per serving and tasted great. Goody helped us start the process of developing consumer-facing messaging to emphasize those key points in partnership with a Boston-based creative agency called SapientNitro, where Chad Portas served as director of design.

Chad, of course, was my creative partner from the beginning of Bai. I had always wanted him to come aboard full time, but he was thriving in his agency work and wasn't prepared to relocate his family to New Jersey. We engaged SapientNitro as Bai's agency partner so I could continue collaborating with him. At the time, we were working on an idea for a caffeine-free version of Bai for kids, and Chad and his team at SapientNitro came up with amazing creative concepts to launch the brand extension. That experience inspired me to press Chad again about coming on full time.

"I need you—and Bai needs you," I told him.

In early 2014, I finally convinced Chad to join Bai as our chief creative officer, giving him his first opportunity to be a member of an executive team. This designation was important because it signified for the company the value of our creative efforts, and it let Chad know that I had faith in his vision for our brand.

Understanding that he didn't want to uproot his family, I allowed Chad to continue working from Boston and to bring along James Cho, his director of design at SapientNitro, to fill that same role at Bai. Unfortunately, our kids' drink project was a little too ahead of its time—we realized that we needed to build the main Bai brand more before we could successfully launch an extension for children. But even though that project never came to pass, Chad was up for the challenge of taking our brand to the next level creatively. And, boy, did he ever.

Chad Portas (former chief creative officer of Bai):
James and I opened the Boston office in a WeWork space—just the two of us in what was basically a little closet, elbow to elbow. The first thing I worked on was giving Bai a true voice and personality. When thinking about how to develop Bai's voice, I would say, "Bai is the drink you'd want to have a drink with." We took that approach to our first outdoor advertising campaign in New York and came up with some sassy stuff, with headlines like "Tell Your Tastebuds to Stop Sexting Us" and "Wet. Juicy. Ready. But Not in That Way." They got a lot of attention in the press, some good, some bad. Most brands wouldn't have gone with that kind of tone. It may have been a little juvenile sometimes, but it definitely made some headlines. I think my favorites were "Flavor So Fresh You'll Want to Slap It" and "Flavor So Juicy You Could Sell It to a Tabloid." Those are two lines that stood the test of time.

Chad, the creative force behind Bai (2014)

As Chad began to define and highlight our brand voice, it became apparent that there was one more missing piece to our executive team. We were just starting to embark on our national distribution with Dr Pepper, and we needed a high-level marketing operation to push the creative team's concepts into action to introduce the brand to new consumers across the country. That's when I turned to my former mentor at Godiva, Michael Simon, who by this time had ascended to the position of chief marketing officer for Panera Bread in Boston.

Michael and I stayed in touch in the years after my consulting work with Godiva wound down. I always valued his wisdom and experience, and I would often tell him I wanted him to make the jump to Bai. Now that the time had come to invest millions in a full-throttle marketing budget—including digital and outdoor advertising, public relations, social media, shopper marketing, field marketing, and market research—I had to know I could trust the guy who was spending that money. I went after Michael again, and this time he accepted. I was thrilled to be able to work closely with Michael, whom I respected greatly and who had been so influential and supportive throughout my career. Michael's move from a $2.5 billion restaurant chain to an upstart beverage brand at the end of 2014 made some news and gave Bai an extra shot of legitimacy in

Celebrating with Michael, my longtime friend and colleague, at his son's bar mitzvah (2015)

the industry's eyes. And it solidified the Bai executive team that would lead us into our debut on the national stage.

With our executive team filled out, I felt I had assembled a group of like-minded drivers who would fight alongside me to protect and propel Bai. Our executive suite was not built through a careful review of résumés or some formula devised by corporate headhunters—of the six of us, only Ken and Michael carried the traditional credentials that you would expect of senior executives for a multimillion-dollar beverage business. We sometimes joked that we were like the Island of Misfit Toys from *Rudolph the Red-Nosed Reindeer*. Our leadership team came together at different stages of our lives and careers, with an array of experiences that might not have seemed like an ideal mixture. But how people look on paper has always been less important to me than what I perceive to be in their heads and their hearts.

I trusted my instincts to bring people into Bai whom I thought would care deeply about creating something special and who would be committed to moving forward rather than falling back into the comfort of doing things the way they had always been done. Not everyone I hired wound up thriving at Bai, of course. But those who did—including our executive team—were the ones who embraced the exceptional opportunity we were given to build our brand and put our souls into our work. The most valuable lesson I learned in Bai's early years was to identify and compel the best people to join the fight. Basementality involves seeing greatness in others, often when they haven't identified it in themselves, and unleashing them toward their edge.

192 - BASEMENTALITY

BASEMENTALITY

STAND TOUGH ALONG THE WAY

You can't find success surrounded by suck-ups. If you want to change the world, go out and find people who will fight for you and against you. Those willing to stand up and stand tough. Those who will stand up for what they believe and stand against others, even if it's you. It's not easy to find special people like this. It's not like they have "black sheep" on their résumés. In fact, sometimes the best people won't have résumés at all!

CHAPTER 8
PUTTING THE CULT BACK IN CULTURE

In November 2013, Christopher Brown, a sales manager for the POM Wonderful pomegranate juice brand, walked into a Chicago-area Jewel supermarket just after the store opened. Scanning his competitors on the shelves, Chris noticed a display of Bai, a brand he had never seen before. Intrigued by the packaging and product description, he Googled "Bai" on his iPhone and found that we had posted an ad on a beverage industry website for a district sales manager in the Windy City. He applied on the spot and then bought a bottle.

About an hour later, Pete Eisenmann, our brand-new regional sales manager in Chicago, saw Chris's application and called him. Chris told him he saw the brand in store, tried it, and loved it. Pete didn't quite believe him at first and asked where he found it.

"The Jewel in New Lenox," Chris said.

Pete laughed to himself. That was the first store where he and Ken Kurtz had placed product early that morning on our brand's first day in the market. Chris was very likely the first person in Chicago to ever purchase a bottle of Bai.

It seemed like Chris was destined to work for Bai. But first he had to get an interview, which turned out to be a bit of a challenge.

I was coming out to Chicago to join Ken for store visits and a meeting with a buyer at Walgreens, so Pete arranged for Chris to talk with us. But our schedule got off track from the early morning, and Chris wound up spending the day in his car, following us from location to location as Pete texted him with updates about our availability. Eventually, I had to get a plane back to New Jersey and never had a chance to meet with Chris. But Ken was impressed with Chris's persistence in following us around since 8 a.m. and squeezed him in for a quick meeting in the lobby of a hotel near O'Hare Airport that evening.

Chris nailed the interview. Ken offered him a job the next day.

The tale of how Chris became a part of our team—and his subsequent success in our organization—was an example that I repeated often when explaining how Bai's culture was forged by people with unusual levels of passion and determination to create change. Bai brought out the best in Chris and other like-minded people who wanted to use their skills and talents to do something more than earn a paycheck and move product from a warehouse to a supermarket shelf. In turn, Bai developed into a remarkably inspired company filled with people on a journey to create something special for the whole team. The soul of our company was built upon the souls of people like Chris.

Even though I had a grand vision for Bai's future from the outset, it took time for our culture to develop. I will never forget the day in 2012 when one of our employees, a creative director whose talents I greatly admired, came into my office and told me he was quitting. The biggest problem, he said, was that Bai had no culture. I was not only surprised by his assessment, but I was angered and hurt by it. In my mind, we had made tremendous strides in establishing our culture as a bold, scrappy, and tireless group of dreamers with a vision for greatness. Hell, would I have been willing to dump less-than-perfect product down the drain time and time again if we didn't have a culture that demanded excellence?

When this guy whom I held in such high regard told me our culture was lacking, my initial reaction was to be pissed off at him for being short-sighted and quitting on us. However, in reflecting on the conversation, I realized I had been taking for granted the notion that everyone at Bai felt the same way I did. When I really let his message sink in, I recognized that I needed to do a better job of establishing a culture that inspired everyone on our team and created a shared sense of pride and attachment. I had to help everyone see what I saw.

After Ken Kurtz arrived to lead our sales team in late 2011, Bai's growth accelerated at a dizzying pace. As our sales team expanded around the country, our home base at BaiQuarters also transformed in terms of the people and the physical space. The development of our administrative, production, and marketing operations brought lots of new faces into BQ. And as we gobbled up square footage from neighboring suites to accommodate our growth, I became fanatical about wanting our headquarters to become a physical manifestation of Bai's passionate culture.

We brought on a small in-house team of tradespeople (which we called Bai Design) focused on building out BQ and making it into more than just an office. I loved starting my days by walking the floors of BQ with Abbey Brown, our dedicated office manager who oversaw the Bai Design team. Abbey was an invaluable collaborator in my quest to find inventive ways to use our space to tell Bai's story. We met first thing every morning when I was in town to examine the progress of our many ongoing projects and start dreaming up new ones. Even though I frequently challenged Abbey with ideas and demands that seemed impossible, she always came through.

We built offices and furniture from glass, concrete, and reclaimed wood, creating an open, modern aesthetic in the midst of a worn-down industrial neighborhood—a metaphor for Bai's emergence in an industry whose biggest players were looking backward at their glory days. Then we took that idea a step further by making BQ visitors feel like they were traveling through the past to enter our space. Abbey found a 1970s-era Coke vending machine that an old woman in New Jersey had put up for sale on eBay. Our team refinished the front panel to make it look like it came from a vintage Bai machine, then installed it as a new front door to our office. To gain access to BQ, you had to find a secret button hidden in the machine's change dispenser to make the door swing open. That's when you stepped into the future of the industry.

We found lots of ways to celebrate our brand and our team throughout BQ. We adorned our walls with topographic maps of coffee-growing regions from around the world, paying homage to our signature ingredient, the coffeefruit. We hung pictures of our team members to honor their efforts. We created a huge graphical timeline of Bai's history so we could tell our story to new employees and visitors. Ice-cold Bai was available to everyone, and music was playing at all times. We started traditions like "Wearable Wednesdays" and "Flavor Fridays," when our employees wore Bai-branded T-shirts designed by Chad Portas and his creative team. We built a kitchen and coffee bar for our employees to enjoy meals and breaks together in a familial setting. I even hired an in-house barista named Jay Miller (also known as Java Jay), a guy Ray and I had gotten to know when Jay worked at Whole Foods in Princeton. Jay saw us in that store week after week, forging our relationships with the managers and working diligently to get Bai a bigger footprint, and he jumped at the chance to be part of our team.

I loved seeing our team respond to the emerging look of BQ, and I enjoyed working with Abbey, our designers, and our tradespeople to transform the space. I couldn't wait to get to work every day, whether I was going to BQ or I was on the road.

When I met a new employee, I didn't talk about tactics or metrics or day-to-day responsibilities—I imparted our vision for the industry and how we would create a new future by outworking and outcaring everyone else. Bai offered the solution to the diet dilemma that no other beverage had been able to conquer. We had the great flavor and authentic ingredients that consumers wanted, without the sugar and calories they detested. We were launching a bevolution to redefine the beverage industry around better products—and I wanted everyone on our team to be as inspired for the fight as I was. I know that my language was R-rated and that I sometimes

I always wore my heart on my sleeve (and my wall) at Bai (2016)

came off as angry, but that's because I believed so strongly that we were in a real fight with an industry that was built on a foundation of sugar and artificial ingredients. If I dropped an f-bomb (or six) in a conversation, it was an honest expression of how much I loved my company and how deeply I cared about our work.

There can be power in a word like "fuck" that goes beyond pure shock value. I never said it to scare or intimidate anyone. I was always trying to convey what was in my heart. I was expressing the depth of my passion for Bai, which couldn't be constrained by politeness. I was holding them accountable to my expectation that everyone, myself included, had to give maximum effort at all times.

Unlike my father, Ken, who regularly berated his employees and family members and then brooded about his hurtful behavior, my intensity was rooted in optimism and enthusiasm. I cursed more often out of excitement than anger or frustration. But even in times when I was upset, I made the effort to explain the context for why I would get so fired up. I did it because I was a die-hard evangelist for our brand and our cause. I was determined to take a word that had so often been thrown at me in a hurtful way and instead use it in an empowering way. I wanted to capture the attention of the people on our team and inspire them to take on Big Sugar and redefine our industry. I wanted to make them fucking great!

Still, I needed more help to grow our culture beyond the people I interacted with on a day-to-day basis. In 2013, we brought on John Denny, a veteran marketing executive who grew up in Princeton, to help us accelerate our branding, marketing, and e-commerce efforts. John had worked for large organizations such as the Advance Publications media company and the Saatchi & Saatchi advertising agency, and he's a student of leadership and business philosophies. He was intrigued by Bai's culture when we discussed the prospect of him coming on board, and he became even more enamored with it once he joined the team.

After just a few weeks on the job, John came to me with an idea to identify and codify our company's core values so all employees, not just the ones in BQ, could be inspired by them on a daily basis.

John Denny (former vice president of e-commerce and digital for Bai):
When you walked into BQ, the culture was so thick you could feel it everywhere. I'm a big believer that culture is transmitted like a virus from person to person. And Ben's intensity in translating that culture was so vibrant. But we were growing so rapidly that people who were being added to the team across the country didn't always understand or feel it. Ben had it all in his head.

If you were fifteen feet away from Ben, you would feel the intensity of who he is. But he couldn't be everywhere at once, and we needed to figure out some way to capture the culture and make it more of a permanent foundation of the company.

We had a series of conversations and began to coalesce his ideas. Ben spoke so passionately about how the beverage industry is designed to crush the little guy and how new ideas and opportunities are not allowed to flourish because they don't fit within the vast programs run by the behemoths of the industry. He insisted that as an independent company, you always had to be fighting, or the industry would marginalize you and make you irrelevant.

Intuitively, Ben embodied two principles that had become prevalent in business thinking. One was "intelligent naivete," meaning you approach issues with an open mind rather than a preconceived notion of how others in the industry might think about them. The other was "10X thinking," popularized by Google, which says true innovation happens when you try to improve something by ten times rather than by 10 percent. At Bai, someone might come up with an idea and then Ben would take the idea up ten or fifteen levels and ask, with a perfectly blank expression, "Why isn't that possible?" And you would have to explain to him why the audacious goal he just threw out to you wasn't achievable. That would force you to recalibrate and figure out, "How do I make that possible?"

If a group was having a meeting and a problem came up, we knew that Ben would say something like, "Take that obstacle—the person who's wrapped in red tape, the person who's saying no—and remove it. Get it done now." When everybody in the room knows exactly how the leader's thought patterns work, and they understand his focus on obsessiveness and execution, it creates a dynamic. Before Bai, I was accustomed to company leaders who were incredibly risk averse. If you brought them an idea, the typical response would be, "Well, you can try it, but you know if you screw this one up, it's on you." You get zero confidence, and you walk away with your tail between your legs. You don't do anything because, why take a risk? Bai was so different. Jack Welch, the former CEO of General Electric, talks about the importance of having company leaders with a "bias for action." I've never seen more of a bias for action than I did with the core leadership group at Bai. The bias for action that Ben created along with the leadership team eradicated any sense of bureaucracy. People understood we were on a mission and needed to execute quickly.

Thanks to John and others on the team whose work helped refine the ideas, we published a *Vision & Values* book that we gave to every employee and shared with visitors and partners. It was a constitution for Bai's company culture. We wanted everyone at Bai to commit our values to heart and keep our collective spirit at the forefront as they played their parts in building our company. We declared that our purpose was to create "beverages without barriers" so we could inspire people to rethink what they drink. We spoke of our envisioned future—a world where "great taste" and "good for you" existed hand-in-hand, where people would not have to compromise enjoyment to feel better about what they drink. And the foundation of our efforts to create this future was our five core values:

- **Be Audacious**
- **Be Obsessive**
- **Be Tenacious**
- **Be Authentic**
- **Be Great**

I aspired to embody each of these values every day, and I challenged everyone at Bai to do the same. In the introduction to the *Vision & Values* book, I wrote:

Our company has a soul because we have contributed our own, and the brand now stands for something that we all believe in. If we live it, consumers will follow. Because when you believe in what you're made of, people will believe in what you make.

I knew we had an exceptional product, but I also knew that lots of other good products had come before Bai and more would come after it. Our difference had to emanate from our culture and values. We had to make Bai a movement that inspired our own people and, ultimately, the consumer.

When I talked to prospective employees, I tried to see beyond their résumés and qualifications to get a better sense of their desire and fortitude. We were pushing hard to challenge giant competitors and a system designed to stifle the growth of independent brands—we needed people who had healthy doses of fight and fire in their systems. As our team expanded, those who truly embodied our core values began to rise to the top in terms of their performance. Not surprisingly, they tended to be those who were the hungriest and most committed to their work because they came to Bai at a time in their careers when they needed a new direction or fresh motivation.

Take Christopher Brown, whose perseverance and obsessiveness in following us around the day of his interview are the same traits that made him such a tremendous salesperson for Bai. Chris and Pete Eisenmann made a great team leading our effort to break into the country's third-largest market. When Pete later moved on to help build our presence in Southern California, Chris stepped up as regional manager in Chicago and we didn't miss a beat.

Even though he had been in food and beverage sales for a decade before starting with us, Chris was never trapped in the mindset of doing things the way other brands did them. He actively sought mentorship from Ken and me, and he embraced Bai's mantra of flawless execution by staying on top of our distributor partners to ensure timely delivery of product to our retail accounts and by training our salespeople to excel in their in-store presentations. He was obsessive about keeping our accounts stocked and making sure our product was merchandised beautifully on shelves and in displays.

As he hired new salespeople, Chris drilled our core values into them and motivated them to help make Chicago one of our fastest-growing markets.

I loved Chris's attitude—I wanted a company full of Bailievers like him who would go over the top for our brand. One night, Chris sent me a video of himself and one of his team members driving a van full of Bai to Wisconsin, with sunglasses on just like Chicago's famed Blues Brothers wore on their "mission from God" (sorry if anyone born after the 1980s doesn't get the reference). After that, I started calling him regularly to check on his progress, and he would frequently send me videos of his team out grinding in the market. I was so impressed with Chris that in September 2015, I asked if he would be interested in relocating to New Jersey to work as the brand manager for our new Bai Bubbles line of carbonated drinks. It was a big request—Chicago was his home, and he had a wife and young kids. But I felt that he was ready to take the next step in his career.

Christopher Brown (former vice president of market development for Bai):

I was stunned. The job was to oversee all aspects of the Bubbles brand, not just sales. I told Ben, "I've never been a brand manager before."

And his response was, "So? I've never run a beverage company before. I'm not looking for somebody with experience. I'm looking for you."

I told my wife, Tammy, about the offer. An hour later, I called Ben back and told him, "We're in."

That was on a Wednesday. On Friday, Tammy and I were on a plane going out to New Jersey to look at houses. That Sunday, we signed a lease.

My friends were like, "What do you mean you're moving to New Jersey?" I'd tell them, "I'm outta here, dude. Gotta go chase the dream."

Two weeks after Ben's call to offer me the position, a moving truck pulled up at our house. I took a picture of the truck to capture the moment because that's when it sunk in: "Holy shit, we're actually going." We had never left Chicago. I'm so glad we did.

Chris faced a significant learning curve in his role as a brand manager, just as the company as a whole did when we began rolling out innovations at a breakneck pace starting in 2015. But what he might have lacked in marketing or production insights, he made up for with drive and a desire to learn and improve. Having him in BQ, I could see every day how hard Chris was working to build the Bubbles brand and how much he strove to live up to our core values and pushed others to do the same. I saw him as an example of what I wanted all of our Bai employees to be, and I would continue to tap him for significant roles in the years to come.

***

When I interviewed people for positions at Bai, I would make no bones about the high level of commitment they would need to thrive with our company and the furious pace at which our team had to move to fulfill our mission. Still, for many people coming to work at Bai was a shock to the system. Those who responded to early challenges by redoubling their efforts rather than shrinking under the pressure became some of our highest-performing employees and were recognized companywide for their contributions.

Carolynn Caruso found herself taking on more than expected when she joined Bai in 2013. Carolynn was hired as a part-time receptionist at BQ by my mom, who was managing our recruiting at the time. She had found an ad for the position on Craigslist, and seeing that our office was not far from where she lived, Carolynn thought it would be an ideal opportunity to make a few extra bucks while trying to build her own business as a holistic health coach. That part-time gig wound up becoming a springboard into a new career.

Carolynn's deep-seated passion for healthy living was a perfect complement to Bai's mission. And her work ethic was obvious from the moment she arrived in BQ—she jumped right in and was willing to fill any gap she encountered. Within a few months of coming aboard, Carolynn moved into a full-time position as our first customer care manager.

Carolynn Caruso (former executive assistant to the CEO of Bai):
When I started, Ben's assistant just handed me a piece of paper with some notes on it and said, "This is what you're supposed to do. Don't ever leave the desk."

The vibe of the office was youthful, energetic, and hungry, but there wasn't much in terms of processes and structure. The phones were ringing like crazy, with people saying how much they liked Bai and asking questions about the product or job openings. Sometimes we got calls from representatives of celebrities who wound up becoming investors in Bai, like Justin Timberlake and Zac Brown, or others who wanted our product, like Madonna and Kanye West. Ben told me that Buzz Aldrin, the astronaut from the first moon landing, once called to say he was a big fan of Bai and asked for advice about starting an energy drink using his name.

Every day, something unexpected happened. I knew from the beginning that I had fallen in love with Bai.

Carolynn did what the most successful people at Bai did over the years—she didn't worry about not having formal training in her role or become overwhelmed by the fact that we were building the plane as we were flying it, as the old saying goes. Rather, she dove headfirst into the challenge of creating our customer care department. She impressed me so much that when my assistant moved into a new position, I swiped Carolynn from the operations team and gave her the job. She became my trusted right hand during my last three years at Bai. Not only did she assume the unenviable task of keeping my hectic schedule organized, she became a more visible figure in the company who set a tone of caring and hard work that everyone recognized. As the business became more successful and more hectic, we grew closer as colleagues and friends—and I'm proud to say that Carolynn and I still work together today.

As our employee ranks grew and we started adding people like Chris and Carolynn, who brought tenacity and work ethic to Bai, we recognized the importance of honoring those who truly embodied our culture and our core values. In true Bai spirit, we had grander visions than an Employee of the Month plaque on a wall. We created an employee recognition program called the Civet Society, which became the centerpiece of Bai's culture, the embodiment of our core values, and the inspiration for our team members to pursue greatness in a way that I don't believe other companies in our industry could match.

So what the hell is a civet? It's a weasel-like mammal with a long tail and claws that lives in the coffee-growing regions of Asia. In my research on coffeefruit, I discovered that civets chomp and digest coffeefruit and then poop out beans, which farmers harvest to brew kopi luwak, the world's most expensive coffee. I suspect that, at first blush, most people might find the idea of a coffee harvested from fecal matter to be curious at best and repugnant at worst. But I saw a different side to the civet's story. I saw the civet as a feisty little beast that could turn a simple, plentiful ingredient into gold. To me, the civet is a symbol of excellence, worthy of being placed on a pedestal.

Bai's Civet Society was launched in 2014, commandeering the name from our Southern California sales group that my uncle, Al Krauza, was in charge of earlier on in the company. Originally, Al hired a half dozen young salespeople who worked for us on a part-time basis in SoCal. They followed the Ray and Al model of providing peerless service to a selection of twenty stores. We called this group the Civets, and their leader, Al, had "Master Civet" emblazoned on his business card (and on his license plate).

As our SoCal business expanded beyond this initial small group, we moved away from using the civet's name, but I always kept it in mind for a future opportunity to represent an elite force that embodied the spirit of Bai. That moment arrived as our business rose to a new level, marked by our headcount exceeding one hundred and our product going national via Dr Pepper's distribution network. Our executive team identified five employees who deserved special commendation for their roles in elevating our brand and for exemplifying our core values—being tenacious, audacious, obsessive, and authentic, and pursuing greatness for themselves and their teammates. This group would be the first class of what we decided to call the Civet Society. Induction into the Civet Society came with a financial reward and perks, such as travel and invitations to special events. Most important, it meant that everyone at Bai—from the executive team to your peers—recognized you as being among the best of the best.

I wanted the unveiling of the Civet Society to be mysterious and memorable. We brought the whole company together for a two-day gathering in which everyone attended Communiversity, an annual festival in downtown Princeton where we promoted Bai and then participated in our national sales meeting at BQ. We borrowed an unoccupied space near the BQ offices for the sales meeting, set up five easels that were each covered with a sheet, and told the team a special ceremony afterward would reveal what was hidden under the cloth. Following a full day of presentations by our executive team and sales managers, we excused everyone from the room and set up the grand unveiling.

When the team reentered the room, they had to wade through a sea of fog to return to their seats, aided by beams of light that cut through the mist. Gregorian chants played over the speakers, adding a haunting touch to the moment. Ken, Ari, Barak, Chad, and I stood at the front of the room (Michael had not yet joined the executive team) and watched everyone return to their seats with looks of curious anticipation on their faces. Once they were settled, Ken stepped forward to explain the concept of the Civet Society and the importance of recognizing superior efforts that propelled Bai's momentum. Keeping with our mystery theme, we decided that each induction would feature remarks highlighting the employee's spirit, strength, and impact without identifying him or her until the end, when the sheet was pulled from the easel, revealing the new Civet's name.

Ryan Pancza, a salesman who covered New Jersey, was our first-ever Civet. Ryan said his induction felt like the biggest achievement in his career, even though when we called his name, he really had no idea what the fuck was going on! He was joined in the inaugural class of Civets by Candice (who flawlessly managed the creation and delivery of our point-of-sale materials), Al (the one-time Master Civet who helped launch Bai in California), Lauren Reilly (who was critical in building our field marketing team), and Jason Brumbach (our operations and warehousing MVP). As each Civet was announced, we pulled the sheet off the easel and revealed their portraits, which were raised to the rafters of BQ like championship banners in a basketball arena. We then took the group into another room, and they recited an oath to Bai's core values, which we translated into Latin, and sipped ceremonial vials of Sumatra Dragonfruit to complete their investiture into the realm of Civetry. After the meeting concluded, the whole company played a raucous game of dodgeball until the building management shut us down for being too loud.

That first Civet Society ceremony might have seemed a bit over the top, but we were just getting started. Over the next three years, we inducted twenty-three more Civets, including Chris, Carolynn, Pete Eisenmann, Kat Haddon, Eric Kellems, and others who were part of Bai from its earliest days, as well as team members who came along later and quickly made a significant impact.

Carolynn Caruso (former executive assistant to the CEO of Bai):
Being inducted as a Civet was a moment I'll never forget. All of the executives were in the front of the room pointing at me, and I remember thinking, "Holy shit! They said my name!" The whole experience

rearranged my molecules—it was life-altering to be recognized in front of the entire company, to be appreciated for everything I had done.

Each year, we amped up the Civet induction presentation until it became a full-blown spectacle. The annual sales meeting transformed into the Bai UnConvention, moving from BQ to the Fillmore, an industrial-style, 25,000-square-foot theater and entertainment venue in Philadelphia. The UnConvention included daytime activities, such as tours of BQ for our remote employees, scavenger hunts, target shooting, and other team-building exercises. The evening at the Fillmore included a cocktail reception, dinner, and live entertainment, including highlights such as a gospel choir

Civet Society scavenger hunt in Philly before the Bai UnConvention (2016)

and a team of singers and dancers who were disguised as venue staff but then surprised our team by shifting from waiting on tables to belting out a killer rendition of the Imagine Dragons' song "Believer." Each year, before kicking off the Civet Society inductions, I delivered a state of the company address to rally our team around our mission and goals. The UnConvention became the most anticipated night of the year for the Bai family, an opportunity for our team members from around the country to spend time together in person and celebrate the culture that we all helped to build and shape.

As Ken was fond of saying, "It's about what you do when no one's looking." A true Civet was someone who spent the extra time and walked the extra mile to make sure their job was done at the highest level because they took pride in themselves and in Bai.

Ed Buczacki, who helped build major beverage brands such as Nantucket Nectars and Vitaminwater before joining Bai in 2011, epitomized the leadership and caring we expected from our Civets. Ed, who also had worked for Coca-Cola and Dr Pepper, was hired as our Mid-Atlantic regional sales manager but quickly moved into a critical position as director of sales operations. In that role, he worked closely with staff across all of our departments and mentored many of our employees who didn't have as much experience and knowledge about the industry, helping to raise our collective game. Ed led by example and poured his heart into every day he worked at Bai, earning his place in our second Civet class.

Ed Buczacki (former director of sales operations for Bai):
I played sports my whole life and was always a leader or captain of my teams. I wanted to continue to do that in my professional career and the Civet Society gave me that platform. Ben and Ken inducted everyone into the Civet Society, but they really let us build it and make it our own, which was great. That's why I prefer entrepreneurial environments to

working for big companies. When you get involved early on, it becomes your company, too. If you treat it like a job, it's just going to be a job. But if you treat it like your own, you develop a real passion for the business. That's what I loved about the culture at Bai.

I also loved the relationships I ended up building with Ben and Ken, and with Ben's family outside of the business. Ben always said he admired my sense of the beverage industry—the fact that I could see trends and sell the brand so well. But what I always admired about him was his ability to take the company on his back. He worked so hard at raising money and carrying the responsibilities of those investors. I always told Ben, "We couldn't do what we do if you didn't do what you do." He preached the dream in a way that I never could. But he always valued the people who were alongside him. After the announcement that Dr Pepper was buying the company, I gave Ben a huge hug and said, "You did it!" And his reply was, "No, WE did it."

As the UnConvention grew larger each year, the Civet Society ceremony became even more theatrical. Instead of having our executive team members give introductory remarks about the new inductees, we hired an actor to play our hidden "Voice of God" and deliver booming, impassioned inductions over the sound system. We crafted cryptic inductions that cast our Civets as warriors, champions, and forces of nature. During dinner, the background music would suddenly be interrupted by a crash of thunder that heralded the next announcement of the newest Civet. No one knew when these announcements would come during the evening or how many there would be. The name of a new Civet was revealed at the end of each induction only after an excruciatingly long, dramatic pause intended to keep everyone on the edge of their seats, wondering if their name was about to be called.

We brought each inductee on stage to be welcomed by our executive team and take their moment in the spotlight in front of their peers. We tried to capture the spirit of each Civet in their inductions, and of course, we never shied away from colorful language when we felt it was necessary to make our point. For example, this was our induction for Chris:

> *In a simpler time, they were called "leatherheads"—pioneers of what is now America's favorite sport. Tough guys who wore soft helmets and barely any pads, going to war on muddy, shitty fields—sticking thumbs in eyes, stomping on hands, breaking bones. All in the pursuit of victory.*
>
> *Today's warriors of the gridiron have fancier equipment and stadiums. Some even get to go to Disney World if they win it all. But inside them still burns that same "kill 'em all" spirit. That same drive to knock over whatever stands in between them and greatness. The same fire that burns inside this badass Civet.*
>
> *This Civet takes on any position, lines up against any opponent, and relishes every battle. Every challenge is met head-on—with an attitude that says, "This is my house, muthafuckaaaaa! You're gonna be sorry you ever showed up." This Civet is our Monster of the Midway, our MVP.*
>
> *This Civet is .... Chris Brown!*

Civets often told me that their inductions were indelible highlights of their careers, and our managers frequently said they were determined to see their employees onstage one day being honored as Civets. To me, the Civet Society was a manifestation of the dreams I had for Bai—it was a home for people who, like me, saw Bai as more than a product or a job. It was for the people who were willing to take risks in their lives and wanted to inspire others to come along on their adventure. We hired some people because we saw a glimmer of promise that could grow into greatness—people such as Durale Harper.

Durale was homeless just a few years before we hired him as a salesperson in the Dallas area, and he quickly proved that he embodied Bai's core values. When we developed large Bai-branded coolers and challenged our salespeople to sell them into retail accounts, Durale was the first to place one in a Target store. When I asked how he accomplished the feat, he told me, "Well, someone said it would be impossible—that's why I did it."

After he became a Civet in 2016, as his family was building a new home, Durale left me a voicemail that I'll never forget.

Durale Harper *(former territory development manager of Bai)*:
Five years ago, I was down and out, with no place to go, and no one to rely on. Two years ago, I met you and Ken in Plano, Texas, and my life has changed. I'm so grateful and so thankful that I took a leap of faith and came to Bai.

Raising a glass to the new members of the Civet Society (2016)

This company has been one of the best things that has ever happened to me in my life. Today I reached a milestone that five years ago, I thought I would have never achieved, and I owe it to you and this company.

I just want you to know that I will never quit, I will never give up, I will continue to rise.

One of the most important effects of establishing the Civet Society, was to stoke the competitive spirits of everyone on our team, not just those in sales. I know many people were disappointed, and sometimes angry, when they did not become Civets, but I felt strongly that admission had to be highly selective to represent the best of the best at Bai.

Tom Parker, who joined Bai in 2014 as our assistant controller, told me after being inducted that he had desperately wanted to be a Civet, though he had never admitted it to anyone. Tom played a vital role in improving the efficiency and effectiveness of our financial systems as well as helping us achieve critical savings in our spending on goods and services. He was typically the first person in the office every day, and though he may not have had the sexiest position in the company, he earned his selection by caring as much and working just as hard as anyone who had been named a Civet before him.

Tom Parker (former controller of Bai):

Becoming a Civet was absolutely the highlight of my professional career. When my name was called, I remember looking down, shutting my eyes, and just smiling.

When I got on the stage, Ben said, "Your life's about to change."

I told him, "It already did the day I joined."

I texted my wife Katie afterward and told her. She was the one person who knew how badly I wanted it. My hands were shaking to the point that I dropped my phone and cracked the screen. It was an amazing, amazing night.

When we inducted employees into the Civet Society, I felt a strong emotional connection to them, as though they were extensions of my own family. I loved getting to know their families and having them visit BQ to see where our shared dreams had taken root. Having Danna and the kids, as well as my parents and sister, intimately involved in Bai since its inception, I always thought of the company first and foremost as a family business, and I hoped that others felt the same way.

Tom Parker (former controller of Bai):

In fall 2016, I was at work early as usual when I saw a call from my sister around eight in the morning. Typically, I wouldn't answer the call at that time because she would just be calling to complain about my other sister. But I did answer it, and that's when she told me that our mom had just passed away suddenly. I just lost it.

There were a few people in the office who hugged me, and Barak walked me outside to get some fresh air. Then Ben pulled into the parking lot, dropped his bag on the ground, and made a beeline to me. I've never had a hug that hard. He just didn't let go. And he stayed with me until Katie got there. We sat and talked on the stoop outside BQ. It's really hard to put into words how much that meant. When Katie got there, I went to give her a hug and turned around to see that Ben had absolutely vanished

That night, I emailed Ben to thank him, and he said, "When you started hugging Katie, I knew it was time for me to go." I can't think of another CEO on the planet who would do that for someone.

***

The Civet Society and the UnConvention were the most prominent examples of our efforts at Bai to establish a company culture centered on the principle that no ideas were too outlandish and that no goals were unachievable. They gave us a platform to celebrate the dreamers and fighters—the black sheep—among us and to inspire everyone to embrace our core values. To further strengthen our cultural connections, we came up with another idea that quickly developed into a Bai tradition.

While driving with Carolynn up to our Saxonville, Massachusetts, office—which we opened in 2014 after Chad joined Bai—I started thinking about ideas to promote camaraderie among our team members. A few months earlier, we had created silicone slap bracelets as giveaways with a hidden USB thumb drive at one end and the phrase "Join the Bevolution" emblazoned across the middle. I never told anyone that I carried a copy of our capitalization table—the ledger of ownership of all Bai shares, including our outside investors and our employees who held equity—on that USB drive. Several times every day, that bracelet would catch my eye as I was writing or lifting a cup of coffee for a sip, and that would remind me of the responsibility I carried for everyone who had a stake in Bai—my family, my employees, and my investors.

As my hand gripped the steering wheel on that drive with Carolynn and the bracelet stared back at me, I wondered if we could create something similar for all of our staff, to serve as a symbol of the goals we were chasing. But rather than another bracelet, I envisioned dog tags—I loved the notion of everyone embracing a daily ritual of putting on their tags as they headed into battle for the day. I had always likened our business to a war, in that we were fighting our competitors hard for space on store shelves and in consumers' hearts. I thought having everyone wear dog tags would unite us.

I asked Chad, who is a veteran of the US Army Special Forces, about the idea, and he loved it. Together, we devised a plan to create two tags, one inscribed with the phrase *A Posse Ad Esse* (which is Latin for "From Potential to Being") and the other marked with a sales goal. Members of the sales team would have tags with their individual goals for annual case sales, while everyone outside of sales would have the overall company goal on their tags as a reminder that everyone played a role in achieving that figure. Then Candice and Carolynn worked their magic, getting silver tags made for everyone in the company and delivered within forty-eight hours.

The idea had an instant impact. Everyone knew their number and would be ready when called upon to recite it and explain their plan for how to accomplish their goal. Even though I never explicitly told everyone they needed to wear the tags on a daily basis, when I was talking to one of our team members, I always checked to see if the tags were hanging around their neck—and to my delight, they were.

I relished my own ritual of putting on my dog tags and my slap bracelet every morning before I headed to work, as though they provided armor for the day's battles. I was proud to see how our team members dedicated themselves to doing the same and expressing their sense of ownership of our company mission. We later decided to make gold tags for the Civets as another way to drive home the special nature of being inducted into that group. Each year at the UnConvention, everyone received new tags with updated goals, and our newest Civets traded in their silver for gold.

We endeavored to find other ways to express Bai's distinctive company culture, including producing a series of videos that highlighted some of the themes from our annual UnConventions and key moments in Bai's history. Sometimes those videos captured moments that were small but significant, like seeing my son, Jack, walk through the office one day and realizing how much both he and Bai had grown alongside each other, or like listening to the voicemail from Durale expressing his gratitude for being part of the Bai journey. These videos, which became part of every new employee's onboarding experience, captured the spirit that drove me to work my hardest every day and that I hoped everyone in the company shared.

LIVE THE BEVOLUTION: Visit the *Basementality* website (Basementality.org) to watch these and other videos to experience the Bai culture in depth.

Even with all these efforts, we sometimes struggled to maintain a consistent companywide culture because we expanded quickly and had many employees spread around the country. But when I look back at my Bai experience, I know that our company culture was absolutely essential to our success in the marketplace. In fact, it was a critical factor in our ability to sell the company at a significant premium when we realized we needed to align with a bigger player in the industry. I can confidently say that we cared more than anyone else and worked harder than anyone else, and that's how we built the fastest-growing brand in the business. We created and stoked a culture that stood for something much grander than bottling and selling a great drink. The essence of Bai was dreaming big, defying expectations, marshaling your passion and heart, creating a better world, and making memories that would last a lifetime.

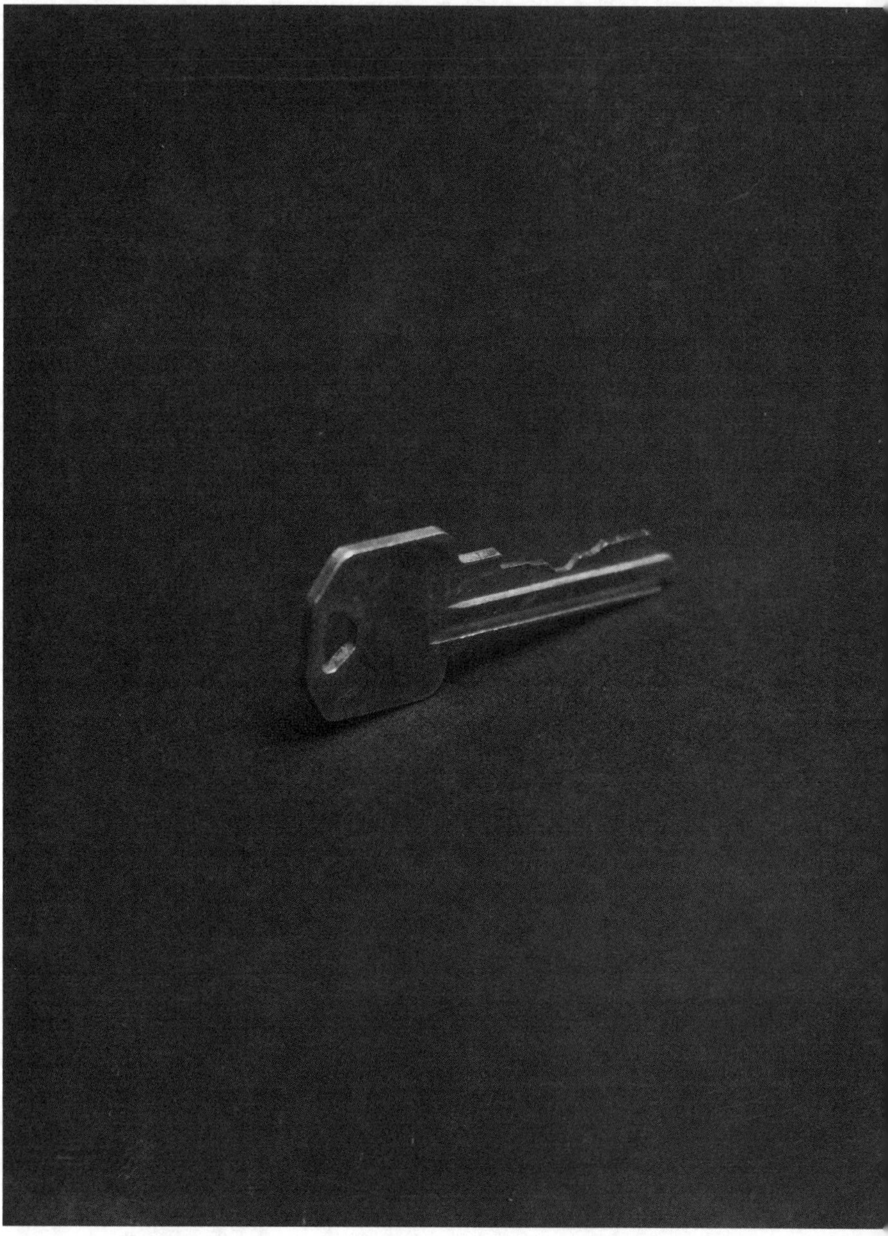

BASEMENTALITY

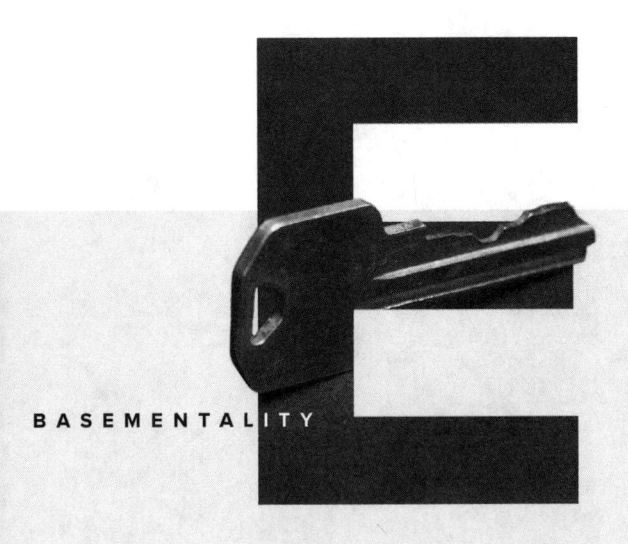

EMPOWER A CULTURE

Inspire others to a way of life, by delivering passion and belief, setting a furious pace, and teaching lessons learned through the good times and the bad. A culture rooted in Basementality is not cultivated by those who play it safe. It has to be a cult that unlocks shared vision. It means tough talk and vocal leadership. It's about creating an authentic place for the surefooted. The black sheep's culture must have myths and symbols and cool shit people want to wear and celebrate all day.

CHAPTER 9
THE END IS IN SIGHT

You might think that Dr Pepper's CEO, Larry Young, who had spent his entire thirty-five-year career in the soda business, would have been turned off by my assuredness that the industry needed a major overhaul. But it was quite the opposite. Larry and I forged an immediate connection, despite having divergent perspectives on our business, as well as very different upbringings and career paths.

Larry is proud of sharing the fact that he comes from humble roots and diligently climbed the traditional beverage industry ladder. He's a hardworking farm boy from Missouri who loves hunting and trucks and grew up drinking sweet tea. Larry started in the beverage business when I was just hitting my teens. His first job was as a truck driver for Pepsi-Cola General Bottlers, and he worked his way up the ranks to become that company's president and chief operating officer. He moved on to serve as CEO and president of Dr Pepper/Seven-Up Bottling Group, which was acquired by Cadbury Schweppes, and then he led the spinoff of Dr Pepper Snapple Group from Cadbury in 2008.

Larry was a Big Soda guy through and through. Even though I had spent the past five years railing against his core products, he greeted me with a warm, friendly demeanor that I couldn't help but admire. He had a plainspoken approach to business, and I could tell that he understood our brand and was a fan of what we were doing. In 2015, after getting a look under the hood of Bai's business and discussing our future plans, Dr Pepper's executive team wanted to make a further investment. Larry initially offered $80 million for a minority stake, but I told him we didn't need that much. Although I wanted some additional funds to invest in growing our business, I didn't want to sell more of a stake than we needed to. We settled on $15 million in exchange for a 3 percent stake in Bai, which valued our company at $500 million just as we were entering our fifth full year in business.

***

I'm often asked about the speed of Bai's trajectory over the seven years from its founding to when I agreed to sell the company to Dr Pepper Snapple Group. I understand how most people would view that time as a whirlwind, as we went from a startup selling cases out of the trunk of my car in Princeton to a national brand in a relative blink of an eye. But from the inside, those years felt like a long and challenging—yet exhilarating—climb because I was on call seven days a week and constantly thinking about next steps and new ideas to drive the business forward.

Although they wouldn't seem like they go together, two words define the experience: "impatience" and "discipline." These are two of the foundations of my Basementality.

My impatience was rooted in my frustration with the beverage industry. I resented the reality that the fate of new brands was largely in the hands of a distribution system that was dominated by the country's three largest soda companies and was slow to embrace true innovation. I knew we had a product that answered the diet dilemma and that people enjoyed immensely, but I was frustrated when distribution companies—even our own partners—didn't appear to share the same drive and vision for Bai that I did. It's natural that a company founder would care more than anyone about his or her brand, but I still took it personally when I felt our distributors could have given Bai more attention and worked harder on our behalf. I thought about Bai from morning until night and wanted everyone involved in the business to do the same.

At the same time, I believed in the methodical, disciplined approach that Ken had established upon his arrival, which focused on creating a consistent look of success for Bai at retail and establishing proof of concept in key selected markets before continuing to expand. Creating that proof of concept was painstaking work and was necessary to give our own team and our distribution partners the ammunition to push Bai into new markets and retail outlets. So although I often felt like a caged animal, aching to break free from the constraints of the industry's structure, I also understood that we needed to be disciplined in how we moved forward.

As we were building our network of independent distributors, I reached out to Dr Pepper's brand management team to gauge the company's interest in carrying Bai. The number three soda company behind Coca-Cola and Pepsi had built a portfolio of independent "allied brands," including Fiji Water and Vita Coco, that it distributed alongside the company's own brands, such as Dr Pepper, Snapple, 7UP, Canada Dry, and Schweppes. Dr Pepper operated its own distribution routes and forged partnerships with other wholesalers to create a network that covered most of the country. In 2011, Ari Soroken and I traveled to Dr Pepper's headquarters in Plano, Texas, to make our first pitch, and a year later, after Ken Kurtz came aboard, Dr Pepper agreed to give Bai a trial run on 150 trucks in its New York and New Jersey distribution area.

Given our progress on our home turf during our first two years of business, as well as Ken's arrival to help build our sales force, both we and our Dr Pepper counterparts were optimistic that the additional distribution power would substantially elevate Bai's presence in the New York and New Jersey area. We kicked off the test run by inviting Dr Pepper's local distributor representatives on a cruise around the Hudson River and gave them our most impassioned presentation about Bai's potential. And the results were powerful: Bai's sales grew consistently each month in the New York and New Jersey markets, encouraging Dr Pepper to give us another opportunity to launch a test in Northern California, which went equally well.

We continued to work diligently with our other independent distributors elsewhere in the country, but we started to see a path to national distribution with Dr Pepper given our success in our test markets. In 2013, we decided to buy out our existing Southern California distribution contract with a major independent wholesaler to show that we were willing to go all-in with the Dr Pepper network. This was a risky move, because if Dr Pepper decided not to move forward with a national agreement, we would have lost distribution in a key market plus the money we spent on the buyout. But the gamble paid off, as Dr Pepper agreed to sign Bai as an allied brand and kick off national distribution at the start of 2014.

After four-plus years in business, we had secured a deal with one of the most storied names in the beverage industry as our new national distribution partner. But I knew this was not the time to get comfortable or complacent or to expect that our presence on Dr Pepper's trucks around the country would instantly rocket us into the stratosphere. We continued to aggressively invest in growing our sales force because we needed to intensify our focus on excellent execution in the field now that Dr Pepper's distribution network would expose us to more retail outlets. We had to retain the discipline and fundamentals that brought us to this point as our presence expanded across the country. Yet even as we had tremendous runway in front of us in terms of growth in the enhanced water market, I felt that Bai could become more than a single-category player. And I must thank my son, Jack, for providing a huge splash of inspiration on that front.

***

Jack has always loved carbonated drinks. Because we didn't buy soda in our household, we purchased a SodaStream machine to make our own sparkling water in our kitchen. One day in spring 2014, Jack decided to experiment by filling the SodaStream with Bai Sumatra Dragonfruit. It was a great idea, but the problem was that those machines are meant only for water, and at twelve years old, Jack didn't have the patience to let the freshly carbonated contents of the bottle settle long enough before he released it from the base of the SodaStream.

In the living room next to the kitchen, I heard a gunshot-like bang and a scream from Jack. I bolted into the kitchen to find my wide-eyed son—along with our newly painted white walls, cabinets, and ceiling—covered in red liquid. Our kitchen resembled the iconic prom-night bloodbath from the movie *Carrie* but with a much sweeter aroma. Once I knew that Jack was okay, I asked him what he was thinking. He said that he simply wanted to make a Bai with bubbles.

After cleaning up the mess, my aggravation began to fade. I thought, "If he wants a carbonated version of Bai, we should do this the right way."

A sparkling line of Bai seemed like such a no-brainer that I couldn't believe we hadn't thought of it earlier. Now that the idea was in my head, I demanded that we go full speed ahead. I returned to the same approach we took with the original version of Bai—I called Paul Sapan and Chad Portas and put them to work on making it taste good and look good. Within three months, Bai Bubbles was born—a ridiculously fast turnaround, considering that a new product launch from a large beverage company typically takes twelve to eighteen months. Paul crafted seven flavors of Bai Bubbles, which we named using the same approach of paying homage to coffee-growing regions: Bolivia Black Cherry, Peru Pineapple, Gimbi Pink Grapefruit, Waikiki Coconut, Jamaica Blood Orange, Indonesia Nashi Pear, and Guatemala Guava. Chad and his creative team designed a beautiful label for the sleek 11.5-ounce cans that we used for Bubbles, perfectly complementing the look of the eighteen-ounce bottles we used for our original product line. Our operations team, including my brother-in-law, Nic Amato, who had joined the company earlier that year, was tasked with getting Bai Bubbles produced, and Ken's sales team began to sell our distribution and retail partners on the potential of our first carbonated brand extension.

Being able to bring Nic into Bai—and eventually reward him and my sister for their hard work after the sale to Dr Pepper—was tremendously meaningful to me. Nic is one of the most honest and devoted people I've ever known. After our Brewed Awakening venture failed years earlier, Nic took a full-time gig with an industrial supply company, plus night shifts cutting produce at a local supermarket, to help provide for Candice and their kids, Max and Chloe. He pitched in with every business I started, including Bai, whether that meant helping to renovate office and storage space or taking countless bags of used bottles home to his recycling bins because, in our earliest days, we didn't have any other way to dispose of them.

If you're lucky enough to have someone like Nic in your life, you want him around as much as possible. I had tried numerous times to get him to join Bai full time, but he was concerned about both he and Candice working for a startup while raising two young children. Yet even though Nic worked nonstop in his daytime and side jobs, he was never too busy or too tired to help his brother-in-law when I needed it. The only questions he ever asked were, "What do you need? And when?"

Nic Amato (brother-in-law):
After seven years, I was let go from my job with the supply company. I called Candice to give her the news as I was driving home. Probably twenty minutes later, Ben was on the phone saying, "That's it—you're coming to work for me."

I agreed to take the leap.

One of my first projects was Bai Bubbles. We had to go to a co-packer in Wisconsin to produce it, which was a bear, but that's where we found the facility that met all of our needs. Ben wanted the can to look and feel a certain way and wanted the production process to be done in a certain way. We certainly could have found easier ways to do things, but he would not stray from his convictions. He had a vision and he stuck to it. And wouldn't you know it, that's what helped catapult the brand.

I went back and forth to Wisconsin for about two years, making sure we put out the absolute best product we could. I would be at that facility from six in the morning to eight at night to ensure that everything was perfect until the next production run, then I would get a call at two or three in the morning to come do a tasting—and I'd drag myself back to sample every flavor. I needed to make sure everything was perfect, not just because it was my job, but because I was doing it for my family.

To introduce Bai Bubbles to Dr Pepper and some of their affiliated distributor partners, we hosted a launch party in a secluded bar in the Chinatown neighborhood of New York City. We wanted to convey the sense

Unveiling Bai Bubbles with Danna, Candice, and special guest Flavor Flav (2014)

of being in an old-time speakeasy so our distributors would feel like they were getting an exclusive look at the unveiling of a hidden gem. To emphasize the great taste of the product, we brought in Flavor Flav, the Public Enemy hype man and reality TV star, to take pictures with everyone under banners reading "Bubbling with Flav" and "For the Love of Flavor." We launched Bai Bubbles in the New York market in September 2014 before beginning national distribution at the start of 2015. Bubbles was an immediate hit, providing an alternative for people who loved sparkling drinks, didn't want the sugar and calories of traditional sodas or the artificial sweeteners of diet sodas, and craved flavor that was missing from sparkling waters.

With Bubbles about to pop on a broader scale, we were able to look back on 2014 as a huge year in the history of the company. Our annual revenue soared to $48.1 million, from $17.1 million in 2013, on the strength of our national distribution agreement with Dr Pepper, the growth and improved effectiveness of our internal sales team, and our steady progress in e-commerce. Bai began selling on Amazon at the end of 2011 and had become the fastest-growing beverage brand on the site, thanks to efforts led by John Denny to effectively target consumers who were seeking healthier foods and beverages. Our aggressive bets on Amazon allowed us to quickly outpace long-established brands, including the Big Three, in e-commerce. We became an example of how emerging companies could leverage new technologies and strategies to threaten the goliaths of the industry. By late 2016, according to the consumer research firm 1010Data, "for every dollar being spent on sweetened beverages online, Bai is getting 45 cents, while the other 40-plus brands all fight over the remaining 55."

In 2014, Bai was included in *Inc.* magazine's rankings of fastest-growing U.S. private companies, and at the start of 2015, we were ranked number thirteen in *Forbes* magazine's list of America's Most Promising Companies. Even though I was proud of these accolades, the award I remember most clearly from 2014 was one I didn't win. Ernst & Young selected me as a finalist for its Entrepreneur of the Year Award for the

New Jersey region, and I was up against mostly technology and health care executives. The New Jersey winner would go on to the national Entrepreneur of the Year competition, and given Bai's swift ascent at that time, I felt very confident about my chances of advancing. I was so confident, in fact, that as the winner's name was about to be announced at the New Jersey awards banquet, I smiled at Danna and Ari, who were seated on either side of me, and started to rise up from my chair to head toward the podium. But I quickly dropped back into my seat as the name of the CEO of a bakery company was announced instead.

I was floored. Not only did I lose out to someone else in the consumer goods business, I lost to someone who wasn't even a company founder. The winner was honored for expanding a company that had been founded by someone else nearly two decades before he came aboard. I was a little embarrassed at my presumption that I would be walking away with the big trophy that night, but more than that, I grew offended by the judges' conception of entrepreneurship. In my mind, a true entrepreneur is someone who comes up with an idea and builds it from the ground up, guided by a dream—it's not someone who takes over an existing company, no matter how much they grow the business.

After that night, I looked differently at how the term "entrepreneur" was used in the business world, and I've pushed back hard against the notion that anyone who succeeds in business can bear that title. To me, a true entrepreneur is someone who grows an idea from nothing and builds it into a thriving business that makes a difference. Growing an existing business to new heights is certainly difficult and commendable, but it's not entrepreneurship in its purest sense.

***

After our first year of national distribution with Dr Pepper, Bai entered 2015 poised to continue our explosive growth. More consumers were familiar with Bai, but we still had a long way to go to become a household name. To help us move forward, I turned back to the guy who helped me start my career two decades earlier with the Godiva Theater Café and Chocolixir, Michael Simon. Michael had spent the past five years as chief marketing officer at Panera Bread and had twenty-plus years of experience guiding major consumer brands. When I convinced him to make the jump to Bai's executive team, I knew I had the person I could trust to manage our first investment of millions of dollars in national marketing campaigns.

Michael initiated market research efforts to better understand the demographic of our consumer base, revealing that millennial customers were a significant driver of our growth. We called them "Conscious Authentics" because compared with older consumers, they wanted to know more about what was inside their foods and beverages, and they placed a higher priority on quality ingredients. They were willing to pay a premium for products like Bai that were aligned with their interests and values. The research also revealed that Bai only had 7 percent aided brand awareness among consumers, meaning only seven out of one hundred consumers recognized the brand if they were shown a bottle of Bai. The fact that we had grown to a nearly $50 million business in just five years with such a small portion of our prospective consumer base knowing we even existed was a testament to the tremendous growth opportunity before us.

Michael's experience in planning and executing marketing campaigns was an ideal match with the efforts of Chad's in-house creative team. We began to roll out digital and out-of-home advertising campaigns featuring our whimsical and provocative brand voice, enhanced our social media presence, and we made our first foray into the entertainment world by sponsoring the Zac Brown Band's *Jekyll + Hyde* North American stadium tour. Zac and I had become friendly a couple of years earlier when he discovered Bai and reached out to us. I loved his music and admired how his band crossed traditional genres to appeal to country, rock, and pop

On the Zac Brown Band tour sponsored by Bai, one of our most fun family adventures (2015)

fans. That summer, I attended concerts with my family and members of the Bai team in several cities, which was a huge highlight for me personally. We launched a drink recipe contest, with the winner getting a VIP experience at one of Zac's concerts, and we made free song downloads available with purchases of Bai.

I was thrilled that Bai gained more exposure by teaming with Zac, of course, but the most fulfilling part of our partnership was sponsoring the Zac Brown Guitar Project. Through this effort, we commissioned five emerging artists to design guitars that Zac autographed, played live in concert, and then auctioned off to support Camp Southern Ground, his nonprofit summer camp for children of all backgrounds. Though Bai had engaged in community projects in the Princeton area, this was our first opportunity to support an important cause on a broader scale and connect in a different way to our mission of helping to improve lives.

Michael Simon (former chief marketing officer of Bai):

Most entrepreneurs don't have a lot of money available early on to do market research. Guys I've worked with like Ben and Ron Shaich, the founder of Panera, were able to build businesses based on their judgment, which was generally very good. The challenge, as the business gets bigger, is that growth is harder to achieve. I'm a big believer that insight can help inform better decision-making. At Bai, we had a lot of people guessing who our core customer was. I always try to answer two questions when I enter a new business: Who are our target customers? and, What drives their behavior? We also needed to find ways to articulate our brand's purpose—I call it our "Why We Exist" approach. I believe that to engage and drive loyalty with a customer, you've got to have more than a transactional relationship. It's got to be more deeply emotional and connective.

For Bai, our tactical messaging focused on one gram of sugar, five calories, and great taste, which was important because it gave consumers a reason to believe in the product. But we also worked on positioning the brand to bring more inspiration to what we were doing and to connect emotionally with the consumer. I told the team it would be a bit of a journey because I've seen some companies move too quickly toward getting to their emotional purpose. Initially, we had to tell people that Bai is a drink that tastes good and is good for you. But later, the goal was to move to a path where we could make deeper connections between the brand and consumers. If we could get someone to be healthy by changing what they drank, that could also be a catalyst for even more change in their life so they could become their best self.

Under Chad's creative direction, we launched our biggest effort to boost our brand awareness with an ad campaign called "None of This Makes Sense," which played off the odd truth that Bai is good for you but still tastes amazing. The linchpin of this campaign was our first Super Bowl commercial, "Horse Whisperer," featuring a swaggy hip-hop equestrian trainer who seemed out of place at a quaint stable but could easily make his horse "fancy prance" on command. The ad played in the New York, Los Angeles, and Chicago markets and helped us gain our biggest mainstream attention to date.

While we were beginning to ramp up our marketing efforts and refine our brand positioning, our relationship with Dr Pepper was getting stronger. As a new allied brand in Dr Pepper's system, Bai quickly became an important growth engine for a company whose flagship soda brand was feeling the pain of consumers' mounting disillusionment with sugary beverages. Dr Pepper's senior management team came to BQ in spring 2015 to take an in-depth look into our business and hear our vision for the future of the industry. I pulled no punches when expressing my thoughts about the decline of soda and the increasingly important role that Bai would play in the industry as the standard-bearer for a new generation of beverages that delivered what consumers were clearly telling us they wanted.

Larry Young (former chief executive officer of Dr Pepper Snapple Group):
My earliest encounter with Bai was when we were doing a test with the product in our distribution network. I was out on a market tour and ran into a young man from our team who was putting up a Bai display in a Wegmans.

He said to me, "Mr. Young, if you ever buy a brand, this here is the one you ought to buy."

And I laughed and said, "You want me to buy Bai?"

The brand kept on going from there, and I met Ben when we went to BaiQuarters for the first time. He invited me over to his house, and when there was not a bunch of other people around, that's when I got to see what kind of a guy he was. The first thing he did was introduce me to his entire family—I even had to get down on the floor and play with the dog. I could tell not only that he had a tremendous passion for his business and what he was building, but he was also balanced. And that's hard to do. You don't find many people in this business who are balanced. I just fell in love with him from day one.

With Dr Pepper's investment, the early success of Bai Bubbles, and our increased understanding of our consumer base, I gained more confidence in Bai's prospects. Bubbles, in particular, awakened my sense that Bai could be much more than an enhanced water product. I believed our distinctive combination of great flavors, low calories, no artificial sweeteners, and antioxidant infusion from the coffeefruit was a recipe that could be extended into multiple categories. I began to refer to Bai as a Total Beverage Solution, meaning that we could offer better options for consumers in enhanced waters, carbonated soft drinks (including sodas), teas, and even unflavored waters. And I didn't see any reason to wait in rolling out our innovations.

In August 2015, we launched Bai Antiwater, an effort to blend hydration and functionality by infusing super-purified water with electrolytes in addition to antioxidants. We called it the "next generation of hydration," or H2.0. Antiwater was a struggle from the outset. We had some production glitches in our initial rollout, and we didn't have an overwhelmingly enthusiastic response from our distributors or retailers. But I was undaunted. I felt it would only be a matter of time before our business partners and consumers saw the benefits of Antiwater, and in the meantime, I continued to push our team to roll out more innovations.

Our next entrant into the market, in February 2016, was our line of four fruit-flavored Bai Superteas. Several months later, we introduced Bai Cocofusions, a collection of coconut waters combined with other fruit flavors, in an effort to leverage the popularity of Molokai Coconut, which had become our second-best seller after Brasilia Blueberry. Before 2016 was out, we also rolled out Bai Black, a line of sparkling beverages with traditional soda flavors, including cola, citrus, root beer, ginger ale, and cream.

By the time our innovation explosion was complete, we had more than thirty different Bai-branded flavors on the market across six categories. My vision for our Total Beverage Solution was that each category would take its appropriate place in stores alongside its primary competitors—Bai in the enhanced water section, Bai Bubbles with the sparkling waters, Bai Superteas in the tea section, Bai Cocofusions with the coconut waters, Bai Antiwater among the still water brands, and Bai Black in the soda aisle. We needed to make the Bai brand ubiquitous—for any kind of drink a consumer wants, we would have the answer.

This approach, however, proved to be a major challenge after we swiftly pushed so much innovation into the market. Initially, distributors and retailers reflexively considered all the Bai products to be under the same umbrella and began combining our base Bai flavors with Bubbles, Superteas, and the others on shelves and in displays. Although we were happy to expose consumers to our variety of options, we did not want to confuse them. Lumping all of our products together had the unwanted effect of cannibalizing some of our base Bai sales, which accounted for the vast majority of our business. We also were missing opportunities to meet consumers where they shopped to introduce our new products. For example, if Snapple or Arizona Iced Tea drinkers were searching for a lower-calorie alternative without artificial sweeteners, they would not look in the enhanced water section next to Bai or Vitaminwater. Similarly, most soda drinkers would not be exposed to Bai Black if it wasn't in the soda aisle. Some of our distributors and retailers began to embrace our vision for the Total Beverage Solution, but others didn't come around as quickly as I would have liked, and I pushed them hard to understand my way of thinking.

Ken Kurtz (former president of Bai):

As we were building our infrastructure and instilling the right disciplines in our sales team and our distributor partners, Ben became the mad scientist. That's when the real pressure on the business began. He's a great innovator, but you have to understand that we were still a relatively new brand, and we were still getting our route-to-market systems flush with Bai. Then all of a sudden, we have these new lineups to introduce. So the distributors are saying, "Good concept—we'll talk to you in six months, and maybe we'll test it out in the marketplace to see how it does." Our response was to go to our national retail accounts and big regional accounts, like Target and Walgreens, to get them to buy in to what we were doing. Then we would say to our distributors, "Test it out? The retailer's ready to go—we have four thousand accounts ready to roll it out."

We jammed a lot of things down the distribution system's throat way before they wanted it. It was very tough for them to turn down new business in a large number of accounts when their business was not growing elsewhere. So as we put a lot of products into the marketplace over a short period of time, the system started to bottleneck.

Perhaps it might have been wiser to introduce these new product lines more gradually to give our distributors and retailers more breathing room to incorporate them. But at the time, all I saw was a bloated industry system that was behind the curve in terms of giving consumers the innovations they wanted. The industry needed to be challenged to change its ways. Dr Pepper's distribution network—the company-owned routes and their independent affiliates—still generated the bulk of its business from traditional and diet soft drinks, even though the growth in those products had evaporated. Who was this brash guy from New Jersey to tell distributors affiliated with a $6 billion beverage powerhouse that they were betting on the wrong horses?

My attitude might have seemed like arrogance to some—or many—in the industry, but I honestly believed I could see that the consumer landscape was shifting far faster than the industry was reacting to those changes. My forcefulness was fueled by the love of my brand and the people who had dreamed and fought alongside me to bring it to life. Yes, I had an edge—but it was sharpened by my determination to protect what I loved. I needed my team to know that I had their backs and that I had the best interests of our brand at heart. I needed them to know that I would fucking run over anybody who tried to stand in our way because I felt that's what they needed in a leader. The industry was starving for disruption, and we were delivering it at an unprecedented pace. A true disruptor is not just someone who creates a new product, but someone who can instill in people a vision for a new future when they can't see it for themselves. I was committed to being the voice of our bevolution.

By the time we were rolling out our wave of innovations in 2016, Bai's annual revenue had skyrocketed to $120 million. Even with the difficulties we faced in getting our full portfolio accepted into Dr Pepper's distribution system and embraced by retailers as a single brand across a family of categories, our business was booming. But I could sense shadows lurking around the corner.

Our strategy in building Bai to this point was to establish proof of concept deep in the marketplace by focusing heavily on certain geographic regions and select retail outlets. This enabled us to achieve triple-digit growth in annual sales, while still creating opportunities for significant continued growth as we increased our product portfolio and our presence in the national marketplace. However, I recognized that we were getting to the point where our ability to scale was more dependent than ever on our distributors—both Dr Pepper and our independent partners—to prioritize and support Bai's growth. Without a swift and substantial increase in distribution firepower, we risked Bai becoming a brand that would not live up to its enormous potential.

For as much support as we had received from Dr Pepper in taking our distribution national and investing in our business, at the end of the day, its legacy brands were still the priority for its distribution system. Those brands were standing in our way. Bai Supertea was not going to be a priority over Snapple as long as Snapple was the name on the outside of the truck making deliveries to stores.

As my vision for Bai's Total Beverage Solution crystallized, the reality was clear—we either needed to create our own distribution system or become fully part of one of the existing systems and create change from within. These were the only options for Bai to fully realize its potential. And even for someone like me, who loves to dream as big as possible, I knew that launching our own distribution system was not a realistic option.

To save my beloved brand from becoming marginalized, the time had come to put Bai up for sale.

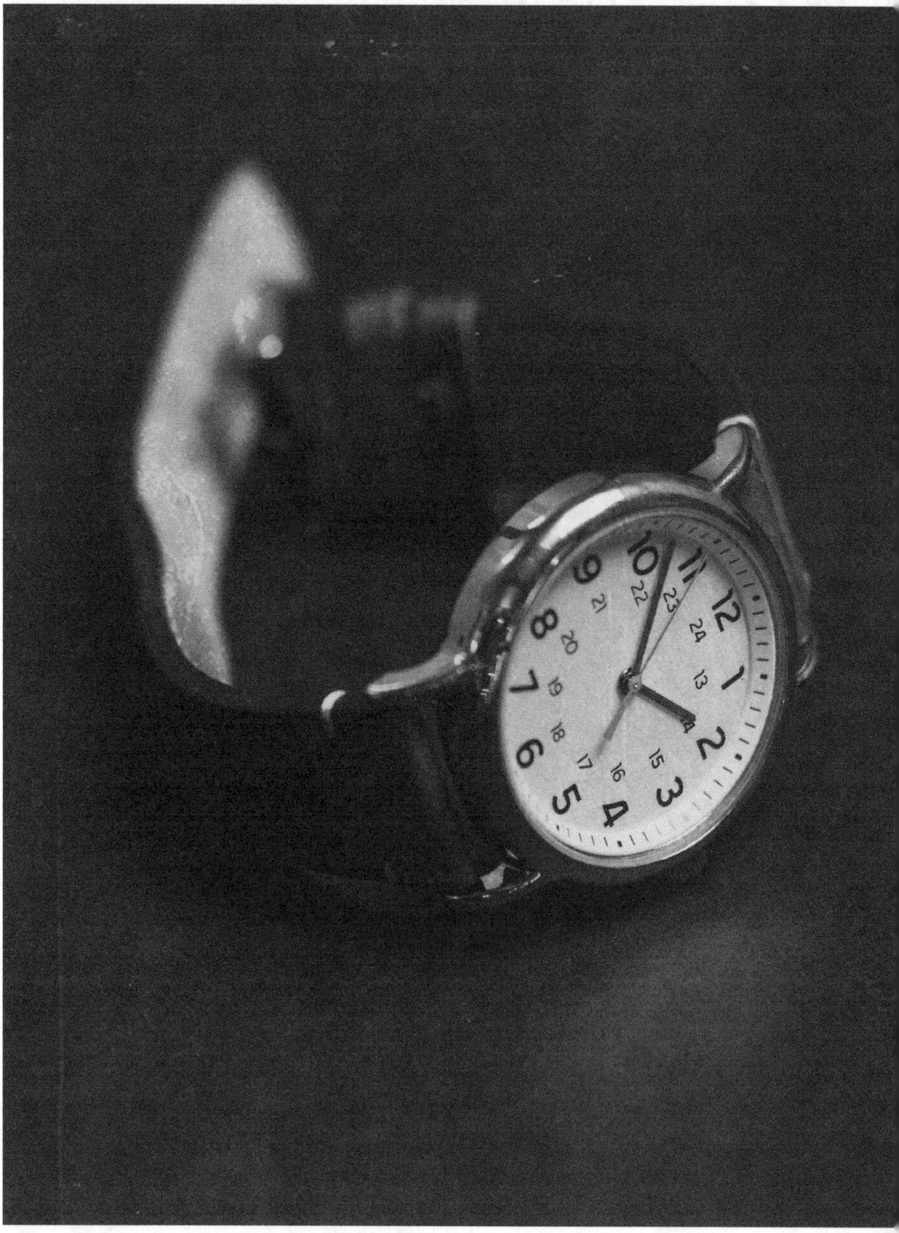

BASEMENTALITY

DON'T HESITATE

Do the work in front of you, day in and day out. And keep everyone around you motivated to do the same. But never let that dull your instincts for reaching your endgame. Listen for the final whistle long before it blows. Figure out where the finish line is when no when else can spot it. With your Basementality, seize the buzzer-beating move when others are still figuring out how to play the game.

CHAPTER 10

I'VE GOT NOTHING LEFT

The decision to put Bai up for sale in spring 2016 was agonizing—and it was the start of the most exciting and tumultuous period of my career.

Over the previous three years, as Bai's sales more than doubled annually, people within the industry would often tell us we should capitalize on our momentum and sell the company. We even had exploratory discussions with a couple of prominent consumer packaged goods (CPG) and beverage companies that reached out to us about a possible deal, but neither offered proposals that would benefit the company and our investors from strategic and financial standpoints.

I was in no rush to consider an exit. Fortunately, we had a great group of investors who were not putting any pressure on us to sell—in fact, I knew that many of them genuinely enjoyed being a part of the ride and took pride in telling people they were Bai investors as our brand was exploding. And I was having so much fun running Bai. We coveted our independence and relished punching up at the Big Soda giants, even as we forged our distribution alliance with Dr Pepper. I loved dreaming and fighting alongside our team and feeling our collective belief in Bai's mission. I couldn't imagine giving up control of my baby, especially as we were just starting to embark on expanding the brand across categories.

But ultimately, I had to be honest with myself about the reality of our industry and our need to align with a company that had the distribution power to take our brand to a higher level. At the same time, I knew the industry's big players were aware of Bai's progress and potential for further growth and that we likely would have a significant opportunity to reward our team members and investors whose support was critical to building our company. The best-case scenario in my mind was finding a partner who wouldn't see Bai merely as a tool to prop up its growth and offset the slowing growth or declines of the other brands taking up space on their distribution trucks. I wanted a true partner who would see Bai as I did: as the catalyst for a massive change in the industry to release the stranglehold that sugar, calories, and artificial ingredients held on beverage consumers for too long.

Through Ari Soroken's hard work, we had built a solid relationship with JPMorgan as a commercial lender. In 2015, JPMorgan's investment banking team pitched us on the idea of an initial public offering, arguing that our growth history would create a ferocious appetite among investors and allow us to raise considerable funds through the stock market to fuel our expansion. But we were wary of the constraints that accompanied being a publicly traded company—namely, having to answer to a board of directors and shareholders who would place a premium on short-term profits and dividends. Looking back at some of our most significant decisions, such as pivoting fully to our five-calorie platform or walking away from Walmart's initial offer to carry Bai at reduced prices, it was hard to imagine being able to make such critical moves so quickly if we had the specter of shareholders' reactions hanging over our heads. Going public also wouldn't solve our core problem of not owning our own distribution system. So when we came to the crossroads in evaluating the future of our business in spring 2016, rather than focus on an initial public offering, we asked JPMorgan to help us explore options for potential deals with larger beverage or CPG companies.

After giving JP Morgan the green light to pursue a deal, our executive team worked intensively to develop a compelling presentation that would illustrate our perspective on the industry and Bai's defining role in its future.

We set the scene by charting the decline of Big Soda, which began in the late 1990s and ultimately resulted in $15.4 billion of consumer sales moving out of traditional and diet sodas over the following two decades. The first wave of change was attributable to what we called the sugar dilemma, as consumers turned to diet sodas to avoid sugar and calories.

But within a few years, consumers developed an increasing distaste for the artificial sweeteners used in diet sodas, shifting more dollars toward functional beverage brands like Vitaminwater that purported to deliver healthier alternatives. Yet Vitaminwater and other brands with perceived health benefits still contained sugar. This left consumers facing a diet dilemma, which is when Bai arrived to lead what we called the industry's smart age. Bai provided the answer to the diet dilemma by creating beverages with five calories, antioxidants, and no artificial sweeteners, all without sacrificing flavor—a combination that no other brand executed as successfully as we did. With this presentation, we positioned Bai as the premier brand for a new generation of drinkers, particularly our core consumer base of millennials, whose changing tastes would further disrupt the beverage industry for years to come.

Through some of our own relationships, in addition to JPMorgan's outreach efforts, we met with several giant US and international companies that were interested in exploring a deal. As our leadership team met with some of the biggest names in our business and made the case for why they should consider aligning with Bai, we didn't focus solely on industry trends, consumer demographics, or the ingredients inside our bottles. We brought these executives into BQ so they could walk the halls, see our people at work, view our timeline and pictures on the walls, and feel how our core values of tenacity, audacity, obsessiveness, audaciousness, and greatness were celebrated throughout our offices. We wanted to give them a genuine view of our culture and a more intimate sense of our team's commitment to fighting for our bevolution. When I stepped up to give my perspectives on Bai, I spoke about our ardent belief that we were changing the world.

We saw the beverage industry as a reckless playground where Big Sugar toyed with the weight and health of consumers without providing options to truly benefit their well-being. People spent their hard-earned money on the products we created, and as torchbearers for the future of the beverage industry, our team at Bai felt we had a responsibility to give them better choices without diminishing their enjoyment.

I realized going into this process that some of our suitors would be taken aback and possibly offended by my remarks. I'm sure that our perspectives on the industry scared some of these companies away from the idea of aligning with us. But it was critically important that we presented our authentic selves. I knew that we were attempting to sell a culture that was never going to mix with some or most of these companies, but I needed to force them to ask themselves: Can we handle this brand? Can we handle its culture? Can we handle its innovation? Both sides needed to understand the answers to those questions because I was not simply looking for a sale—I wanted an adoption.

If we had to become part of a bigger company to secure our future, I wanted it to be one that would embrace our vision as its own and that would make Bai a central component of its business strategy. I wanted to give my baby to a parent who could take the best care of it, and the only way to find that kind of match was to give them an honest sense of who we were and why we did what we did every day. Ultimately, I believe the strength of our culture was a predominant factor in our ability to elicit significant offers from the companies that put in bids to acquire Bai.

Ari Soroken (former chief financial officer of Bai):
For years, we never focused on or thought about selling the company. You can't think about selling a company and, at the same time, fully focus on getting shit done daily—making long-term decisions on contracts, employees, and leases and dealing with all the other things that go into running a business. We never wanted to be in that position, and we had

a hard time embracing the fact that maybe one day we would have to sell the company. Then, when we eventually did decide to sell, I don't think we realized how quickly it was going to happen once we committed to it.

Word got out quickly through the investment banking community and some publications, so we had to move fast. The last thing you want is for the process to languish or go sideways, and plenty of things can influence it, like a market downturn or another acquisition. Once it starts, it's a locomotive that you can't stop. The bankers did everything they could to make it a frothy, competitive process. Honestly, we still felt that if we didn't get a price that was fair to our investors, we didn't have to sell.

It was an incredibly fast-paced, exciting process. Each company that expressed interest sent in their lawyers, investment bankers, and accountants, who all wanted to see information presented in their own ways. We had armies of people coming through BQ. We spent six months answering questions, but it didn't seem that long because it all happened so quickly. Each of the suitors had the right to ask hundreds and hundreds of questions. There were many times when we would go into New York City with our investment bankers and meet with the accountants and bankers of a suitor, who would walk us through fifty slides of questions they had prepared. Eventually we had to put a hard stop to the questions because we realized some of those companies might not have been intending to purchase us but were doing competitive research. Even at that point, we were still questioning if this was really going to happen. Are we going to get an offer? What does that offer need to be for us to accept it? Everyone from Ben to our investment bankers had wildly different opinions.

When we started the sale process and began to engage with prospective buyers, Dr Pepper was the one major player that wasn't initially involved. The company had shied away from making aggressive acquisitions in recent years, like its major rivals, but I wanted Dr Pepper to be in the mix—in fact, I thought they would be the best potential acquirer given our history and Larry Young's belief in our brand. However, I thought that they might need a little push and that we needed to whet their appetite a bit more by letting them hear that other companies were beginning to circle around us. I knew that this strategy struck a nerve when Ken and I were summoned to Plano, Texas, where a very unhappy Larry and Marty Ellen, Dr Pepper's chief financial officer, met us for lunch at the Capital Grille, their favorite restaurant near their corporate headquarters.

Marty fumed at us for not involving Dr Pepper in the sale process. Although I certainly understood his position, after a few minutes of tongue-lashing, I started to get upset myself. Dr Pepper had the most to lose if another company acquired Bai, as we accounted for a significant piece of its growth after becoming an allied brand. Over the past few years, Dr Pepper had lost other fast-growing allied brands—including Vitaminwater, Monster, Rockstar, and Fuze—that were either acquired by rival companies or, in Monster's case, switched distributors after going public. Were Larry and Marty prepared for the same thing to happen with Bai? If not, why were we spending time arguing about whether we should have notified them about the sale process instead of focusing on the opportunity that was in front of all of us?

"Look, Marty, I get that you're upset, but let's face facts," I retorted, matching his forceful tone and pointing over at a small crowd mingling at the restaurant's bar. "We're the beautiful woman at the bar that everybody wants to take home. Don't yell at me because I didn't invite you into the process when you should have noticed that all the other guys are looking at us. You need to take me home, Marty!"

Larry chuckled at my analogy, while Marty and I each continued to seethe at the table. I would not have spoken to another prospective buyer like that, but my emotional reaction was actually triggered by my affection for Dr Pepper and, specifically, Larry. I didn't want any animosity between our two companies. As I considered the potential bidders for Bai, I didn't think any others would be as good of a fit as Dr Pepper, particularly because of my relationship with Larry. I remembered that, just a few months earlier, I had texted Larry to ask if he would be willing to record a video message for us to play at our UnConvention. Minutes later, he texted me back with a video recorded at his desk on his assistant's iPhone. Larry gave our team an earnest rallying cry, encouraging them to keep fighting for our bevolution and to keep punching Dr Pepper and him "right in the nose." I was struck by how quickly he responded and how enthusiastically he challenged us to forge ahead with disrupting the industry's status quo.

Sitting at that table in the Capital Grille, I realized that I admired and liked Larry so much that if we had to be adopted by another family, I wanted him to be the one sitting at the head of the table. He understood our mission and had always supported it, even though his own company was often in our crosshairs. I believed that acquiring Bai and making it the most important brand in the industry could be the capstone of Larry's legendary career.

After Marty and I calmed down, the four of us finished our lunch. As Ken and I got up to head back to the airport, I took Larry aside and said, "You really should be the one to buy this company. This should be your legacy." Shortly after that meeting, Dr Pepper formally entered the process.

Ken Kurtz *(former president of Bai)*:

I never felt for a day in my life that I've had to work for a job because I love what I do. And that was especially true at Bai. But when we were looking at potential acquisition offers, it became highly, highly stressful. For months, instead of being locked in on growing the business and the culture, it was more about getting our management presentation right, which obviously was incredibly important. That was a really challenging time because that's not who and what we were. We weren't about diving into all the analytics of every aspect of the business to justify its worth—we knew its worth based on the growth that we saw and based on our consumer and retailer feedback.

I know Ben felt the pressure, and Ben knew I felt it too. Early on in the process, I remember him pulling us all together for a huddle. There were lots of tears and also lots of jokes—basically, he was trying to ease everybody's stress by saying, "I don't give a fuck how this goes, even if we don't sell the company." It was a great moment. But there was still a lot of tension during that time.

Not long after Ken and I had lunch with Larry and Marty, offers began to come in. Of the six companies that visited BQ to express interest in an acquisition, three submitted formal bids (including Dr Pepper), two communicated their interest informally, and one dropped out of the process. Some of the offers were overly complicated, with an initial payment followed by earnouts paid over time if Bai hit certain performance goals after the acquisition. I was not interested in any offers that depended upon earnouts because I believed our brand offered a strong enough proposition that a buyer should be willing to make its full commitment up front. I was dubious that we could ever achieve the full value of any deal based upon earnouts because, as part of a larger company, our ability to achieve sales goals to trigger those payments would not solely be in our own team's hands.

Our executive team was involved in meeting with and presenting to all of our suitors, but I handled the sale negotiations alone. Although I had great belief in Bai and I understood our company's value in the industry, this was still the most challenging experience of my life—so much so that I contracted shingles, a painful viral infection that can be caused by excess stress. By this time, Bai had around four hundred employees, most of whom had equity in the company, and I was committed to getting the highest price possible for Bai to reward their efforts. At the same time, I knew that selling the company would bring significant change in the lives of everyone on the Bai team, myself included, and I wanted to make the best strategic decision for all of our futures. Also, while I was lucky to have supportive investors who did not pressure me for their returns, I still carried the weight of $60 million of their money on my shoulders and wanted to repay them handsomely for their faith in me. And with all that on my mind, I was dealing with valuations that would have been unfathomable just seven years earlier when I was selling Bai out of the trunk of my car with my stepfather, Ray.

I had built the fastest-growing brand in the business alongside an amazing team, and now I was responsible for determining its future by making the biggest deal of my career. I felt not just the future of Bai's employees and investors in my hands—I felt like I held the fate of the industry, too.

Over several weeks, the field narrowed to the three formal bidders, and I negotiated terms with each. I remained steadfast that we would not take a deal that hinged upon earnouts. One of the bidders, which I had viewed as a serious contender, dropped out when its leadership team got cold feet about making such a bold acquisition, even though its CEO was enthusiastic about a deal. At that point, I needed to choose between the two remaining bids.

Dr Pepper offered $1.7 billion in cash up front to acquire Bai, a remarkable departure from its previous strategy of eschewing large deals in favor of building through allied brands. This was a very strong offer, and it was a testament to Larry's faith in Bai as well as an acknowledgment that our brand was vital to Dr Pepper's growth. The other bidder made its best offer at the same price. That offer, however, included earnouts, and the company did not own a route-to-market system, which made the proposal even riskier because it would require a separate distribution deal that would still leave Bai fighting to gain a third-party wholesaler's priority attention. Plus, that company did not have Larry Young at the helm—a factor that was just as important as the dollar figures on the offer sheet. Strategically and financially, the best option was clear.

Ari Soroken (former chief financial officer of Bai):
As the offers came in, Ben kept them close to the vest. I knew he wasn't going to do a deal that required holding money back for an earnout—they had to pay full price up front. There's so much strength that comes from pride of ownership, so he was able to say, "Fuck you, this is the way it's going to be, and if you don't like it, then don't take it."

One Sunday night, I got a call from Ben, asking me to meet him at Winberie's, a pub in downtown Princeton. The place was deserted. Ben was in the back corner, unshaven, with the collar up on his coat, looking like he'd just been beat up.

I asked him, "What's going on?"

He said Dr Pepper wanted to buy us.

I said, "I figured that. What's the number?"

He took a deep breath and said, "They're coming in at $1.7 billion."

I started looking for a high five or a fist bump. "That's great!" I said. "That's amazing!" He looked at me like I was crazy.

I think it took a long time for him to get comfortable with the fact that there was an offer on the table that investors would probably be pissed off if he didn't accept. I remember trying to convince him it was a good thing. Even when we left there, I thought maybe he still wasn't convinced.

The next morning, on Monday, November 14, I accepted Dr Pepper's offer. It represented a life-changing reward for so many people involved with Bai, myself included. Still, it was gut-wrenching to accept a deal to sell the company I loved so much.

Agreeing to Dr Pepper's offer was just the first step, albeit an enormous one, in getting the deal done, so I was not feeling much joy or relief. I felt secure that it was a solid offer and that Dr Pepper was the most ideal partner, but even though I'm not typically a second-guesser, I admittedly still had questions running through my head: Did we pick the right time to sell? Is that the most we can get for our investors? Am I really ready to hand my company over to someone else?

Compounding the stress of a sale process that ran through the spring, summer, and fall of 2016, we still had to run a business that was in hyper-growth mode. Our sales were on pace to double again to $250 million that year, we continued to expand our staff, and we were rolling out innovations at a furious pace. We also made a huge splash in October when we revealed that Justin Timberlake was joining Bai as an investor and as our first chief flavor officer.

Justin's appointment to this new role, which was covered by major media outlets around the country, meant he would contribute to flavor innovations, product launches, and marketing campaigns for our brand. Justin was a perfect public face for Bai, as he was an authentic consumer of our product, he was a member of the millennial generation that was our main customer base, and of course, he had mass appeal as a singer and an actor. After spending time with him, I found Justin to be a smart, down-to-earth guy who was deeply interested in the beverage business—he launched a tequila brand in 2009—and who had great ideas about product development and marketing. Combining our brands was a natural fit, and our new partnership made me even more excited about Bai's potential to break into the upper echelon of consumer brands in 2017.

But first, we needed to seal the deal with Dr Pepper—and as we soon found out, it would not be a leisurely jog to the finish line. After accepting the offer in principle, we had a one-week exclusive window to negotiate final terms, so Ari and our legal team dove into the task alongside our investment bankers. It was a feisty process, as Dr Pepper's executives and lawyers negotiated aggressively with our team over every last provision in the sale agreement. Ari and our team did an excellent job of clearing almost all the hurdles put in front of them, and I was grateful for their efforts to slog through all the details of the deal. Around four in the afternoon on Sunday, November 20, Ari called to tell me to come into New York to our lawyers' office because there were just a few issues left on the table to finalize.

"You're ready to sign," Ari told me.

I drove in from Princeton with anticipation and dread churning in my stomach. I looked forward to ending the grueling sale process, but I lamented the fact that I was about sign away my ownership of such a special company. When I arrived at the lawyers' office, Ari and our legal team had been there for forty-eight hours, save for a few short hours of sleep, and there was a big spread of food beside a conference table strewn with papers and binders. The fluorescent lights of the conference room highlighted the weariness and strain on Ari's face from grappling over every letter of contractual fine print. For three hours, we waited to hear back from Dr Pepper's lawyers on a few unresolved issues.

Then our lawyers gave us some surprising news: the Dr Pepper team had gone "pencils down." At first, I thought this meant Dr Pepper was walking away from the deal altogether. I was stunned. How could a few relatively minor disagreements torpedo a deal that we had worked so hard to achieve? I knew that Larry was the guy I wanted to buy my company, but during these negotiations, it wasn't his voice we heard on the other end of the phone. I started to get angry and offended about how the Dr Pepper team was handling the deal, and I took it personally when I thought that their team was trying to withhold money that our stakeholders deserved.

Our lawyers explained that pencils down just meant that the Dr Pepper team would pick up the discussions again in the morning, but I still felt unnerved. I went out with Ari to grab a beer and blow off some steam. By the time we took our last sips at the bar, it was 11 p.m. and too late to head back home because we needed to be back in the lawyers' office first thing in the morning. We went back to the hotel where Ari had been staying for the past two nights, and I booked myself a room. I had expected to arrive at the lawyers' office that afternoon, sign the papers, and head back to Princeton that evening, so I didn't bring a change of clothes, and on Monday, I wore the same hoodie and jeans in which I had arrived the day before.

As we were heading to our rooms, I wondered, "What happens if they don't buy the company?" For as much sadness as I felt about selling Bai, I knew the deal made business sense, and I didn't want it to collapse. I worried that I had risked everything by not formally accepting the terms before the Dr Pepper team put their pencils down.

Then I remembered that we did have another potential option. We had negotiated with our other bidder up to the last minute before taking the Dr Pepper deal, and they wanted Bai badly enough that they were able to match the $1.7 billion figure, though not all up front. They were deeply disappointed when our bankers told them we had taken another offer. The Dr Pepper deal was clearly better for us, but now I was worried that it was at risk. And I knew that at ten the next morning, our one-week window to negotiate exclusively with Dr Pepper would expire, and we would be free to reengage with the other bidder. What if we could get them to come back with an even better offer?

"If we can make it to ten," I said to Ari, "the bankers can talk to them."

The next morning, when the clock struck ten, our lawyers called Dr Pepper's team and asked where we stood. Their answer was firm: they would not yield on the unresolved issues, and they gave us until 1 p.m. to accept the existing offer. If they had said we had to take it or leave it immediately, I would have accepted it on the spot—remember, I had already signed the papers the evening before. But Dr Pepper left the window open for another three hours, so we pounced on the opportunity to see if a newer, better offer might materialize.

Our bankers immediately jumped on the phone, trying to work some last-minute magic. The other bidder was thrilled to be back in the mix and was willing to match $1.7 billion up front and add an earnout on top of it, so the deal would potentially be more lucrative. Now we suddenly had a more serious counteroffer to consider—but the clock was ticking fast. I could have easily skipped my cup of coffee that morning, as I had more than enough adrenaline pumping through my veins as I received updates from the bankers and huddled with Ari to consider our next moves.

As a businessman, I understood that I needed to exhaust all options before agreeing to a final deal. But I was struggling to understand why the Dr Pepper team would allow these issues, which seemed relatively minor, to push our negotiations to the brink like this. Then my phone buzzed, and I saw Larry's name on the screen. I picked up and heard his familiar drawl on the other end.

"Hello, Ben," he said. "I gotta tell you something. Fuck these lawyers and these bankers. We don't need 'em. We can get this deal done ourselves."

We spoke for a few minutes, with Larry making his case for why Dr Pepper was the best partner for Bai. It was just what I needed to hear. Even though I got swept up in the excitement of navigating a high-stakes corporate cat-and-mouse game that morning, Larry's call reminded me of what I already knew in my heart: he was the guy I wanted to adopt Bai. I agreed that it was time to finalize our agreement.

"Larry," I told him, "you had me at hello."

After I hung up with Larry, our bankers updated me that the other bidder needed more time to figure out how to raise the money to fund the richer offer. But I couldn't afford to risk losing the Dr Pepper deal by waiting to see if the other company could arrange financing, and I didn't want to walk away from Larry. I knew he had fought hard to get his executive team and board of directors to accept the idea of spending an unprecedented amount of money to acquire Bai. Look, he wasn't being charitable—Bai had fueled Dr Pepper's growth over the past couple of years, and his shareholders might have rebelled if another fast-rising allied brand left the system. He didn't want to spend $1.7 billion for Bai—he had to do it to keep his company competitive. But I appreciated that Larry saw our value, and his support of our brand and our team felt genuine and very meaningful to me.

I told our team to call off the discussions with the other bidder, and we turned over the signed documents to Dr Pepper's lawyers. The deal was done.

Larry Young (former chief executive officer of Dr Pepper Snapple Group):
When you look at the history of Dr Pepper, there are so many brands out there today that we had built with our distribution network and then lost when they were sold. When we found out Ben was going to sell Bai, it was a sad day. Our team thought we were going to lose Bai too. But I thought, "We're not gonna lose it. This one's too good."

It was a hard sell, though. We'd never done a deal like that. If a bigger company like Coke or Pepsi had bought Bai, the purchase price would be a blip because their market cap is so huge. But when a company like us pays $1.7 billion, that's 10 percent of our market cap. We had investors freaking out, and our board was nervous, but I just wasn't going to lose Bai. I felt that much for the brand. Ben had the huge passion and created the brand, but I was its biggest cheerleader.

We had a long process going back and forth on the deal. Any time you've got bankers and lawyers involved, you can get really close to destroying friendships with people. But we finally came up with a number, and I said, "That's it." Ben and I had a good conversation on the phone. We decided to just get it done. A lot of times you don't need bankers and lawyers to do this stuff—they think they need to be there, but they'll usually mess it up. Ben and I just said to each other, "C'mon, let's go!"

The reality of agreeing to sell Bai was a shock to my system, but it was tempered by the fact that I genuinely felt the right person was buying my company. Larry had become a real hero to me. He was willing to take the risk of acquiring Bai, and he fought hard for the deal when his executives and board of directors balked. He was a powerful Fortune 500 CEO who could have easily played it safe and let Bai slip away because the asking price was too high. But he demonstrated his faith in me by betting his company's future on the business that sprang from my dreams—and he did it with a smile on his face and a warm embrace. I felt a strong kinship

Larry deserved his own set of Bai dog tags for adopting our brand (2017)

with Larry from the first time he visited my home, and that bond only grew stronger as our business relationship developed. I loved Larry, and even with my trepidation about selling Bai, I felt he was the one person I could trust with my baby.

***

After I had initially agreed to Dr Pepper's offer—a week before we formally signed the deal—I gathered Danna, Jack, and Shayna at home and told them the news. We hugged and cried and hugged some more, with our feelings of jubilation offset by a sense of loss at the thought of no longer owning the company that was such a big part of our family's lives.

Then I went into BQ, pulled Ari, Ken, and Barak Bar-Cohen together, and told them, "Fellas, I just sold this company for $1.7 billion."

We had a long group hug, and the tears flowed as the pressure that had been hanging over us for six months finally started to dissipate. I also invited Michael Simon and Chad Portas to come down from our Saxonville office and asked Paul Sapan to fly in from California. The next day, I shared the news with Michael, whom I had known longer than anyone else involved in the business outside my family. Then I took Chad and Paul on a walk outside BQ, thanked them for helping me bring Bai to life back in 2009, and told them about the deal. Each of these conversations was powerful and moving, with a sense of elation balanced by the bittersweet realization that everything was about to change.

I also conferred with Chad about how we should announce the deal to our team after it was finalized. We put so much time and effort into building our company's culture that a simple email or press release would not suffice to express the significance of Bai's journey, the true sense of family our team had developed over the years, and my vision for our brand's future in full partnership with Dr Pepper. Chad developed the concept for a video we called *Adoption*, which compared Bai's evolution with that of a child who emerges through the fragile first years of life and finds strength and promise in the arms of a loving guardian.

Chad summoned Brian Tice, our video producer in BQ, to come up to Boston and work with him in secret on the video as we negotiated the terms of the deal. Brian is a talented, self-taught filmmaker and photographer whom Danna discovered when he was installing audio/visual systems at our house. She recommended that we use him at Bai, and he wound up helming several of our culture videos, first as a freelancer and then a full-time employee. Brian and Chad both had an innate sense for how to communicate my love for Bai and how to celebrate our moments and milestones. They outdid themselves with the *Adoption* video, which concludes with a scene of a man (Chad in a cameo) on a beach holding a child (Chad's son Gus) on his shoulders and unzipping a Bai jacket to reveal a Dr Pepper T-shirt underneath.

The closing lines, which I narrated, say, "There's a beautiful future that's right in front of us—one full of friendship that's been forged into family. So close your eyes with us. Imagine the possibilities. And let's change the world together."

That video still gives me chills to this day, as it immediately brings me back into the deluge of emotions that so many of us felt during the sale process.

TAKE THE ADOPTION JOURNEY: Visit the *Basementality* website (Basementality.org) to watch the *Adoption* video.

After we reached the final agreement on Monday, November 21, it took several hours for the paperwork to be completed. I called Danna and walked her through the drama of the morning and let her know that the deal was done, which felt quite surreal to both of us. While sitting through the paperwork process, Ari and I called Ken and Barak to come to Manhattan. We met them for a drink and an early dinner at Lure Fishbar, a classic seafood restaurant with an ocean theme that seemed like an appropriate backdrop for raising a toast to the Dr Pepper deal—the most epic catch of our lives.

After dinner, I headed home to Princeton and asked Danna to invite Haim Blecher and his wife, Shari, our close friends and the first investors in Bai, to our house so we could give them the news in person. Haim and Shari were already there when I arrived home, and the four of us went down into the basement—where else, after all, would be more fitting to let them know that our lives were about to change? I played the *Adoption* video for Haim and Shari and then told them that we agreed to sell Bai to Dr Pepper.

As we all celebrated, I fell into a long embrace with Danna, tears streaming down my cheeks, and I said to her over and over, "I'm so tired. I've got nothing left."

Danna Weiss (wife):

I haven't seen Ben cry very often, but he did that night. He was so exhausted. He told me he kept thinking back to when he was planning to go to Europe after college—he couldn't really afford to go, so every day, he would take the change from his pockets and dump it in this old water jug to save up for the trip. One night during spring break, when all his friends were down in Florida or Mexico partying on the beach, he was sitting with his parents counting the change from that jug. Now he had gone from counting quarters to being able to tell his family and friends he sold his business for $1.7 billion.

It was such an emotional night for everyone. Haim was crying as well, and I think Shari was in a state of shock. Sharing that moment with our friends—being able to thank them for being our first investors—meant so much to Ben. I was in shock, too, and at the same time, I felt so relieved that it was finally out in the open because it was such a big secret we had to keep until the deal was done.

There was no time to rest after we finalized the sale agreement. That evening, as Brian and Chad completed the final edits on the *Adoption* video, our companies' communications teams put the finishing touches on a press release that would be published the next morning before the US stock markets opened. We sent an email to all Bai staff in the New Jersey and New York area, as well as employees from our Saxonville office, mandating that they come to BQ first thing on Tuesday, November 22, for an important meeting.

That morning, after everyone, including Danna and my parents, were gathered in the screening room at BQ, we played the video. When the Dr Pepper shirt was revealed, the room erupted in shouts, applause, and again, tears. We then emailed the video and public announcement to the full company to share the news with our colleagues around the country who couldn't join us at BQ.

That morning was such a whirlwind. I shared countless hugs and handshakes with everyone at BQ, and my phone absolutely blew up with texts, calls, and voicemails from employees, investors, friends, and business associates. It's impossible to remember the details of all those conversations in the dizzying moments of that morning, but I certainly remember the bursting sense of accomplishment and pride I felt in seeing how many lives had been enhanced by a company that, just seven years earlier, was little more than an idea Danna and I dreamed about with our kids on the brown chenille couch in our old town house.

As our team celebrated at BQ, Larry and Marty held a conference call with investors and Wall Street analysts to discuss the details of the deal and explain why Bai inspired Dr Pepper to depart from recent history and make a big bet on acquiring a growing brand. I wanted to honor their faith in us by having our team give them an enormous welcome at BQ. By this point, our office manager, Abbey Brown, was used to my outrageous last-minute requests, and working with my assistant Carolynn Caruso and others, she pulled together a huge party for that afternoon. When Larry, Marty, and other Dr Pepper senior executives arrived, our team was lined up on both sides of the long hallway entering BQ, cheering and high-fiving them as the OneRepublic song "Future Looks Good" blared over our sound system.

As the Dr Pepper and Bai teams celebrated, Brian took a fantastic photo of Larry and my stepfather, Ray, laughing and embracing each other like old friends. A few days later, I had that picture blown up and hung in that same hallway. In the months after that celebration, I loved looking at that photo and thinking about how much I learned from each of those men at different stages of my life and how grateful I was for the fact that they worked so hard to help me achieve my dreams.

Ari Soroken *(former chief financial officer of Bai)*:
I had bought Ben and Danna two big six-liter bottles of champagne as holiday gifts and told them, "Put these away—one day, we're going to celebrate with them."

Danna brought them into the office after Larry and Marty arrived. It turned into a raging party. People were making speeches and crying—the day was so emotional and such a high. My mother was in town because it was two days before Thanksgiving, so she came to the office with my wife Janine and got to witness the whole thing.

At one point, she said to me, "Okay, so this is what you've been doing for the last seven years."

The party did, indeed, rage into the evening, and the next day, our crew was a little haggard. But aside from one employee (who shall remain nameless) losing his breakfast at my feet, the team rebounded and got back to work. The euphoria surrounding the announcement, however, didn't stay with me all day.

That evening, Danna and I joined our executive team for a dinner with some of our major investors. I was thoroughly fatigued by this point, and I felt a bit detached from the festivities. Some of the investors shared lovely remarks about being associated with Bai and thanked our team for guiding the company to the point where we could celebrate such a lucrative deal. When my turn to speak arose, I was honest with everyone.

"I just made a lot of money, as did all of you," I said. "But this is not the happiest day of my life."

Some of the people around the table looked surprised by my remarks, and I hoped I didn't put a damper on the evening, but I had to be truthful. I was exhausted and feeling wistful about the journey that had brought me to that moment. Even though I was pleased to be partnering with Larry, and I certainly appreciated the financial security that the deal brought my family, the idea of Bai being part of the Dr Pepper corporate family was not a dream come true. I was determined to make the best of the situation, and I believed Larry had good intentions to nurture our brand, but I also knew that our new reality could never be as fun or energizing as the previous seven years had been.

The Thanksgiving holiday afforded me a break to relax a bit—though I can't say the same for Danna, who managed to host a holiday dinner for fifteen, with no help from me, to top off one of the most intense weeks of our lives. This was the first time in more than six months when I felt like I could sit still and take a deep breath, and it gave me an opportunity to reflect upon the enormity of our accomplishment.

When I started Bai, I knew that Coca-Cola's $4.1 billion acquisition of Vitaminwater's parent company, Glaceau, in 2007 was the bellwether for beverage industry deals—both in terms of the size of the purchase price and the recognition by Big Soda's goliath that consumers were heading in a new direction. For every startup beverage company with ambitions to be the next big thing and for every distributor that helped to introduce a brand into the marketplace, the Vitaminwater deal loomed as the holy grail. Once the Bai brand took off and we entered our sale process, we were no exception. I'm competitive enough that I wanted to get as close as possible to that $4.1 billion price tag so Bai's sale could be regarded in the same echelon as the Vitaminwater deal. But there are several factors that led me to conclude that our deal was better than—or at least as noteworthy as—Vitaminwater's, even if our headline price was not as massive.

To scale our business to the point where we could command a sale price similar to Vitaminwater's, we would have needed to raise additional capital in the tens of millions of dollars, which would have substantially diluted the shares of investors who had been with us from our earliest years. By timing Bai's sale when we did, we were able to reward our most loyal investors with significant—and in some cases, astronomical—returns without having to seek additional funds from them or from new investors. Bai sold in its seventh year of operation, compared with Vitaminwater selling in its tenth year, and we achieved a sale price of nearly $2 billion despite never having turned a profit because we reinvested all of our revenue back into the operation to push our sales into hypergrowth. Also, our sale did not require us to make any buyout payments to distributors, whereas Coke's Vitaminwater deal included $200 million in fees to terminate existing distribution contracts.

But comparing our sale with Vitaminwater's deal does not provide the full perspective of our amazing accomplishment. The Small Business Administration reports that only about half of new businesses in the United States survive five years or longer—and according to data analyzed by the Kauffman Foundation, just 125 to 250 of the 552,000 companies founded each year will ever reach $100 million in revenue. When Bai eclipsed $100 million in revenue in 2015, we reached a level that only 0.02 percent to 0.04 percent of new companies ever attain. And in terms of realizing a return for our investors, we stood alone in our industry. The business research firm CB Insights tracked more than two hundred worldwide "unicorn exits"—a term for private-company acquisitions or initial public offerings valued at $1 billion or more—across all industries from 2009 to 2019. The Bai deal was the only unicorn acquisition in the food and beverage industry during that decade.

The term "unicorn" definitely seems appropriate to me because I look back on my Bai experience as something of a fairy tale. I've often said that I was the right entrepreneur who came along at the right time with the right product—who also needed a lot of luck along the way. There is no single factor that I can point to as the secret to our success. Was it because

Tony Chiurco was able to persuade several of his friends and colleagues to invest in an ambitious entrepreneur? Was it because Paul Sapan came up with just the right blueberry and coconut flavors? Was it because Ken Kurtz was looking for a job when we needed someone to run our sales team? Yes, yes, yes—and then some.

My job was to put Bai in a position to capitalize on our team's hard work and good luck by keeping everyone focused and motivated and by giving us all a dream to chase and a mission to accomplish. The fact that I was able to do so while forging relationships with wonderful people and having a hell of a lot of fun every day for seven-plus years is what made my Bai experience feel like such a storybook.

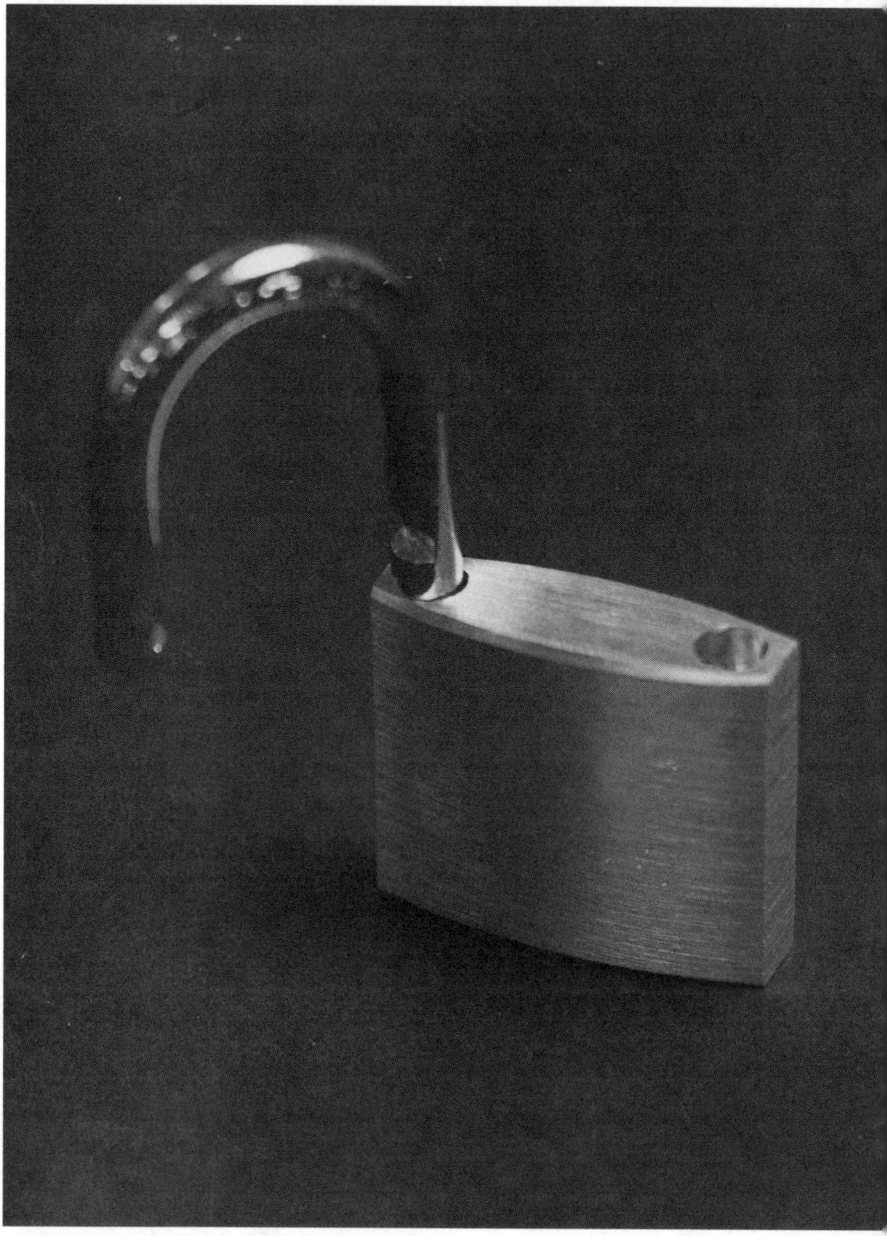

BASEMENTALITY

GIVE EVERY OUNCE & MAKE THEM FEEL IT

There's one common edge that all winners share, in all walks of life. They see plays develop before anyone else. They then do shit no one else dreamed possible. Go your hardest every minute, whether you're making the smallest moves or setting up for the winning play. Your feel for the game will get better every day. And your teammates will know you're leaving it all on the field. Because when the final whistle blows, a true black sheep brings nothing back to the locker room.

CHAPTER 11
THE AFTERMATH

In the two months leading up to the sale's closing on January 31, 2017, Bai's executive team met frequently with Dr Pepper's leadership to plan for our formal adoption. Larry Young bestowed upon me the title of chief disruptive officer and pledged that he wanted me to continue running Bai with the same tenacious spirit I always had. The rest of our executive team was to remain in place as well, so we felt optimistic that we would be able to run our organization as we saw fit, but now with the benefit of Dr Pepper's distribution system and a 20,000-strong workforce treating Bai as a high-priority, company-owned brand.

I believed we were getting off to a good start when Larry endorsed our plan to pounce on an expensive, headline-grabbing marketing effort: our first national Super Bowl commercial, starring our new chief flavor officer, Justin Timberlake. About 90 percent of the commercial time for the Patriots versus Falcons game already had been sold by December, at a rate of roughly $5 million per thirty-second spot. When we learned there were still some open slots, I thought it was the perfect opportunity to boost our brand awareness by marrying Bai with a famous face in front of more than 110 million consumers just as we were about to amplify our distribution with our new corporate partner.

On a Saturday in mid-January, just three weeks before the big game, I called Chad and told him I wanted to do another Super Bowl commercial—this time for the whole country instead of a few select markets. A few hours later, he came back with a concept to showcase our brand by connecting Bai to Justin's biggest hit from his NSYNC boy-band days, "Bye Bye Bye." Chad's idea was simple, offbeat, and brilliant—to wink at Justin's past and slyly acknowledge his emergence as a respected entertainer, while clarifying for any still-confused customers that our brand name was not pronounced "Bay" or "B-A-I."

Justin's team recruited Christopher Walken to join him for the spot, which wound up on numerous media outlets' best-of lists for that year's Super Bowl ads. The commercial, which we dubbed *Jentleman*, kicked off with Walken sitting in front of a crackling fireplace, reciting some of the song's lyrics in his trademark quirky delivery, ending with a twist: "It

"Ain't no lie" when Justin Timberlake and Christopher Walken promote Bai in a Super Bowl commercial (2017)

might sound crazy, but it ain't no lie, baby. Bai Bai Bai." He then looks over at Justin—sitting beside him on a leather couch, nattily dressed in an ascot and pocket square—who silently affirms the sentiment before the song's chorus kicks in and a bottle of Ipanema Pomegranate appears onscreen with the tagline: "5 Calories, No Artificial Sweeteners, and Tastes Amazing. #BaiBaiBai."

Chad Portas (former chief creative officer of Bai):
When Ben read the first script I wrote, he loved it and said he wanted to show it to Justin right away. But I felt we had to come up with some more concepts. I wrote a few more scripts over the weekend and then, on Monday, pulled in two creative directors on our team, who wrote another ten scripts. Ben and I flew out to California on Wednesday and presented the concepts to Justin and his manager, who both loved the "Bai Bai Bai" idea. We all started riffing and ideating, and it started to take form.

We flew back east on Friday, then back to Los Angeles on Monday to shoot the spot. It all came together in record time—ten days from the moment Ben called me, we had a fully produced Super Bowl spot. That would be unheard of, just impossible, in the ad agency world. Being able to move that quickly and be that nimble is something you can only do with an in-house creative team and a CEO who believes in creative.

The best part is that it worked—the commercial was really well received and was considered a hit. For me, that was the single most exciting and rewarding moment at Bai in seven years with the brand.

I hoped the burst of positive publicity from the Super Bowl ad would help kick off Bai's next phase of hypergrowth as part of the Dr Pepper team. Going into 2017, I had convinced myself that Bai's adoption was the start of the second half of our marathon—there were another thirteen miles to go before we could truly accomplish the goals of our bevolution. I wanted to believe that we would, indeed, be allowed to run the organization independently and lean on Dr Pepper for strategic resources and support.

In my mind, we were beginning a journey toward our brand becoming Dr Pepper's new flagship. My vision was that, in the not-so-distant future, Bai would be spoken of in the same breath as Coke and Pepsi as one of the industry's most iconic brands. I didn't want to become just one of many products clustered under Dr Pepper's corporate umbrella. I believed that Bai would lead a historic change in redefining the beverage business and pushing Big Sugar off the streets. To be honest, I didn't have a game plan for how a seven-year-old brand that had $250 million in sales in 2016 could essentially take over a $6 billion corporate giant from within. But I knew that I was ready to dream and work and fight to figure out how to make it a reality. And that's when the first cracks in our team began to form.

As I looked at the slate of innovations that we rolled out in 2015 and 2016—Bubbles, Antiwater, Supertea, Cocofusions, and Bai Black—I recognized that we needed to slow down and do a better job of incubating those product lines in order to achieve my vision of Bai becoming a Total Beverage Solution. Though we were now a national brand that was part of a giant corporation, we had to focus on the same strategy that drove our first wave of hypergrowth: creating greatness on a small scale and then expanding upon it. We needed to be the same tenacious team we had always been and do the things that no one else thought we could do. We had to recommit to the mentality we had in Bai's earliest days when we were still working out of my town house. To grow even bigger, we needed to act like we were small again.

As I told our team, we had to go back to the basement.

To inspire this effort, I decided to actually build a room we called the Basement in BQ. Having always used the office as a physical representation of our culture and mission, I wanted to create a big symbol to show our team my commitment to going back to basics and assembling the building blocks for the next phase of Bai's growth. I wanted to return to the same environment where Bai was spawned—with no windows to stare out and no music to distract me—to regain the thrill of building something from the ground up. Both Bai and I needed to be reborn.

We took over a space behind our research lab that formerly housed an artist's studio, and I challenged Abbey Brown and our construction team with converting it into a secluded war room to serve as the home base for our efforts to root our innovations in the marketplace. The problem was that BQ didn't actually have a cellar, so we had to create the appearance of one. We built a stairwell in our research lab that led up to a walkway decorated with portraits of famed innovators like Steve Jobs, Nikola Tesla, and Thomas Edison, but with red X's over their mouths to signify that we were no longer looking to the past, only toward the future. We referred to them—affectionately, of course—as "fucking has-beens." At the end of that walkway was a heavy door that required a digital fingerprint for entry, and on the other side of the door was a brick and stone stairway that led down to the Basement.

At the same time, Bai was swiftly thrust into the realities of transitioning into corporate ownership. The Dr Pepper presence in our business was inescapable. They began integrating our back-end financial and HR systems into theirs, examining our supply chain processes, and reviewing our sales forecasts, marketing budgets, overhead costs, and every other aspect of the business. A handful of Dr Pepper employees were embedded in BQ to oversee transitions. Larry, Marty, and other Dr Pepper executives traveled to BQ for monthly business review meetings with our leadership team, and our executive team found themselves on countless conference calls with their counterparts in Plano, discussing our day-to-day workings. Most painfully, we had to eliminate dozens of positions, mainly in sales.

It's natural that any company would assume operational control and start cutting costs after spending $1.7 billion to acquire another business. But this certainly did not feel like the independence we were promised, and it frustrated the hell out of me. I feared that Dr Pepper was more comfortable leading Bai into a future of slower, safer, manageable growth, with less imagination and no desire to challenge the status quo in our industry. As a result, I started to withdraw from the rest of the executive team, and the Basement became my new sanctuary. I spent far less time in my office and more hours in this new incubation space, working on ideas for how to better support our innovations to unlock our Total Beverage Solution.

The centerpiece of this effort was what I called the Baiosphere. The strategy behind the Baiosphere was the same one Ken had instilled when he came aboard at Bai: identify a set of key retail accounts in an important market, provide the highest levels of execution and service in those stores, and build proof of concept for your brand on a manageable scale before expanding. That's how we built our base Bai brand, and I wanted to do the same with our innovations. I identified the Dallas market—right in Dr Pepper's backyard—as the ideal location to launch our first Baiosphere, and I pulled Christopher Brown out of the Bai Bubbles brand management role to become our point person for executing this new strategy.

We selected two hundred Target, Walmart, and Kroger stores in a thirty-mile radius in the Dallas area and hired a team of twelve salespeople called the Guardians of Flavor to service those accounts. Their mission was to establish all of our brands in their appropriate locations within the stores—Bubbles with the sparkling waters, Supertea in the tea aisle, and so on—and achieve incremental sales of each new product line without cannibalizing our base Bai brand.

Elsewhere around the country, we continued to see the various Bai brands displayed together at retail, stifling the growth potential of our innovations. But in Dallas, the Baiosphere quickly began to show results. With our extreme focus on building each product line in those two hundred stores, sales of our innovations and our base Bai were all rising, and we began to see a halo effect in the market: sales increased in stores that were nearby but outside of the Baiosphere radius, thanks to a greater overall brand awareness.

The Basement at BQ, where we incubated the next phase of our bevolution (2017)

Working with Chris in the Basement in the first few months of 2017 energized me as we started planning for future Baiosphere rollouts around the country that would ultimately drive a huge wave of growth across all of our product categories. I was starting to see our bevolution come to life.

Every Monday, Chris jumped on a 5:30 a.m. flight from Philadelphia to Dallas and spent the week in Texas—sacrificing precious time with his wife and three young children—to lead our Guardians of Flavor as they worked to unearth our Total Beverage Solution in a way that no one else in the company was doing. At a time when others at Bai were questioning our direction, Chris rallied behind the Baiosphere concept with the same fervor he demonstrated years earlier when he caught my eye by tirelessly working to launch our brand in Chicago. I saw in Chris the same fight that brought me to where I was in business and in life. Having the opportunity to work closely with Chris and mentor him—to feel the energy of his dedication to the Baiosphere and the company as a whole—helped buoy me as I struggled with the changes that were emerging under Bai's new ownership. As I worked to set a new course for Bai, I saw Chris as a future leader of our company, and I was honored to dream and work alongside him inside the new Basement that meant so much to me.

Christopher Brown *(former vice president of market development for Bai)*:

I was always the kid who struggled to respect the authority of the crappy teacher in school. I was naturally defiant when I didn't believe in or respect someone. I was always told that I was an idealist or a dreamer, and I was reminded by every guidance counselor that if I stayed on the same path, I would only amount to meeting my minimum potential.

For years, the world conditioned me to think that I was just destined to play guitar in the corner of a smoky bar forever. Then I had kids, and I had to get to work. I found the beverage business in my early twenties—it was a tolerable career path, where I felt that my people skills and creativity could benefit me. But it led me to multiple bosses who were just like my guidance counselors back in school. Then I found Bai and Ben, the dreamer who was openly fighting the system. With the Baiosphere, he wanted me to build a new sales team that shared our desire to change a broken system. Armed with his belief in me and finally having someone encourage my way of defiant thinking, I was unlocked.

Outside the Basement, however, Bai was rapidly transforming into a much different place, and my disconnect from the rest of the operation was widening. Our team was inundated with changes, as Dr Pepper's ownership meant that we had to begin conforming to its processes and procedures. I was chasing a vision beyond what anyone else could see at that moment, and I thought that would be enough to motivate my leadership team to keep running alongside me. By committing to the idea of going back into the basement and building out the Baiosphere initiative, I believed we could recapture the focus and drive of Bai's early days to help us chart our path forward. We missed our sales targets in the first few months of 2017, but that didn't bother me—we always set overaggressive goals to motivate our team to work as hard as possible. I was more concerned with upholding our disruptive brand mission and solidifying our long-term direction.

Larry loved the concept of the Baiosphere and began to use the Total Beverage Solution term on conference calls with investors. But the rest of Dr Pepper leadership hated it because my plan to roll out Baiosphere programs and create dedicated sales teams in additional markets required considerable overhead. My expansion plans for the Baiosphere pushed the conflict into overdrive.

Frankly, I didn't care about line-by-line monthly review meetings and achieving corporate synergies, which put me squarely at odds with Dr Pepper's leadership, as well as our own. I was pushing Dr Pepper's people away as they were trying to fold Bai into their system. I reminded Larry that he made me his chief disruptive officer, and I embraced the title by telling him and the rest of his leadership to leave us alone and let us do our thing. But I was the only one at Bai kicking and screaming in that way—the rest of our executive team was struggling to support my rebellious attitude while trying to figure out how to blend our disparate cultures and organizations. For the first time, I felt like they didn't have my back.

Ken Kurtz (former president of Bai):

The Dr Pepper deal changed our lives, but I think in a lot of ways, it did take the air out of our team. Although it was great in some ways, a new reality also set in. That's when our shift in focus began. Ben is *always looking five miles down the road, and he had a new vision of where he wanted to go. But I was looking right in front of me. Everything was different. Now we were sitting in meetings with Dr Pepper's executive team, going through numbers over and over again. Instead of being cheerleaders out in the field and getting in front of our customers, we had to sit in meetings trying to justify to Larry and Marty where our business was, why it was where it was, and what we were going to do about it.*

It was a huge turnoff for Ben to have to answer those questions. I think he was also incensed that I would give the Dr Pepper guys that amount of quality time to answer those questions. But in my thought process, if Bai was going to stay as Bai, we had to engage with them because if we pulled away too much, they would wind up putting in even more controls over our organization. And that's what ended up happening. We weren't hitting certain aspirational targets, so the noose became tighter around our necks, and the situation became a lot more uncomfortable.

At the beginning of May, Barak Bar-Cohen became the first member of our executive team to leave Bai, telling me that he didn't want to work for a big company like Dr Pepper, preferring instead to pursue his own entrepreneurial path. I was angry and disappointed, feeling like he had abandoned our mission. In fact, as I watched our leadership team try to navigate our new corporate environment, I questioned whether any of them still believed in our bevolution.

Just two days after Barak's departure, we held our annual UnConvention, which offered an opportunity to reignite our company culture and, in my mind, remind Dr Pepper's executives of why we were such a special organization. Larry, Marty, and others from Dr Pepper joined the three hundred–plus attendees who came to Philadelphia from around the country. In my speech, I acknowledged that our transition into corporate ownership had been a bumpy one and that many people at Bai may not have been as excited for the UnConvention as they had been in previous years. I conceded that I deserved some of the blame for that, as I had not been as visible or as outspoken in leading and encouraging our team in recent months. Then I explained that I had been sequestered in our new incubation space, developing the Baiosphere initiative as the launching pad for our brighter future.

"That's why we built the new Basement in BQ," I said in the speech. "It's the symbol that represents our need to go back home to get us to our future. I firmly believe that, and it's why I'm going to work even harder now to make it happen."

I concluded by challenging the Dr Pepper team to "let these scrappy motherfuckers from the Basement do we what do best."

Although the speech was well received in the room that night, at least among the Bai employees, it did not ease the tensions I was feeling from both Dr Pepper's leadership team and our own. I felt like I was beating my head against a wall in trying to convince them that we needed to turn our collective attention toward nurturing and expanding the Baiosphere concept.

Michael Simon, who had worked in large corporate environments before Bai, was working hard to assimilate into the Dr Pepper system and iron out confusion about our path forward, but he and I no longer saw eye to eye. He exited about three weeks after Barak, unable to find a balance between new owners who wanted things done their way and a founder who was challenging them at every turn. Michael and I had been friends and colleagues for more than two decades, and although he left Bai on good terms personally, I hated the fact that our business relationship had taken a sour turn.

Finally, in mid-June, just over four months after our adoption was finalized, the friction between me and the Dr Pepper team sparked into a raging fire. At our monthly review meeting, the discussion turned toward possible changes in retail pricing and packaging for Bai Bubbles, and I disagreed vehemently with the ideas that were being proposed. But when

I looked around the room, I recognized that I was the only one fighting on our side. I'm sure that Ken, Ari, and Chad felt like siblings trapped at the dinner table between a pair of squabbling parents. My focus at that point was squarely on the Baiosphere, and I felt that the Dr Pepper team didn't understand the importance and the urgency of the work I was doing. I was trying to drag them into a future that they couldn't see. What they saw, instead, was me being difficult and refusing to fall in line.

Those review meetings were typically open, with people stepping out of the conference room for phone calls or restroom breaks, so I took a call and then went back to my office to try to calm down. I fully intended to return, but I just couldn't bring myself to go back into that room. The meeting went on for another hour and a half without me.

Afterward, Chad and Ari came into my office and told me that Larry was enraged by the end of the meeting. They recounted that he slammed his fist on the table and shouted, "I came all the way from Plano, Texas, to be in this meeting, and he walks out and doesn't even come back in? Who does that guy think he is?"

When I heard that, I was crestfallen. I looked up to Larry as a father figure, and I hated the idea of disappointing him. I truly felt terrible.

I called Larry with the intention of explaining myself. He picked up on the first ring, and before I could utter a word, he said, "Ben, I just can't talk to you right now because I might say things I don't want to say. I'm just too angry right now."

I told him that I understood, and we both hung up.

The next morning, Ken and I flew to Minneapolis to meet with a buyer at Target. As soon as we landed and got off the plane, my phone rang. It was Larry. The anger was gone from his voice, replaced by a palpable sadness.

He told me I was fired.

I wasn't completely surprised by Larry's decision, but it was still jarring to hear him say it. I had never worked for anyone else except for my brief bank job right after college. Now, on the heels of the greatest success of my career, I was being fired from the company I created.

"Ben," Larry said with a gentle understanding, "you don't love Dr Pepper. You love Bai."

"You're absolutely right," I said. "Larry, I love Bai with every fiber of my being. And I will never love a soda company like I love Bai. But that doesn't mean I wasn't working hard for you."

We spoke for a few more minutes and agreed to reconnect shortly to figure out the process of managing my exit. After I hung up the phone, I told Ken what had just transpired. Not really knowing what to do next, we did what we always did—we went to work. Ken and I drove to Target headquarters and had a productive meeting with the buyer to secure business for 2018, even though I knew I wouldn't be around to see it through.

That evening, we flew to Orange County, California, because we had a meeting scheduled for the next morning with Bai's regional sales team, which was intended to be the kickoff of a series of meetings with our sales teams around the country. As might be expected, by the time that meeting started, my mind was no longer focused on the agenda.

The previous twenty-four hours had been a maelstrom of emotions, especially when I called Danna and the kids to give them the news. As I replayed the events in my head, in some moments, I understood Larry's point of view, but then I would have flashes of fury about being pushed out of my own company, which were then overtaken by sadness at the end of a once-in-a-lifetime journey. When I got back home to Princeton, I gathered with the family and consoled Jack and Shayna, who were devastated by the prospect of not being able to hang out at BQ with so many people they viewed as their own friends and family.

They couldn't come to grips with no longer being a part of the amazing company they had grown up with. I tried to keep a brave face and not make it too obvious that I felt the same way.

In negotiating with Dr Pepper about how to deliver the news of my exit, I was adamant that I be allowed to say goodbye to my team in my own words. I felt I had earned that right. Larry graciously allowed me to do so, for which I remain profoundly grateful. We agreed to make the announcement on Wednesday, June 21, one week after he told me that he had to let me go.

The night before the announcement, Larry called, and we had a long, emotional conversation, setting aside the tensions of the past few months. I had so much respect for that big cowboy, yet I had been so disrespectful to him. No one would have blamed him if he rejected my request to bid farewell to everyone, but he didn't do that. I know that he made what he thought was the best decision for the business by letting me go, but he also showed me how much he cared by the way he let me exit with pride and dignity.

Larry Young (former chief executive officer of Dr Pepper Snapple Group):
It was absolutely the right thing to let Ben say goodbye to his team the way he wanted to. We couldn't have done it in any other way.

I think we both knew it was time to make the change. I hated to see him not be Ben, the guy I met and loved and enjoyed being around. All of a sudden, he was stressing out, not acting like himself. It wasn't good for him. That creativity and talent should be focused on something other than this infighting and pressure. I thought, "I can't do this to him—I can't let this eat him up." He needs to take that attitude and spirit and make bigger, more beautiful things—because that's what he's good at, not trying to run a big corporation.

The next morning, we gathered the entire company on a conference call, and sitting in my home with my family and some of my closest colleagues, I read a lengthy statement, telling the team that my Bai journey had come to an end. I thanked everyone for their commitment, passion, and friendship;

for being willing to dream alongside me to make history in our industry; and for filling my life with such joy over the past eight years.

"I am not leaving you," I said. "I have not abandoned you. And I hope you are better than when you found Bai. Because all of you have done that for me."

A couple of hours later, I went into BQ for the last time. Dozens of our team members were lined up on both sides of the long hallway entering the office, just as they had when Larry and Marty arrived on the day of our adoption announcement. I was humbled by their applause, hugs, and tears, and I tried to spend at least a few minutes with as many people as possible. We then retreated into the BQ screening room, where Chad cued up a magnificent new video called *GoodBai*, which he and Brian had produced, working through the night. My eyes welled up as scenes of my family—Danna, Jack, Shayna, my parents, Candice, and so many members of my extended Bai family—filled the screen. The video ended with the same words I used to conclude my remarks to the team that morning: "Bai ... For Now."

When the video concluded, I stood and faced the room, silently taking in the sea of faces of people who had been by my side for years. Someone called for me to make a speech, but I couldn't do it.

"That's it," I said, with my voice cracking. "I left it all on the floor."

BE PART OF THE FAREWELL: Visit the *Basementality* website (Basementality.org) to watch the *GoodBai* video.

After I walked out the doors of BQ for the last time, I needed a break from everything that reminded me of Bai. That would not prove to be so easy. After the news about my exit became public, I received countless phone calls, texts, and emails from Bai employees, investors, friends, and colleagues within the industry—all of them wishing me well and many wanting the inside scoop on why I was no longer part of the brand I created.

It was nice to hear from so many people whose lives I had touched, but I was not interested in going down memory lane. At least not outwardly. In my head, though, I couldn't help but keep running through my last few months at Bai and reexamining why everything seemed to go off the rails so quickly.

There's no question that I carried lessons from my past into every one of my businesses. My first taste of success with Godiva Theater Café inspired me to run hard with Brewed Awakening and Five Alarm Brew, chasing my dream to become a major player in the coffee industry. The pressures and ultimate demise of those ventures pushed me toward a new path that led to the creation of Chocolixir. When my involvement in that business ran its course, I created Boosta Shot with the idea that, like Chocolixir, I had identified a way to fill a need in the marketplace. Boosta Shot's failure, in turn, served as a reminder not to overcomplicate things—a particularly critical perspective for Bai's early years in trying to figure out how to position our product with consumers.

Through all those years, even though each of my previous experiences informed the next ones, I was always focused on looking forward, not backward. My life in business has been marked by a consistent pattern—I would leave it all on the floor, catch my breath, and go out there and do it again.

But in the days and weeks following my departure from Bai, I found myself in the unusual position of being preoccupied with my past. I went through an intense mourning period, feeling angry at Dr Pepper for not letting me lead the way I wanted to and feeling embittered about the way my relationship with Bai's executive team devolved in the months after the sale was completed.

For several weeks after my firing, I just could not escape the black cloud that was lingering over my head. I thought I had assembled a team of like-minded black sheep who were aligned with my quest to continue building our brand into an industry-changing phenomenon.

When our executive team—a group of guys I admired and loved—struggled with figuring out how to operate in our new corporate environment, I took it so personally. Then after I was fired, I felt betrayed that Ken, Ari, and Chad didn't walk right out the door behind me. I thought we had left our mission unfinished and our vision unrealized, and I didn't understand why they would want to stay behind to work for a soda company that didn't share our mission. Even though we had achieved an unprecedented success story with Bai, I could only focus on what we didn't accomplish.

That's why it hurt so much when it came to an end.

**

The few months after I was fired from Bai afforded me something I never had before: time. Freed from the day-to-day pressures and demands of running a business, I was able to gain some perspective on what I had undertaken over the past eight years.

I knew that we had to sell Bai to protect the brand's future, and I understood that Larry wasn't going to just shove Dr Pepper, 7Up, and Snapple off the shelves to make way for Bai even though I made it quite clear that I wanted him to do just that. With time and reflection, my bitterness about my exit from Bai and my relationships with our executive team started to dissipate. I came to appreciate that Ken, Ari, and Chad had their own personal, financial, and professional considerations and that I wasn't offering them a new business idea and a new chase if they walked away from Bai because they were pissed off that I got fired. Rather than fixating on what I saw as the missed opportunities for Bai's future and the fact that we never finished the marathon we were running in my mind, I grew prouder of what we achieved—and prouder that I was able to lead that journey alongside my family and everyone else I loved who contributed to the Bai journey.

One of the most eye-opening moments of my post-Bai life came more than a year after I left the company. For an assignment in her eighth-grade English class, Shayna had to write an essay about an important moment in her life, and to my surprise, she chose to focus on my firing from Bai. I knew that my kids were upset when it happened, but I didn't understand the significance of my firing to Shayna because she didn't talk much about it. However, in reading her essay through tear-filled eyes, I realized that the end of our family's time with Bai had as deep of an impact on Shayna as the growth of the company had on Jack years earlier, when he expressed his resentment about the business taking me away from him.

Shayna grew up with and alongside Bai, bounding from preschool to elementary school to middle school as we rocketed from a local business to a national company to an industry superstar. Bai was part of her identity, and as Shayna wrote in her essay, she didn't want to lose that:

A million thoughts ran through my head once I found out. But my immediate thought was, "My dad got let go. My dad is no longer the CEO at Bai. My family will never be a part of Bai again." I tried to stay as strong as possible and didn't cry. Bai was my family's baby, and it got taken away from us. My dad left the room once he told me, so I got time to comprehend what I had heard. My whole life I've grown up with Bai being a part of my family. It all started in my old town house basement, where my parents created the idea and it grew from then on. It took a few minutes but then I finally rolled out of bed, walked into my closet, and put whatever I saw first on. I was so flustered by the news that I completely forgot to brush my teeth. I walked downstairs into the kitchen and saw my family sitting at the dining table, looking just as miserable as I was.

But even as she reflected on a hurtful experience, Shayna looked toward to the future. In the essay, she described the four of us driving past the town house where Bai started and Jack putting Andra Day's song "Rise Up" on the car stereo. "Rise Up" was the theme of our 2016 UnConvention and became a rallying cry for our team. For Shayna, hearing that song represented hope during a dark moment.

I didn't realize how much my family related to the song until this day. Nothing will stop me and my family. Nothing. We will rise from this bump in the road, no matter how bad it was…It felt like we were at the bottom of an endless pit, and we would never be the same. But deep down inside, I knew we weren't. I knew we would end up okay.

Just as Shayna understood that the end of our time with Bai would not be the last of our family's adventures, I recognized that something unimaginable had occurred: I was no longer obsessed with the brand. During my time running the company, if I was out shopping with Danna and the kids over a weekend and didn't see Bai in a prominent position, or if I came across even one bottle with a crooked label, I would lose my mind. That fanatical attitude is what made Bai and me successful, as I was convinced that even the slightest glitch would bring us down as a company. I was so fucking dramatic about it because I truly felt like we needed to be perfect. But clearly, there's a downside to that behavior—that type of rage and intensity is unhealthy and might have killed me if I had kept it up.

Today, if I'm in a store and see Bai looking less than perfect on a shelf or in a cooler, I'll feel a twinge of disappointment and think to myself, "I hope they do a better job there." I'll always love Bai, and I'm still immensely proud of it. Unlike before, now I can just walk away from a torn label or a messy shelf without my blood pressure soaring.

Looking back, I have such appreciation for the people who supported me in those difficult days and weeks after my firing. My family, of course, was right by my side, including my sister, Candice, who immediately resigned from Bai. My assistant, Carolynn Caruso, was right behind her out the door of BQ. And my longtime mate, Simon Richmond, gave his notice shortly afterward, telling me he simply didn't want to work for Bai if I wasn't there. Simon helped me dust myself off and start thinking about new ideas for the future, and he got me excited about getting into business again.

Although I didn't miss the stress and workload that came with running a startup company, I quickly realized that I missed the feeling of running toward something. That feeling drove me when I was concocting ideas for how to sell coffee in movie theaters twenty years earlier and continued through every business since then. I especially missed the feeling that I enjoyed more than anything while I was running Bai—being surrounded by people who were willing to chase what started as my dream and who summoned their energy and imagination to make it their dream too.

Danna Weiss (wife):

After Ben was let go from Bai, I thought we might finally have a chance to relax, kick back and live the good life. But who was I kidding? I'm living with a man who can't sit still.

Ben has this unbelievable ability to get people to take risks and leave things behind to follow his dreams. C'mon, he even convinced a Mormon to leave Utah to come work for him! People just get caught up in his infectious ideas, and next thing you know, they're off and running. Now he has new people working alongside him, plus those who came back to him. And so, here we go again.

No matter what directions I travel in the future, I will always be inspired by and grateful for the incredible experience of creating and building Bai. Several months after my exit from the company, I was in our local Wegmans supermarket with my stepfather, Ray, and we walked past a Bai display. Without a word, we stopped and looked at it together. After a few seconds, I threw my arm around Ray's shoulder.

"It doesn't seem that long ago that we were lugging these bottles out of the trunk of my car, trying to get into this store," I said.

Ray nodded and smiled. His hair is a little whiter these days, and his hearing has gotten worse, but in that moment, he instantly became ten years younger. I saw the same sparkle in his eyes that he had a decade earlier when he walked the floors of that store, dragging a cooler behind him, talking baseball with the beverage buyer, and trying to convince him to take a chance on carrying his son's new drink.

Watching Ray happily transport back in time, if just for a few seconds, helped me understand why my Bai journey—even at its toughest moments—was so magical. Creating a successful business and making a lasting impact on my industry are accomplishments that I'm enormously proud of. Doing that alongside people I love and helping change their lives for the better? That's priceless.

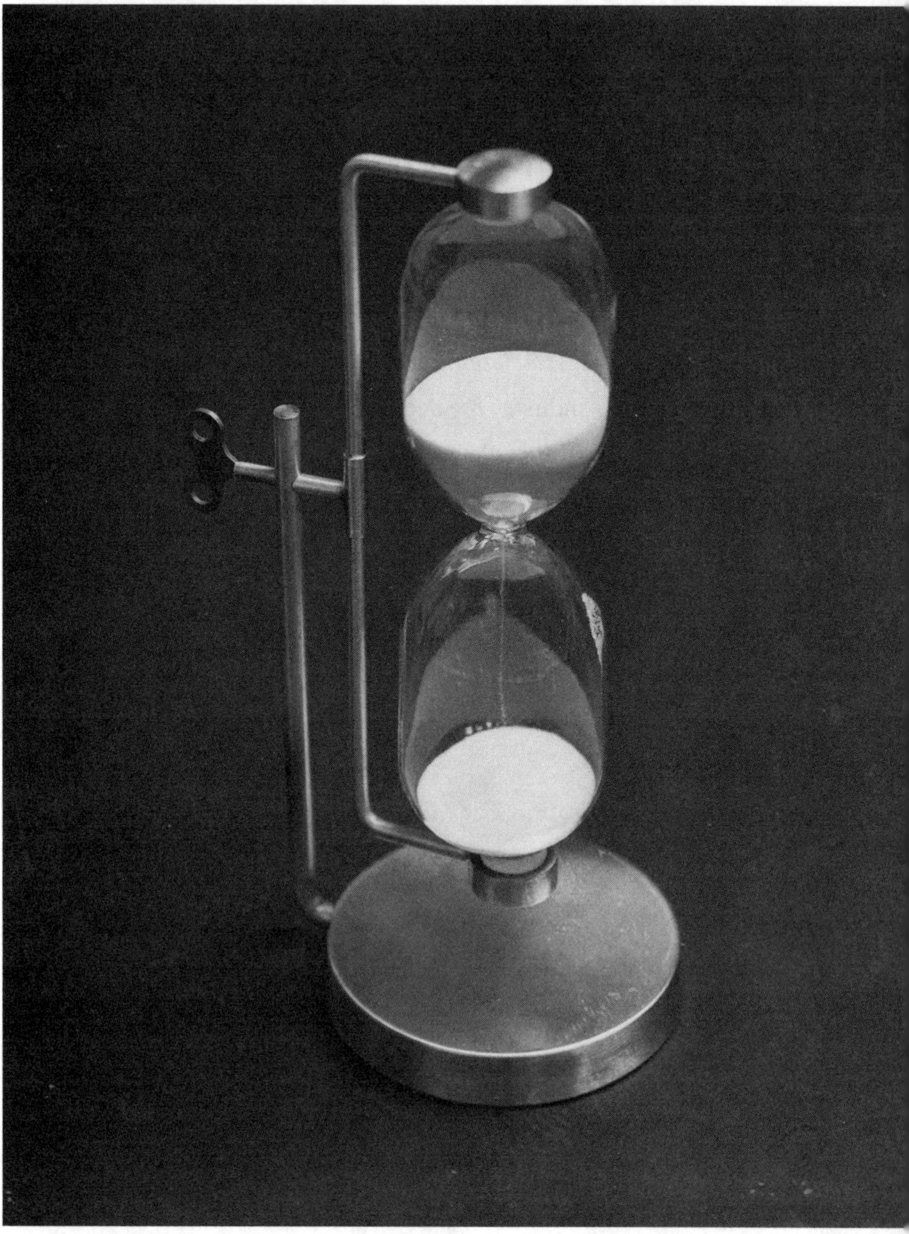

BASEMENTALITY

EXPECT THE QUESTION

Even after a huge win, you'll ask yourself: Was it all worth it? Why do you feel such a great sense of loss? Is this black sheep headed out to pasture? Fuck no! Whether it's a day, a month, or a year from now, you need to get up, look up, and find inspiration to go again. The black sheep will never retire. You'll be back in the basement soon. And that invisible hand will be right behind you to guide you. Because it's a part of you. It's your edge.

JACK WEISS
EPILOGUE

More than two years after my dad's last day at Bai, he's standing in another basement. To be more specific, he's standing in a tunnel leading into a basement. Around him are thousands of rocks hand-packed behind thick steel mesh that holds back the earth. Dim lights show the way.

He feels that ever-present force guiding him to chase a new horizon. He looks over his shoulder at us, his family, with a familiar look on his face. We lock eyes and I nod. I know where he wants to go, and I want us all to go there together.

Beside him are some familiar faces. There's Ken, Chris, Goody, Simon, Chad, and others from the Bai days, once again looking forward. And there are new faces—former bankers, lawyers, and corporate salespeople who are unbound from the constraints and traditions of their old environments. Now they're charging ahead, channeling their inner black sheep.

Behind the heavy, speakeasy-style door is our new brand. Our new fight. It beckons us on. It's about to come to life in a new basement. He takes a very long, deep breath. He feels the invisible hand closer than ever, urging him to find the edge on the other side of that door. Together, we'll step into the future, led by a man with permission and purpose.

Crook & Marker is born. And the bevolution continues ...

ACKNOWLEDGMENTS

My sincere thanks to everyone who supported this book project in so many ways, including participating in interviews, providing feedback on drafts, contributing their creative talents, and more. This includes our "book team" of Simon Hammond, Daniel Goodfellow, Chad Portas, Mike Boos, Brian Tice, Adam Davis, Terri Gillespie, and Alyssa Adoni, as well as family members, friends, colleagues from Bai and Crook & Marker, and others who have been a part of my career journey. We did not have room to quote everyone who was interviewed for the book, but your memories and insights were invaluable to the process of writing this book.

PHOTO CREDITS

Book jacket and pages 5, 26, 44, 86, 90, 120, 140, 162, 173, 192, 199, 210, 214, 220, 242, 270, 294: Photos by Brian Tice

Book jacket: Bai® and the Bai bottle are trademarks and property of Keurig Dr Pepper

Pages 10, 279: Courtesy of Eric Quiñones

Page 12: Photo by Andy Sapp

Page 35: Courtesy of Pat Schlaefer

Pages 38, 64, 73, 96, 105, 154, 190, 233: Courtesy of Danna Weiss

Page 137: Courtesy of Simon Richmond

Pages 180, 229, 260: Courtesy of Kat Haddon

Pages 186, 189: Courtesy of Ben Weiss

Page 274: ©Bai Brands LLC, 2017

INDEX

Amato, Candice, 30–37, 41–42, 64–66, 74, 149–50, 152, 169, 209, 218, 228, 287, 291

Amato, Nic, 65–66, 69–70, 73–74, 76, 81, 227–29

Amazon, 230

Bai Brands
    Annual sales of, 22, 151, 166, 230, 239
    Bai Antiwater, innovation of, 236-37, 276
    Bai Black, innovation of, 237, 276
    Bai Bubbles, innovation of, 204–05, 227–30, 236–37, 276, 278, 283
    Bai Cocofusions, innovation of, 236–37, 276
    Bai Superteas, innovation of, 236–37, 240, 276, 278
    Baiosphere, initiative of, 278–81, 283–84
    BaiQuarters (BQ) of, 153, 157, 159, 169–71, 174, 179, 197–200, 205, 208–10, 216, 235, 247, 249, 252, 261, 264, 276–77, 283, 285, 287, 292
    Basement of, 276–81, 283
    Certified tasters of, 115, 150
    Civet Society of, 207–16
    Coffeefruit use by, 20–22, 89–91, 94–96, 107–09, 129, 150, 159–60, 171, 187, 198, 207, 236
    Core values of, 31, 175, 200–04, 207–09, 213, 217, 247
    First delivery of, 97–100
    Name meaning of, 21, 91, 109
    Super Bowl commercials by, 235, 273–75

Switch to five-calorie line by, 22, 158–61
Total Beverage Solution of, 236–37, 240, 276, 278–79, 281
UnConvention of, 210–12, 216, 218, 251, 282, 291
Bar-Cohen, Barak, 179–85, 208, 216, 261–62, 283–83
Basementality, 17–18, 37, 53, 79, 114, 118, 168, 191, 224
Blecher, Haim, 128–31, 262–63
Blecher, Shari, 128–29, 262–63
Blendtec, 76, 79, 83–84
Boosta Shot, 16, 82–84, 89, 91, 149, 288
Boston University, 39, 47–49
Bradley, Bill, 123–26
Brewed Awakening, 53, 61–76, 78, 80, 82, 92, 228, 288
Brown, Abbey, 197–98, 264, 277
Brown, Christopher, 195–96, 203–05, 207, 209, 213, 278–80, 297
Brown, Zac, 11–13, 206, 232–33
Brumbach, Jason, 209
Buczacki, Ed, 211-12
Buffett, Warren, 118

Café Cinema
see Godiva Chocolatier

Caruso, Carolynn, 205–07, 209–10, 217–18, 264, 292
Chiurco, Tony, 132–36, 268
Cho, James, 188
Chocolixir
see Godiva Chocolatier
Civet Society
see Bai Brands
Coca-Cola Co. (Coke), 15, 21, 23, 53, 92–93, 103, 112, 126–27, 155, 197, 211, 225, 259, 266–67, 276
Costco, 144–48, 150, 165
Crook & Marker, 17, 297

Denny, John, 200–02, 230
Direct store distribution (DSD), 116, 155, 157, 166–67, 173
Dr Pepper Snapple Group, 15–16, 23–24, 131, 157, 187, 189, 208, 211–12, 223–26, 228–31, 235–36, 238–39, 245, 249-67, 273, 275–78, 280–89

Edison, Thomas, 277
Ellen, Marty, 250–52, 264–65, 277, 282, 287
Eisenmann, Pete, 195–96, 203, 209
Ernst & Young Entrepreneur of the Year Award, 230–31

Five Alarm Brew, 59–62, 67–68, 72, 288
Flavor Flav, 230
Fuze, 250

G. Housen, 156–57
Godiva Chocolatier, 54–59, 75–82, 89, 91, 189, 232
  Chocolixir and, 76–82, 89, 91, 149, 232, 288
  Godiva Theater Café (also Café Cinema) and, 53–59, 75, 232, 288
Goodfellow, Daniel, 185–87, 297

Haddon, Kat, 107–08, 116, 124, 146–49, 169, 209
Harper, Durale, 213–15, 218

Invisible hand, 52–53, 297
Izze, 93

Jobs, Steve, 277
JPMorgan, 246–47

Kellems, Eric, 76, 79–83, 149–52, 169, 209
Krauza, Al, 207, 209
Kroger, 278
Kurtz, Ken, 165–68, 170–84, 191, 195–97, 203, 208, 211–12, 214,
225, 227, 238, 250–52, 261–62, 268, 278, 281–82, 284–85, 289, 297

McCaffrey's, 143–44, 158–59
Metzger, Sam, 68–73
Miller, Jay, 198
Muchnick, Jill, 29, 47–48, 153
Muchnick, Natie, 57, 72, 153

Nantucket Nectars, 211
National Amusements, 54, 56–57

Odwalla, 93, 175
Oza, Rohan, 126–27

Pancza, Ryan, 209
Parker, Tom, 215–16
PepsiCo., 15, 23, 93, 112, 155, 223, 225, 259, 276
POM Wonderful, 175, 195
Portas, Chad, 15, 18, 21, 91–95, 187–89, 198, 208, 217–19, 227, 232, 235, 261–63, 266, 273–75, 284, 287, 289, 297

Reilly, Lauren, 209
Richmond, Simon, 92, 100, 136–38, 292, 297

Sapan, Paul, 21, 91–95, 106, 150, 227, 261, 268
Schlaefer, Pat, 30–32, 38–39, 50, 64, 71, 104, 148–49, 153
Schlaefer, Ray, 22, 32, 34, 39, 47, 66, 81, 101–06, 109, 116, 124, 129, 143, 148–49, 151–54, 169, 178, 198, 207, 253, 264, 292–93
Schultz, Howard, 125
Simon, Michael, 54–58, 75–80, 82, 189–91, 208, 232, 234, 261, 283
SoBe, 93
Soroken, Ari, 19–20, 22–23, 110–115, 117–18, 134, 146, 149, 152, 154, 156, 169–70, 172, 179–80, 182, 184, 208, 225, 231, 246, 248–49, 254–58, 261–62, 265, 284, 289

Target, 168, 214, 238, 278, 284–85
Tesla, Nikola, 277
Tice, Brian, 261–64, 287
Timberlake, Justin, 206, 255, 273–75

UnConvention
    see Bai Brands
Unicorn exits, 267

Vitaminwater, 21, 92–93, 107, 112, 126, 155, 175, 211, 237, 247, 250, 266–67

Walken, Christopher, 274
Walmart, 165–68, 176, 246, 278
Weiss, Danna, 19–21, 29, 41, 47–49, 53, 56–57, 59–63, 66–69, 71–72, 75–77, 84, 90–92, 94, 97, 111, 118–19, 124, 128–29, 131–32, 135, 144, 146, 150, 153–54, 165, 168, 178, 185, 216, 231, 261–66, 285, 287, 291–92
Weiss, Jack, 19, 21, 61–63, 66–69, 75, 77, 90–93, 100, 118–19, 124, 128, 132, 218, 226–27, 261, 285, 287, 290, 297
Weiss, Shayna, 19, 21, 63, 80, 90–93, 100, 118–119, 128, 261, 285, 287, 290–91
Whole Foods, 103, 174, 198

Young, Larry, 15–16, 24, 223–24, 235, 250–53, 256, 258–60, 264–66, 273, 277, 281–82, 284–87, 289

ABOUT THE AUTHORS

Entrepreneur **Ben Weiss** founded the antioxidant beverage company Bai in his basement in 2009 and quickly built it into the fastest-growing brand in the industry. With Bai, Weiss led a "bevolution" against giant soda companies by delivering great-tasting drinks without mounds of sugar and artificial ingredients. Dr Pepper Snapple Group acquired Bai in 2017 for $1.7 billion.

After his departure from Bai, Weiss founded Crook & Marker, an organic alcoholic beverage brand that launched nationally in 2019. He is continuing his bevolution with Crook & Marker by challenging traditional beer brands with beverages that offer authentic flavor, variety, and transparency.

Weiss has been featured in major media outlets including *Inc.*, *Forbes*, *Business Insider*, CNBC, and Fox Business. He lives in Princeton, New Jersey, with his wife, Danna, and his children, Jack and Shayna.

Eric Quiñones is a former national business reporter for the Associated Press and former freelance journalist whose work has been published in *The New York Times*, *The Washington Post*, *The Los Angeles Times*, and more. He also served as speechwriter for the president of Princeton University and has held communications leadership positions with Bai and Crook & Marker.